In my experience, Mormon another as adults, with all the complexities adulthood entails. That's what makes *Living on the Inside of the Edge* so refreshing—it's a book by a Mormon adult for other Mormon adults. You probably won't agree with everything here. Chris doesn't care. He just wants you to be an adult. I'm pretty sure God does too.

—Patrick Mason
author of *Restoration:
God's Call to the 21st-Century World*

Chris has managed to write a great primer for Latter-day Saints who desperately need a new way to navigate their changing relationship with the Church. I could have been spared a lot of heartache if I had had this book ten years ago when church started getting really complicated for me. Full of practical advice, it's sure to become a handbook for individuals who struggle with what's in a different Handbook

—Cynthia Winward
co-host of the *At Last She Said It* podcast

Chris Kimball's *Living on the Inside of the Edge* was one of the most difficult reads of my life. As one of those who wants to be an "all in" member, it was not easy for me to watch several of my sacred cows get butchered and carved up into more tolerable beef steaks because the manure in the Church pasture was too much to handle. Yet, to be fair, "all in" hopefuls like me were not the audience for this book and Kimball was crystal clear about that throughout his work.

Despite the personal difficulty of portions of the book for me, the benefits of the read for me were undeniable. It was a poignant experience, including the heartbreaking awareness that the pain, dissonance, and frustration I felt during portions of the book have been Chris's unrelenting companions for decades. My heart was touched with a deepened empathy for the many others who live "inside of the edge." In spite of the differences Chris and I have in our views and approaches to the faith, I found an undeniable ring of authenticity, sincerity, and vulnerability in Chris's writing that made it impossible for me to dismiss or cast his experiences aside.

As I finished *Living on the Inside of the Edge*, quite exhausted, I felt as though I had made a new friend—one who drove me a little crazy, one very different from me in some ways, but a friend that I now hold in profound respect.

—Loren Marks
Professor, BYU School of Family Life and
co-director of the *American Families of Faith*
National Research Project

Every week, I hear from people who have one foot out the door of the Church but actually want to find reasons to stay. For those people, Christian Kimball's book is a lifeline, containing wise suggestions about how to stay for those who choose to do so. There's guidance here on claiming your own spiritual authority, dealing lovingly with orthodox family members, and surviving worthiness interviews. There's advice for how to talk to a bishop who doesn't understand your faith crisis—offered from someone who once served as a bishop but has spent the last 25 years as a back-bencher in a blue shirt and no tie, as he puts it. Kimball employs his liminal position to the reader's advantage, advocating for "middle way Mormons" as a consummate observer and judicious friend.

—Jana Riess
Senior columnist for Religion News Service and
author of *The Next Mormons: How Millennials
Are Changing the LDS Church*

LIVING ON THE INSIDE OF THE EDGE

BCC PRESS

BY COMMON CONSENT PRESS is a non-profit publisher dedicated to producing affordable, high-quality books that help define and shape the Latter-day Saint experience. BCC Press publishes books that address all aspects of Mormon life. Our mission includes finding manuscripts that will contribute to the lives of thoughtful Latter-day Saints, mentoring authors and nurturing projects to completion, and distributing important books to the Mormon audience at the lowest possible cost.

LIVING ON THE INSIDE OF THE EDGE

Christian Kimball

Living on the Inside of the Edge: A Survival Guide
Copyright © 2023 by Christian Kimball

All rights reserved. Printed in the United States of America. No part of this book may be used or reproduced in any manner whatsoever without written permission except in the case of brief quotations embodied in critical articles or reviews.

For information contact
By Common Consent Press
4900 Penrose Dr.
Newburgh, IN 47630

Cover design: D Christian Harrison
Book design: Andrew Heiss

www.bccpress.org
ISBN-13: 978-1-948218-78-8

10 9 8 7 6 5 4 3 2 1

CONTENTS

Introduction 1

WORKING WITH YOURSELF
Differentiation 13
What is the Church 23
Why We Stay 29
Commandments 45
Sex 61
Control 75
Anger 85

WORKING WITH THE INSTITUTION
Magical Thinking 95
Talking with the Bishop 109
The Temple Recommend 125
Callings 137
Membership Councils 145

WORKING WITH THE CULTURE
Church vs Gospel 161

Shibboleths — 169
Orthodoxy — 175
Spirit of Contention — 185
Affiliation — 193

WORKING WITH CIRCUMSTANCES

Tribes and Respect — 205

One Woman's Perspective — 211
Susan Meredith Hinckley

The Inside of the Edge for Single Adults — 225
Mara Haslam

Living on the Inside of the Edge—
A Latter-gay Perspective — 239
David Doyle

Black and Mormon: Activism to Survive — 255
James Jones

Complicated Families: Raising Children on the Edge — 267
Christian E. Kimball

Complicated Families:
Raising Feminist Boys in a Sexist Church — 279
Anne Bennett

Complicated Families: LGBTQ Children — 287
Shari Siebers Crall

Complicated Families: Pushing Orthodoxy as a Seminarian's Daughter — 295
Kajsa Berlin-Kaufusi

Choose The Right — 309
Afterword — 317

INTRODUCTION

Steal This Book! Oops, I can't use that title. That's Abbie Hoffman's counter-culture survival guide from 1971 that almost didn't get published because likely publishers hated the title. If you know the reference, congratulations on your first Easter Egg. If not, you now have an insight into how old I am.

Hoffman's book comes to mind every time I want to describe this book by genre. Like any writer, I want everybody to read *Living on the Inside of the Edge: A Survival Guide*. I think everybody would find something interesting. But I know that's self-aggrandizement on a large scale. This book fits a narrow genre with a limited audience and the better part of me wants to not disappoint or over-promise. So here's some shelving advice. Unlike the majority of books with a Mormon flavor, this book is not theology, not history, not a memoir or biography, not apologetic, not devotional. For a broad category, this is a self-help book. More specifically, I'm thinking about a shelf of books in my parent's house. It was a high shelf, not readily accessible to children. It was the shelf with books like Abbie Hoffman's *Steal This Book*, Saul Alinsky's *Rules for Radicals*, and Alex Comfort's *The Joy of Sex*. Somewhat transgressive counter-culture instruction manuals, usually with catchy titles and covers that made you want a plain paper wrapper. In my most ambitious dreams for this book, that's the shelf it belongs on.

The setting for this whole book is The Church of Jesus Christ of Latter-day Saints in the twenty-first century. "Mormon" is useful as a cultural designation and the most common adjective form and I use it freely and without apology. If "Mormon" troubles or annoys you, there is a lot about this book that will trouble or annoy you. Where necessary to distinguish the institution, I sometimes use the full name but most often simply the Church. Whenever there is no explicit distinction or label, the Church means The Church of Jesus Christ of Latter-day Saints.

Through friends and a small amount of study and larger amounts of public media I am aware that the issues and concerns of differently thinking Mormons have parallels in other traditions, including among Catholics, Evangelicals, and conservative Jews (not an exclusive or comprehensive list, but just the accident of my circumstances). Although I draw on thinking and writing that comes out of those traditions, I have made no attempt to speak to a broader audience. I leave to the better informed any parallels and value that might be found.

Thinking of themes or approaches within the context of The Church of Jesus Christ of Latter-day Saints that might be expected or feared, this is not an extended argument to stay in the Church. This is an inward-looking book and staying might be an indirect effect, in the sense that if you want to stay and you pick up some tools to make it possible and learn that you are not alone, you might be able to hang on a little bit longer. But this is not an argument that you should stay. In my experience there are valid reasons to leave the Church, and valid reasons to stay, but this book is not about either one. This book is for people like me who have concerns about the Church that make leaving a genuine consideration, but have decided or chosen or felt called to stay and now want to figure out how to make it work. This book is about how to make it work.

Nor is this an extended argument to leave the Church. People leave the Church all the time. Some are called or attracted to a better fit or more appealing narrative. Some are pushed out, explicitly or by offensive actions of others. We find the foundational reasons for our original membership are not true or no longer satisfying. Or we see a divergence between the Church's actions and what our own moral compass dictates. For the purposes of this book, it is axiomatic that there are valid reasons to leave and that a purposeful decision to stay must be open to the possibility of not staying. From beginning to end, leaving is an open possibility. But this book is inward looking. However open to the possibility of leaving, this book is ultimately about not leaving, for people who feel called to stay.

Third in the "not this" category, this is not a what's wrong with the Church book nor a how-to-fix-the-Church manual. In some circles it's kind of a sport to criticize the Church. Criticize and draw up lists of what's wrong and how the Church needs to change. If you picked up this book in hopes of being entertained by 250 pages of Church trashing or even organized religion trashing, perhaps you should ask for your money back. This book is survival strategies for the individual. There are very few direct attacks on The Church of Jesus Christ of Latter-day Saints. You might glean some ideas for change in an indirect way. When the thought "it shouldn't be this hard" intrudes, that's a hint at something that could change. However, this book is all about the individual coping in the Church as it is. There's relatively little about what *they* should do. Most of this book is about what *you* can do.

RECOMMENDING THIS BOOK

Word of mouth recommendations are generally a great way to build a market. However, this book is usually one you choose for yourself, having decided you are in the target audience and want to know more. If somebody gave you this book or recommended this book, give some serious consideration to their motives and message. Proselytizing this book is a bit suspect. You would have to know somebody well to ever imagine they would want this book. If you don't know them that well, or they don't know you that well, it's possible somebody wants to fix you. Handle with care.

Notwithstanding the handle with care of the preceding paragraph, it might occur to someone to give or recommend a copy of this book. Please don't do it with the intent of fixing, or encouraging, or as any kind of supposed to or it-would-be-good-for-you gesture. If you want to give or recommend this book, the way to do it is with an "I know you" hand off. I know you and I think you will like it or appreciate it or it will be meaningful or it will make you angry. The recommendation part isn't important. The "I know you" is the key.

ON THE EDGE?

If you think you are on the edge, you're in! Welcome. If someone else is telling you you're on the edge, take a deep breath and count to ten.

The "edge" is notoriously difficult to define and goes by many names, each presenting a different flavor: middle way, disaffected, not believing, doubter, progressive, questioning, heretic, unorthodox, heterodox, skeptic. Have you sat on your hands at church to keep yourself from saying something that would draw side glances? Has it crossed your mind that you might be happier if you never attended another Sunday School class? Has a church leader made you furiously angry? Have you said no to a calling, or debated whether to renew your temple recommend? Are you on a self-imposed sabbatical from church activity, wondering when or whether it will end? Or an externally imposed 'sabbatical' by way of church discipline? Does the Church sometimes feel like an antagonist, like you're wrestling rather than appreciating?

For the purposes of this book it's all good. We're not judging here. This is not a club with tight boundaries.

On the other hand, there are church leaders and family members and neighbors who make a practice of drawing lines, telling others they are "in" ('full fellowship' might be the term they use), or "out," meaning some behavior or belief marks someone as unacceptable. They might be right, but outsider judgments like that are not determinative. There are formal indicators of membership but belonging to the community is almost entirely self-determined.

One of the quickest ways to see the difference between self-determination and the judgments of family, friends, and leaders, is to interrogate attitudes or beliefs about the Book of Mormon. There are many ways to think about the Book of Mormon: as an historic record literally translated, an entirely nineteenth-century creation, a fraud, an expansion on a core historic record, an inspired but not historical book, and a half-dozen more nuanced variations. These different attitudes or beliefs exist, meaning there are real people out there really holding all these different views. At the same time, there is a cottage industry of people telling us that one of these views is legitimate, and everything else is impermissible or flat wrong or reveals character defects in the bearer. This in turn serves as the basis to form a sharp demarcation of who is in and who is out.

The problem with the sharp demarcation is that it is an observable fact that real people holding real beliefs about the Book of Mormon feel themselves to be all-in, or on the edge, or all-out, in ways that do not sync with those litmus-test markers.

For purposes of this book we can be fairly relaxed about defining in and out and edge, because we're not going to attempt to solve any of the differences. We're not going to answer the Book of Mormon historicity question. Instead, we're going to talk about how to cope in a world where your attitude about the Book of Mormon is different from your neighbor's.

As a result, if you think you're on the edge by any definition of "edge" you're in the club. Read on.

A final caution: The word "edge" can suggest the image of a knife blade, an extremely narrow place that everybody is doomed to fall from to the inside or the outside. That might in fact be your experience, but I would urge you to suspend disbelief for a time. In effect this whole book is an argument that the edge is broader than a knife and that it is possible—for some of us, some of the time—to enjoy a robust and extended life on the inside of the edge. The cover illustration was chosen with this argument in mind. The dream is for that lively bright circle of light and energy to become for you, for me, for us, the inside of the edge.

INSIDE OF THE EDGE?

If you've spent any amount of time on the edge you have (probably, likely) braced yourself for a pitch here that you SHOULD be looking in, staying, engaging with the Church, making it work, staying in the boat.

Nope. If you are not in fact looking in, put this book down and move on. Full stop.

A whole lot of people who get to the edge just keep going. Bless them. Bless you. I wish you all the best. I hope you find happiness wherever your journey takes you.

But some of us who get to the edge have reasons to turn in, to plant ourselves on the inside of the edge. It may be the result of family, or tradition, or guilt, or a Pascal's wager sort of caution. It may be a desire to help others or make a difference. It may be an internal sense or revelation telling you to stay. Very often it is a combination of things. For the purposes of this book I boil it down to a "call." By your own measure, by your own judgment, by your own feelings and concerns and even personal revelation, you have been called to stay.

No judgment here about the reason. No argument that there are good reasons and bad reasons. It turns out to be important that you understand your own reasons (more about that later). But for present purposes it is very seldom relevant what they are. If you find yourself on some form of an edge and you feel a call to stay, then know that it is a challenge for most of us, a fraught place, sometimes (yes) like living on a knife edge, and this book is for you. How to cope. How to make it work.

On the other hand, if you're looking for reasons to stay or a persuasive argument to stay, or if the person who gave you this book hopes you will find a reason to stay, this may not be the book for you and there is a fair chance you will find the discussion annoying.

WHY LISTEN TO ME?

This book is opinion, almost from the first word to the last. It is opinion backed by years of experience and hundreds of conversations, but for all that it is anecdotal not statistical. Even acknowledging all this opinion, I would prefer to let my words stand on their own. But my son tells me that as much as he is committed to reading everything his dad writes, for the rest of the world I have to say something about who I am or why you should listen to me. Realistically, that might call for an autobiography or memoir longer than this book. But I can think of four justifications that are easier and shorter to describe.

FIRST VERSION   I was born of goodly parents. It's not a joke. I'm the eminently privileged son of well-educated, white, upper-middle class, multi-generation Mormon parents. Grandson of an LDS Church president. The oldest of seven, with one wife, three children, and eleven grandchildren. Until I was 40 I checked every Mormon box—mission, marriage in the temple, leadership callings, speaking opportunities, temple service, the works. There's a risk that this sounds like "listen to me because I'm an old white man." But privilege is real, and the least we can expect of people with privilege is acknowledgment, and in this case it is intended as a way to say I'm an insider. I speak and write from a lifetime in the church.

I've given up or lost a good bit of that privileged state. In the mid-1990s, while serving as the bishop of the Longfellow Park Ward in Cambridge, Massachusetts, my relationship with the Church came off the rails. Shortly after I was released from that calling, I returned my temple recommend to my home ward bishop and have refused to sit for any kind of worthiness interview ever since. I have now spent more than 25 years on the fringes of the Church. This book is not an autobiography, but it is a reflection of my life and the things I have learned as a survivor on the edge.

SECOND VERSION   In 1995, sitting in counsel with a young gay man, the angel on my right shoulder whispered, "tell him to go elsewhere; tell him that he will not be nurtured as he deserves in this Church in his lifetime." And the angel (or was it a devil?) on my left shoulder said more loudly "you can't do that; you're the bishop, your current assignment is to keep him here as best you can." I did not speak up. I am ashamed of that.

I have spent more than 25 years now pondering what I wish I had done, what I wish I had said, what I now know better. In a sense this book is penance. It is the best I know of what I have learned in the years since my release as a bishop. It is an answer to what I wish I had said and done and counseled and taught.

THIRD VERSION   In 2007 I was diagnosed with a rare cancer that could have ended my life. I endured dramatic surgery and several kinds of chemotherapy that I expected would end my life. I'm still here, on bonus time. I have survived my parents. I have reached the end of a multi-faceted career. Unwilling to engage with the institutional church on its terms, I have no prospects for Church employment or any kind of leadership calling.

This book is the voice of an old man living on bonus time, having nothing to lose, telling the no-apologies real stuff from his point of view and life experience.

FOURTH VERSION In the process of writing this book, I felt I should explain for myself why I stay. As noted in these pages, there are many possible reasons and I have several working in me. One of the most powerful reasons for me at present is that Mormon men and women living on the edge of the Church are my friends, my companions, my circle of trust. They . . . we . . . you . . . are some of the best people I know. This book is a love letter to my people.

WORKING WITH YOURSELF

DIFFERENTIATION

Parent-child is the default relationship of church to member—the church as parent, the member as child. In this opening chapter I propose that differentiation from the church is the most important developmental task we face while living on the inside of the edge.

Putting it bluntly, the charge here is to grow up. That could be the two-word summary of this whole book: Grow Up.

In case *Grow Up* offends, we can use the more technical phrase "differentiation of self." Differentiation of self is a concept commonly attributed to Dr. Murray Bowen (1913–1990), an American psychiatrist and professor of psychiatry at Georgetown University. Differentiation of self is the ability to think as an individual while staying meaningfully connected to others. As Bowen put it, differentiation is a person's ability to "define his or her own life's goals and values apart from the pressures of those around them."[1] The concept has been used interchangeably with the similar concepts of individuation and psychological differentiation.

---

1. Murray Bowen, *Family Therapy in Clinical Practice* (Jason Aronson Inc., 1992).

Given the work of Dr. Bowen and others, a psychologist or family therapist today is likely to describe differentiation from and within the family as one of the most important developmental tasks we face in life. It is a psychological and emotional separation that helps with the process of adult identity formation. It is part of the path of emotional maturity. I propose that a parallel development, i.e., formation of an adult identity separate from but still in relationship with the Church, is necessary to survive and even thrive as an adult living on the inside of the edge of the Church.

Let me illustrate the base case parent-child dynamic, and the living on the edge necessity for differentiation. The following reflection from a woman who grew up in the Church illustrates the parent-child dynamic (used by permission with minor editing for length and relevance; name withheld):

> I was the epitome of a believing, trusting, completely-wrapping-my-life-around-the-doctrine Mormon. This beautiful culture raised me and loved me. I feel forever blessed and indebted to the religious community for that. A debt I felt obligated to pay by doing everything to the letter. I feel I never found my own two feet or sense of self. Which is neither the complete fault of the religion or me, probably just a combination of the two. I deferred everything to the Church, as if it were a trusted parent, my role model. It filled a spot in my life I so desperately needed filled, to feel loved, to give boundaries, to be given a job/purpose. This model, for me, took out the stressful work of self-discovery as a woman. Be a good Mormon, proselytize, get married, have children, spend all free time dedicated to church service. And I have checked all those boxes, some over and over and over again. I feel it has created a person who is fun and social, but also devoid of any deep convictions or passions.

I have three reactions to this reflection:

First, familiarity—I know the feeling, I know people who know the feeling.

Second, concern that many Church leaders and traditional members will think this sounds great! (all except the implied negative). This kind of identification with the Church makes for a loyal, enthusiastic, service oriented, devotionally sound member. They will say "What's the problem anyway?"

Third, a fear that if/when this person finds herself on the edge, she is going to find it nearly impossible to stay there.

That differentiation is necessary, not just nice to have, might be illustrated by the following made-up example:

> Living on the inside of the edge, you go to Sacrament Meeting or a Sunday School class and pay attention. You hear a scripture explained or a principle described or a commandment pushed in a way that doesn't sit right. (You are on the edge, after all.) Wincing, you check it out and find that the explanation or lesson point or principle taught is right out of the study guide or is a line out of a recent General Conference talk or was spoken by one of the self-appointed authorities in the ward (we used to call them High Priests). In any event, it hits your radar as The.Church.Speaks.

If you have not differentiated well, you may find yourself forced into binary thinking.

> I conform my belief to what was just said. I make it work.
>
> **OR**
>
> I leave.

There may be no apparent third option.

If you are working the differentiation path, you should have options:

- Something new to think about.
- I thought that too, once upon a time, but I've moved on.
- I wonder if I should push back?
- What is everyone else getting out of this?
- Is there someone I should nudge and whisper "not me"?
- Is this the last straw? There might come a day when the disjunction between me and what happens at meetings is too much. But is that just about Sunday School, or about affiliation more generally? Hm . . .
- I wonder if there's a counter-quote from a respected source?
- I think I'll have a nap.

What's most important about these options is not that there is a right one but that there are many, and in particular more than two. For purposes of survival on the inside of the edge, binaries are dangerous. Conform or leave is precarious. In or out is an in-your-face challenge. Differentiating almost always opens up options, alternatives, middle grounds, personal choices. Having options and knowing you have options can be essential to survival on the inside of the edge.

Differentiation should give you options. Differentiation can also help avoid a too quick reflex reaction when something goes terribly wrong. If your identity is wrapped up in your church, and something shocking happens with your church, the immediate reaction can be "I have to get out NOW." Differentiation can give you enough space to be reflective, to make good decisions, to choose the best path for you instead of reflexively taking flight.

DIFFERENTIATING SELF

Differentiating is a form of emotional maturity. It is the same work as growing into a role and presence as an adult in the family. Many churches, and in my experience The Church of Jesus Christ of Latter-day Saints no less than most, will not tell you it is possible. Many church programs are designed to encourage and perpetuate loyalty and zeal and little else. It may be that the biggest trick in differentiating *vis a vis* the Church is just believing it is possible.

Dr. Bowen and others have observed that differentiation is not a once-and-for-all or an all-or-nothing concept. Differentiation comes in degrees and most of us work on it our whole lives. In his book *Emotionally Healthy Spirituality*, Pete Scazzero developed a scale to measure differentiation with a wealth of descriptions.[2] Inspired by and with substantial credit to Scazzero's descriptions, here's a way to give shape and substance to the idea of differentiation:

LOW

- Has difficulty distinguishing between fact and feeling.
- Is emotionally needy and highly reactive.
- Seeks the approval of others.
- Has difficulty with "I think . . ." or "I believe . . ." or "My opinion . . ."
- Has difficulty with boundaries.

STARTING TO WORK IT

- Has some ability to distinguish between fact and feeling.

---

2. Peter Scazzero, *Emotionally Healthy Spirituality: It's Impossible to Be Spiritually Mature, While Remaining Emotionally Immature* (Zondervan, 2017).

- Self-determines some elements of self-image rather than reflecting others and tying to compliments and criticisms.
- Is still quick to imitate others and change to gain acceptance.
- Is still likely to talk about principles and beliefs but act in ways that are inconsistent with those principles.
- Decision making is negatively affected by stress.

ADULTING

- Is attentive to thinking and feeling as functions that work together.
- Self-assessment is reasonably aligned with reality.
- Goals are self-determined.
- Expresses opinions without putting others down.
- Allows others to continue at their own varying stages of development.
- Forms and maintains relationships without demanding a common worldview.
- Functions alone and with others.

SAGE (RARE)

- Is principle-oriented and goal-directed. Secure. Unaffected by criticism or praise.
- Is confident in personal beliefs but not dogmatic or closed to new ideas.
- Can listen without reacting and communicate without antagonizing.
- Is able to maintain attentive calm while under stress and pressure.
- Takes responsibility for their own destiny and life . . .

- while remaining attentive to dependence on and responsibility for others.

If you are the Mormon equivalent of a sage, you probably have no time for nor interest in this book. But I would like to sit with you and learn from you. For all the rest of us, there are growth opportunities laid out in these levels and stages of differentiation. There is work to do—not abstract, impossible-to-imagine, reach-for-the-stars kind of work, but practical step-by-step individuation work.

To take another perspective on what differentiation looks like, consider the following descriptions of reasonably differentiated thinking. Even though I don't sit with sages in real life, and don't happen to know anybody who's got it all together, these descriptions characterize real people of my acquaintance. It can be done.

- I have my own principles and goals in life. I have sorted through the commandments and guidance and responsibilities I've been given and determined what works for me. I am secure and confident about this. I listen when the bishop or the president tells me my principles and goals are not their principles and goals or suggest that I'm on the wrong path, but I make up my own mind about it.
- When I make a determination about principles or teachings, I own it. Along the way I consult with others and study out of multiple resources, but once I reach a conclusion for myself I don't ask permission or validation.
- I know what I believe and don't believe about the Church, the history, the leaders, the principles and the teachings. I do listen and take in new information and I'm always learning. My relationship with and interaction with the Church is a consequence of my deeply held principles and my studied beliefs. It is highly un-

likely to change by other people's opinions regardless of title or experience and is slow to change by new information.
- I listen to General Conference with interest and without feeling attacked. I take it in, learning, and at the same time I remain confident in my own principles, my own journey.
- I engage in what is effectively disagreement with my Sunday School teacher without antagonizing them.
- I maintain attentive calm when there is headline news about the Church or about my best friend in the Church. I care on behalf of others, but news seldom affects my own principles and goals or my understanding and beliefs about the Church.
- I am ready to take what comes in terms of God and Heaven and Kingdoms of Glory. My journey is mine to take.
- My journey is not all alone. I recognize dependence on others and act on responsibility toward them.

The next several chapters take up some of these topics, thinking about what the Church is, about why we stay, about commandments and sex, about managing our emotions—matters the church wants to dictate that we ultimately have to decide for ourselves.

JOY IN THE JOURNEY

Compared to letting the Church do everything, tell you everything, take charge of your life, provide the route to joy in this life and eternal bliss in the next, compared to that peaceful confidence, differentiation can seem like a lot of work for little or no benefit. It may not feel good.

I push for differentiation here because it speaks to the purpose of this book. If you want to live on the inside of the edge, you must differentiate. Otherwise, you will break. Whether to the center or to the exit, you will break.

But I also push for differentiation because it is the way of the true disciple. Whether I think of the path as taking up the cross or drinking the cup, or I talk about following the Way or the Tao, or I use the language of discipleship or of joy, I want to be all in. The God that makes sense to me is not particularly interested in me being one more church-clone. The God that makes sense to me is interested in me, all of me. I'm all in for this journey.

WHAT IS THE CHURCH

For many of us, in order to differentiate from the church we must begin with defining the church for ourselves. We have to do this work because there are two extreme versions or images of the Church that exert a strong pull but are not healthy or useful for someone interested in life on the inside of the edge. Most of us need to differentiate from the Kingdom version and also from the Evil Empire version.

The Church of Jesus Christ of Latter-day Saints promotes itself as the Kingdom of God on Earth, the direct expression of Christ's will, the one-and-only pathway to eternal life and therefore the exclusive community of the faithful. This is a church in which every word from the prophet's lips is the word of God. A church where an apostle can say "my word is scripture" and it makes sense. Where members are afraid that turning down a calling is to turn their back on God, in effect rejecting a direct request from Heaven, confident that God has total and absolute knowledge of their circumstances, talents, fears, and needs.

That Kingdom image of the Church exercises a strong pull, difficult to resist. If that is your true image of the Church, why would you want to differentiate?

At the other extreme, there are some whose image of the Church is Evil Empire—an institution that lies and manipulates and abuses and controls, that is only interested in growth and power. If that is your image of the Church, why are you interested in the inside of the edge rather than already beyond the horizon?

But for most people on the edge, the one-and-only-Kingdom-of-God-on-Earth model doesn't fit in total or in all respects. And anyone interested in living on the inside of the edge already recognizes that there is more value and nuanced meaning than evil empire captures.

So what is this church?[1]

There is no one answer, and my answer is not your answer. There are many operative definitions and what's important is that you figure out what "church" or "Church" means for you. In furtherance of that goal, explore the following possibilities for yourself:

- The church is a group of people. The church is a history. The church is a culture. The church is a kinship group. The church is a human institution. The church is a set of principles and ordinances. The church is buildings. The church is community. The church is a language.
- How did the church come to be? Is the church the result of inspiration or divine guidance or a theophany or an ancient book or an angel or a vivid imagination? Was it an event in time? Or multiple events? Or an ongoing process?
- Many recognize that the church has made mistakes. Are mistakes defining? Have there been a couple of doozies in 200 years? Do they happen every day? What

---

1. Note the intentional lower-case "church" here. Very likely the proper form would be to capitalize "Church." However, capital-C "Church" too easily implies or assumes the Church's understanding of itself, and this is a process of stepping outside that paradigm and defining church or Church for yourself.

mistakes are substance rather than just bad timing or rhetorical choice? Do those distinctions matter? Which mistakes of the past still make a difference today? How much credit do you give for good intentions?
- For many the church is a package of truth statements, about the purpose of life, the way the universe runs, the nature of the hereafter, the nature of God. Do you accept some of its perspectives? All of them? Is there one that is enough to be defining, by itself?
- What do you believe or know or sustain? What is your "testimony"? Many people who recognize a testimony related to the church also acknowledge that experiential testimony covers a handful of propositions and everything else is derivative or a consequence of one or two propositions, an if-then sort of conclusion. Does that work for you? Are there elements that are critical and necessary, and others that are nice to have?

Another way to explore the definition of church is in terms of what you get or what you expect or hope for from a church. Again there is not a right or wrong answer and there doesn't have to be one answer. Just your answers. Consider the following:

- Opportunity. It's not what I get but what I give. Church is an opportunity for service. Church is an opportunity to learn from difficult people or people not like me. Church is an opportunity to grow in the most important ways.
- Happiness. Life in the church, living according to gospel principles, brings happiness. Makes me feel safe. Comforts me.
- Salvation. The covenants and the ordinances promise a way to heaven. The church is a path, a way, a passage to eternal life and exaltation.

- Justice. The church is a place to build heaven on earth. It's a big Zion project, mapping the moral, ethical, right way to live. The church gives me hope of a just society in the here and now.
- Community. The church is brothers and sisters I enjoy and want to be with. It's a big extended family. It's a place I like to be.

There is not a correct or incorrect way to work with these thought starters. There is not a correct choice, nor a hierarchy. You do not have to choose one. This is not a test. This is an exercise in deconstructing binaries and thereby escaping them—getting away from true or not-true—and opening possibilities for your own definition of the church. Your perspectives on these points, whatever they are, are likely to change over time. Your perspectives may not be things you can preach or teach or persuade others to believe. Your conclusions may in fact sound like apostasy to some if you were to say them out loud.

Maybe the best you can hope for is a tentative definition of the Church for yourself for the present. But that's good enough. The goal here is not to get it right, but to make it your own.

There is a temptation to see a bunch of bullet points and think this is easy. All you have to do is pick a couple and move on. Perhaps it actually is a simple afternoon exercise in self-reflection, for someone of deep personal conviction, substantial spiritual health, and a philosophical frame of mind. However, that afternoon of reflection is not the way most of us get through the work. The Church projects a strong authoritarian structure, telling us what to do and what to think, and what to think about the Church itself. For many of us who have lived within that system and accepted it as normal for most of our lives, the work of differentiating takes months and years. If we used to deeply, sincerely, believe in the Church as it presents itself and now we don't, that change can also challenge what we believe about ourselves. The work can be painful. On the other hand, that same work of discovery and invention, about the church and about ourselves, can be freeing and exciting and life-giving. The work often benefits from conversation with others (formal or informal talk therapy), and it might require stepping aside for a time. Some of us cannot do the work from within the church and need time apart—a sabbatical without commitments where the church is not always present—to create mental space to do this work.

For some of us, the simple proposition that we can have our own definition and concept of "church" is a learning that comes slowly and painfully. For me it came in a rush. I remember a thunderclap experience, a sudden awakening, with one sentence in my head: "I do not have to accept the Church's definition of itself." However, I also remember ten years of figuring out what that means. I'd like to think this chapter could reduce ten years to something shorter for you. But it would be fanciful to think this chapter could reduce ten years to one afternoon.

The defining-church exercise might lead you all the way to the outside of the edge. You might discover a church you want nothing to do with. You might line up what you want from a church, compare it with what you see in The Church of Jesus Christ of Latter-day Saints, and decide there's not a match. You might take a sabbatical and never come back. This is not a real process if the possibility of leaving isn't included in the package. But the exercise, with all its inherent risk, is so very important to the process of differentiation because it is almost guaranteed to put the church in the category of Other. When you finish defining the church for yourself, that church will probably not be exactly the same as what the Church says it is. More importantly, that church will not be you and will not define you, and you will be an active agent in defining and controlling your relationship with the church.

WHY WE STAY

Many of us get asked "why do you stay?"[1] Often there is a binary nature to the question, suggesting that if you are not all in, then you are out or should be out or will be out tomorrow. However, listening to hundreds of experiences, I find that there are many reasons to stay and many middle-way or inside-of-the-edge ways to stay. I also find that there are many reasons to leave, and that reasons to stay do not always last forever.

It's that last point—the do not last forever point—that merits an extended discussion here. This chapter and this book is not about encouraging you to stay, and not about ranking or qualifying or dissing reasons to stay and reasons to go. Rather, as part of a survival guide, this chapter is about belief and commitment and experience with and about the Church over the course of a lifetime where it seems that very little if anything lasts forever.

As a general observation, it has been my experience that:

---

1. Jump forward to David Doyle's *Living on the Inside of the Edge—A Latter-gay Perspective* at page 239 for a dramatic experience being asked and answering the "Why do you stay?" question.

- There are a number of reasons to stay and no one master reason or best reason.
- Most motives or rationales fade over time. Sometimes that marks an ending, and people leave. Sometimes one formerly sufficient reason is replaced by another newly sufficient reason.
- Within broad categories, most people find their own reasons. Notwithstanding General Conference talks and exhortations from the pulpit, advice from bishops and online discussion groups, it appears that most of us glean helpful ideas but ultimately decide for ourselves.
- People who have reasons to stay generally find it useful or valuable to understand themselves, recognize a life cycle for reasons to stay, and engage in an ongoing conversation.

To avoid a hierarchy of reasons and because it makes for easy one-liners when somebody asks, I use the word *Call* for all reasons to stay. This kind of call is not an assignment from the bishop (although it could be, if you respond to such things), or a personal revelation from God (although it could be, if such a revelation comes to you and you pay attention). This kind of call is simply your own reason for staying. Whatever moves you. Whatever you assess as reason enough for now.

VARIETIES OF CALLS

The first and perhaps only advice here is the Delphic maxim "know thyself." Thinking in terms of coping strategies and long-term survival, the biggest risk is not that you have a bad or deficient reason to stay, but that you misunderstand or deceive yourself about your reason to stay and forget that most good things come to an end.

CALLED BY GOD

If you understand or believe that God wants you in The Church of Jesus Christ of Latter-day Saints, that would seem to be an unassailable position. It is relatively independent of truth claims, historical anomalies or problems, leadership changes, church policies, offenses intentional or unintentional, even changes in life circumstances.

However, two kinds of questions can arise around this sort of call. First is questioning the validity or source of the call. Second is questioning the content.

A call from God might be experienced as a constant, steady, unending state of grace. That probably is an unassailable position so long as it lasts. But the state-of-grace kind of call seems the exception rather than the rule. More frequently people describe a call from God as a specific event, a supernatural external intervention into one's consciousness. As with any specific time and place event, there is a latency problem. What is the effect? How fast does it act? How long does it last? Any such intervention is inherently subject to second guessing. It happened once upon a time. Was it real? Does God really work that way? What if my understanding of God changes? It is not uncommon for religious-minded or God-fearing people to run into doubts, or even a belief to the contrary about an interventionist God. And many people with a rich prayer life and abiding faith report long dark periods. In either case, it is easy for trust in memory to fade.

Then there's the content issue—what is the meaning or content of "in the Church"? The kind of spiritual experience reported as a call might be richly detailed and specific. But rich detail seems the exception. More frequently a call is described as "stay" or "join" or "go" with little detail. For many it is natural to assume that stay or join or go means full engagement in every aspect of the Church the way current leaders define and explain. But what if (a real-life example) the sexism inherent in current temple practices makes continued temple attendance detrimental to one's spirituality or equanimity? Is it possible for "in" to mean Sacrament Meeting but not temple attendance?

There are no global answers to these questions. Sometimes we hear counsel to make a decision and never look back. Of course, that counsel assumes the first decision was the right decision. Just imagine the complexity of a missionary to a potential convert saying "no, not that decision to commit to your old faith, but this new decision—make this new one and then keep it." More to the point, people don't work like that. Years pass, circumstances change, memory fades. Decisions and choices are made in the present. Even the decision to follow an old decision is a present moment choice.

Attention to these issues—both the original call and the subsequent issues and questions—calls for a certain conservatism. "Never change" is an impossible goal. But take it slow, make incremental changes, be patient with yourself and others. Recognize that there will be bumps and shocks along the way, and resist letting one bump determine your whole trajectory.

UNIQUE AND NECESSARY

One strong reason for staying is a conviction that in The Church of Jesus Christ of Latter-day Saints there are unique and necessary saving ordinances. Unique meaning found nowhere else on earth. Necessary meaning the gates of heaven, eternal happiness, family forever, i.e., the ultimate goal of existence, is available only to those who have participated in the ordinances.

The Church of Jesus Christ of Latter-day Saints is a sacramental church and does preach both necessity and uniqueness (by "proper priesthood authority") for its ordinances. This is not self-evident. There are competing claims of several sorts. Nor is it provable by external objective evidence. This is a matter of testimony.

If you have such a testimony, it might seem to be the end of inquiry. However, several issues and questions do come up.

The most obvious issues are the latency and content problems discussed above. The confidence that we call a testimony might be experienced as a steady unending state of grace. However, more commonly people talk about their testimony arising from a specific event. When that is the case, the event is subject to all the bumps and bruises of mortality, with fading memory constantly overwritten by new experience.

With respect to content, the unique-and-necessary testimony might be experienced as a fully detailed recitation, but it seems far more common to have a general "it all makes sense" experience, or a line-upon-line "this much for now" experience. From those somewhat general experiences we often infer a detailed logical sequence—basically the whole story of the Restoration. The problem is that upon reflection or under stress it may become apparent that the inferential process added suppositions and made one or more leaps of logic to move from a general feeling that it all makes sense to a strong unique-and-necessary logical conclusion.

A third issue, what might be termed the history problem, is that the strength of unique-and-necessary depends on divine authority. In Mormon terms this amounts to an exceptional and necessary restoration of the priesthood. A one-of-a-kind restoration of authority, that "whatsoever you bind on earth shall be bound in heaven" (D&C 128:8), is an extraordinary claim. Rarely, it is supported by an independent testimony of each detail of the Restoration narrative. More commonly, it is supported by a chain of logic that depends on every link being correct. The history problem, then, is that in the latter case, the chain of logic case, any gap or inconsistency or revision in the history undermines the logic.

For purposes of this discussion, what's important is not that unique-and-necessary is the right way or the wrong way to go. What's important is that unique-and-necessary is a strong reason to stay but is subject to breaking. Unique-and-necessary is almost unassailable as long as it lasts. For that time, often nothing else matters.

However, the unique-and-necessary perspective has the potential of crumbling when cracks appear.

A cynic would say enjoy it while it lasts. A charitable person would recommend patience and learning to live with ambiguity. The latter is good advice, even though the hard edges and square corners of unique-and-necessary seem incompatible with ambiguity.

In summary fashion:

- If you are living in a unique-and-necessary state of mind, enjoy the reassurance and certainty it brings.
- Keep in the back of your mind that unique-and-necessary has the potential of cracking *and* that it is not the only kind of call discussed in this chapter. If it should crumble on you, life is not over and there is still much to think about.
- Practice tolerance and patience, for yourself and especially for others. Unique-and-necessary is powerful, and people who live within that paradigm sometimes find it hard to imagine or make sense of anybody outside the paradigm.

MEANINGFUL DOCTRINE

Mormonism includes some distinctive doctrines, including *apotheosis*, the idea that humans can become as gods, most easily accessible in Lorenzo Snow's couplet "As man now is, God once was; as God now is, man may be." And the idea of a Mother in Heaven, citing Eliza Snow's hymn *O My Father* with the following lines:

> In the heav'ns are parents single?
> No, the thought makes reason stare!
> Truth is reason; truth eternal
> Tells me I've a mother there.

Historic Mormon thought includes a universalist thread, a millennialist thread, a Zion on earth thread, and the idea of a sociality and ongoing relationships in heaven. Historic Mormonism honors the idea of an open canon and truth wherever it can be found. Mormonism promises that whatever principle of intelligence we attain in this life, it will rise with us in the resurrection (D&C 130:18).

Mormonism also includes the idea of a chosen people and a covenant path to exaltation, and a manifest destiny nationalism about the United States of America. Mormonism includes a strong gender essentialism and a "traditional" concept of marriage. And the promise of sealing a couple "for time and all eternity" (D&C 132:19). Mormonism tends to be strongly works-oriented and sacramental in practice, meaning the ordinances are necessary and salvific.

Some or all of these ideas or doctrines can be very attractive, intellectually, but also spiritually and emotionally. Staying can be a way to align oneself with important doctrines, especially for people of a philosophical or intellectual persuasion. Or staying can be a way of respecting and appreciating a culture, a society of people, an organization, that contains the thoughts and ideas that inspire.

Attachment based on doctrines and beliefs can come to an end or be challenged in a number of ways. There may come a realization that the most attractive doctrines are only part of the whole, and that the entire package deal is not equally desirable or that some parts of the package are in fact offensive. There may come shifts in emphasis such that the most engaging doctrines (to the individual) are obscured or even disallowed in public comment. Changes concerning polygamy and concerning Black people pose serious questions as to whether the changes are about practice or about doctrine. Depending on which doctrines are thought to be most important, there may come a learning or a realization that one or more of the most strongly motivating doctrines are not unique to The Church of Jesus Christ of Latter-day Saints, in terms of historic development or in terms of present-day teaching. There may come a time when meaningful doctrines don't feel meaningful any longer, or alternate views and understandings take their place. There may come a determination that one can hold to important doctrines and beliefs, however they have developed, without the intermediation of a church.

Attachment to doctrine can be very strong, both intellectually and emotionally. Meaningful doctrine is one of the more persuasive ways to answer the question why stay with this Church, among all the possibilities. This may be what church authorities have in mind when they ask rhetorically "where would you go?" Separating from or relinquishing important doctrines can be and often is described as very painful. This is more than an abstract intellectual exercise. However, as noted, attachments do break, doctrines or understandings of doctrine do change, and people do find that doctrine and church are not one and the same. As with every reason to stay, meaningful doctrine is important but not always forever.

MAKING A DIFFERENCE FOR INDIVIDUALS

Some people feel called to stay to make room for others. We talk about expanding the tent or acting as an ally or being an example for others by being present and by speaking up in a way that adds options or introduces additional ways to think about a problem.

Making a difference or being an ally is a legitimate, honorable, even Christ-like reason to stay, but there are some limitations and cautions. One trait to watch out for is developing a savior complex. "Savior complex" describes a person who feels obligated or compelled to seek people who need help and assist them, even if helping is detrimental to one or both. To counter this tendency, common recommendations are to practice the maxim of "first, do no harm" and to consult with the people being helped—ask what they need or want. The result may be that you help in a way that is asked for and in fact helpful, and you get to feel good about it. On the other hand, the result may be that you stand by, not actively making a difference, while others do their thing. And forego the fuzzy warmth of feeling like a savior.

There is often a life cycle to ally-ship. It can be exhausting work, an uphill battle in a culture that doesn't care and sometimes actively resists. People get tired. Sometimes the immediate motivation is a particular individual or group of people who seem to need help. Sometimes they don't want help. And sometimes they get tired or frustrated or just change their mind and move on. You can lose your most direct motivation in a moment of decision by someone else.

And then there's the greener grass problem. As allies tire, it is common to reflect on two things. First, what's in it for me, here in this hard place? Second, look over there where the grass appears greener, where it looks like we could all be happy with much less effort.

MAKING A DIFFERENCE IN THE INSTITUTION

The advocates and lobbyists among us (by type, not necessarily profession) may find their calling in working for change from within.

There are serious debates about how change occurs in a church. Do public statements work better than private letters? Does a march make more difference than quiet reasoning? What are the relative strengths of litigation vs opinion pieces vs careful history vs public outrage? Is what makes a difference on a local level different from what makes a difference on an area or global level? For activists cultivating a public following there is a further question: Do followers make one more powerful or simply more likely to be disciplined or excommunicated?

For all the debate and the several forms of public and private activism, there is a common and clearly legitimate feeling that working for change from within is more effective than working for change from outside. That feeling can become a call to stay.

There are two aspects of the call for change from within to watch out for: the with-me-or-against-me attitude, and general burn-out.

As noted, the unique-and-necessary mindset runs the risk of a particular sort of pride or hubris ("I can't even imagine how anybody stays who doesn't get it like I do"). The calling of an ally comes with the risk of a savior complex. For people interested in advocacy an analogous risk is alienating everybody who doesn't join their cause. Advocates can be passionate. Passion communicates a with-me-or-against-me, ally-or-enemy dichotomy. Certainly, these are extremes and can be avoided with care and attention. Nonetheless they are genuine risks, all-too-easy traps.

More common than alienation is the risk of frustration and burn-out. For an advocate with only one lifetime to give, churches move very slowly. In the twentieth century my friends and I used to talk about twenty-five-year cycles. In the twenty-first century the time frame has arguably shortened and I hear people talking about ten-year cycles. On the other hand, for my own peace of mind I often settle into a "not in my lifetime" perspective. Under any of these time periods for change, the arc of church history is long and only slowly curving. Furthermore, modern practice seems to disavow any outside influence. The Church moves because it is the right thing to do, or because there is a revelation, or because an individual leader decides. The agitator never gets credit. Putting this all together, working for change in the Church might be the archetype of Sisyphean labor.

Working for change from within can be more effective and show quicker results at a local level. However, those results depend critically on the character and interest of the leader of the day. When that leader changes, the work begins all over again.

Working for change is likely to be exhausting and frustrating. That doesn't mean it's always futile or that it shouldn't be attempted. The call is real, the effort laudable. So is the burnout. Maybe not in weeks or months, but sustained advocacy year after year is exhausting.

FOR THE FAMILY

Some people stay for family. We want to be there with our spouse. We want the training and experience for our children. We want to please our parents. We want to celebrate and preserve the eternal bonds sealing ordinances promise.

Sometimes I sense a diffidence while owning up to a for-the-family reason to stay. As though that's not good enough, or embarrassing to admit. To the contrary, family is important. For some of us it is the most important consideration. In my view, for-the-family is a completely legitimate call and deserves massive respect.

The lifecycle problem is a literal one in the case of staying for the family. Families change. In real life examples, I've seen attitudes change overnight when a key grandparent dies. Or a daughter turns 11 and starts noticing the differences in church practices for boys and for girls. Or a son comes home early from a mission in a mix of despair and anger. Or a child dies after 10 days of labored breathing on underdeveloped lungs and nothing makes sense anymore. Or a daughter comes out as bi-sexual or non-binary, or Marxist. Or a spouse goes through their own faith transition and "together" takes on nuances that were not part of the original deal.

Any call to stay, for any reason, will be tested by life changes of the sort described. But staying for the family can lose meaning in a flash.

COMING HOME

I'm told by experts who study religion that religion can be a blessing in people's lives. The claim—and I believe it—is that at least for cases where the God-image is positive and sustaining and loving, more often than not religion is life-fulfilling and makes people happy.

I have friends and acquaintances who will be incredulous at the claim, but for some of us with the right attitude and approach The Church of Jesus Christ of Latter-day Saints can be such a place. Without regard to truth claims or historical triumphs and failures, without reference to policy matters or peculiar doctrines, the Church can be home and family and community. When we feel this way, we may talk about the Church as good. Not true or necessary or unique, but good, valuable, enlivening.

Coming home can be as much a calling as any of the types described above or below. However, as with all the other types, there are lifecycle issues.

One lifecycle issue is that the Church does change. From one year to the next the changes may be small enough to ignore. But over the course of a lifetime the changes can accumulate to the point that the Church no longer feels like home. Making this personal, I grew up in the mission field of a church with fewer than 2 million members worldwide, before the rise of Correlation, when General Conference was a meeting you traveled to or read about months later and temples were a few-times-in-a-lifetime kind of experience. My local ward still feels like home, like the same sort of place I attended when I was 12 years old. However, nothing else about the twenty-first century Church feels the same as when I was baptized or attended seminary. Even the hymnbook is different from the one I grew up with.

A more specific issue for people on the edge is that we tend to be non-conformists and push boundaries. Being home at church may include a large dollop of take-me-as-I-am, notwithstanding general expectations and cultural norms. I am a 25-year veteran backbencher in a blue shirt and no tie, myself. This can be wonderfully freeing, but it is not an unlimited license. I can be home at church as a lovable eccentric. I probably cannot be home at church as an angry agitator.

FOR THE COMMUNITY

The first time I heard "I believe in the Ward" I thought it was profound and unusual. Now I've heard it a dozen times, most often in response to something the big church has done, or failed to do, that made the speaker angry. I still think it is profound but now I know it is a common shared sentiment.

A local ward can be a strong and inviting community. Wards tend to be about the right size to know most everybody, to minister to each other, to make a difference in individual lives. To know and be known—an essential human need. We come together to worship and to support. A call to that sort of community can be deep and meaningful.

Some people hate the small-town experience. Some of us thrive on it. Unfortunately, even for those who thrive on it, the ward as community doesn't always last forever. People move in and out, bishops come and go, buildings need fresh carpet, the kids grow up and go on missions and don't come back except for holidays. People fight. Feelings are hurt. Petty jealousies develop.

The call to the ward as community may not last forever, but for as long as it does that community is something to appreciate and celebrate.

BECAUSE I PROMISED

The promise may be understood as a covenant made in the temple. The promise may be made to a grandmother in her last days. The promise may be explicit or implicit in forming a lasting relationship with a spouse. One way or another, a commitment to stay in the Church can be defining of our being and our relationships.

Promises can last forever. We are strongly encouraged to treat good, uplifting, legitimate, free-will promises as lasting forever. However, real world experience tells us that promises are not always forever. Divorces happen, in marriage and in relationship with the Church. Circumstances change, time passes, people grow and learn and change. There can come a time when it feels like the person who made the promise is a distant memory and no longer in charge of the future. When the present-tense person would not make the same promise. The tension of having made a promise but knowing that you wouldn't make the same promise today is at best uncomfortable and more often devastating. But the tension is real for some of us, and in that case the old promise may not last forever.

FOR THE FUTURE

Some of us are blessed with a vision of the future, a sense of the Restoration as a work in progress. Patrick Mason calls it the "ongoing Restoration."[2] In a thoughtful moment we might say "I believe in the church that is to come." With such a vision, there can be a call to stay around to watch it unfold and to be part of that future.

The characteristics of a call to be part of the future church are much like the unique-and-necessary mindset but forward looking instead of historical. So long as we feel progress in a desired direction we can sustain enthusiasm, perhaps forever. Yet, in addition to all the latency and content concerns discussed above, there are two special problems with staying for the future church—what might be called the fits and starts problem, and the divergence problem.

The fits and starts problem is that the ongoing Restoration does not proceed in a straight line and doesn't even proceed in a constantly improving path. Simple observation tells us the Church tries things, reverses course, tries something else, modifies, and tries again. Faith in an ongoing Restoration requires patience and tolerance and a long perspective.

The divergence problem is that most people blessed with an enthusiasm for the future church have a certain model in mind, a picture of what that future will look like. Even allowing for fits and starts, over time there can develop an ever-widening gap between an individual's model and the reality of the Church's direction. As the gap widens, patience may not be enough and staying with the

---

2. Patrick Mason, *Restoration: God's Call to the 21st-Century World* (Faith Matters Publishing, 2020).

Church may come to depend on a manifest destiny sort of testimony, a trust and faith and confidence that The Church of Jesus Christ of Latter-day Saints is in fact the prophesied gospel that shall "roll forth unto the ends of the earth, as the stone which is cut out of the mountain without hands shall roll forth, until it has filled the whole earth" (Daniel 2:45 and D&C 65:2). This is a very particular kind of testimony and may or may not be how you see the Church.

SUMMING UP

For someone living on the inside of the edge there is no right or wrong reason to stay. There are only your reasons. The plural is intentional. Most people I know who survive for any length of time on the inside of the edge have multiple reasons to stay, both in the present and over time. As a survival guide, what is important is that there are multiple reasons, most of them don't last forever, and losing one doesn't have to be the end of the road.

As for me, I have stayed for more than 25 years now after a large enough break to make staying debatable. Sometimes I stay because it is my church too. Sometimes I stay because Mormonism is my native language. Sometimes it's no more than a familiar hymnbook. But much of the time I stay because people on the edge but staying—the people of this book—are some of the best people I know. We are the company I choose to keep.

COMMANDMENTS

If you are one of the rare readers who tries to make sense of the Table of Contents, or chapter headings, you might be wondering why this Commandments chapter shows up in the Working With Yourself section instead of the Working With The Institution section. Aren't commandments just what the Church tells us they are?

The Church may be an important source of information about commandments but differentiating from the Church means making up your own mind about commandments. This isn't optional; it's a built-in unavoidable part of the work of growing up. To skip over the commandments would be like trying to build an adult-to-adult relationship with your parents while hanging on to all the instances of "because I told you so." Working through commandments for yourself is to make them your own. It means moving from "because we say so" to "this is how I want to live." The result is not guaranteed to line up with the Church perfectly. Nor is it likely to be 180-degrees different. This work is not about accepting or rejecting the Church's teachings; rather, it's about making some version of them your own. If you end up the same in some respects and different in others, or close but not exactly the same, that may be uncomfortable. Comfort and ease are not the ultimate goals here. This is about standing up for your own life.

This is not a sermon, not a lesson in right and wrong, not a path to enlightenment or being a better person, not a list of thou shalts and thou shalt nots. This is not an invitation to nihilism—a rejection of all religious and moral principles because life is meaningless. Or hedonism—the pursuit of sensual self-indulgence. Rather, the proposition here is that commandments are serious business and you have work to do. This is about differentiating, about standing for your own life, making your own decisions. Paying attention to the Church, but ultimately doing for yourself.

GREEN TEA

As an introduction to thinking about commandments, let's talk about green tea. Are you allowed to drink green tea?

A reasonable first reaction is "Do I really care? Stop wasting my time!" Green tea seems like such a trivial issue. Of course, we're using it to set the stage, to exemplify a process. And it's not as though we don't deal with serious matters; the next chapter is all about sex, for just one example. But there is a serious concern reflected in "stop wasting my time." Working through questions about commandments is real work and does not always come easy. For many of us there is a strong temptation to revert to "just tell me what to do already!" or "leave me alone to do whatever makes sense in the moment." Neither one is satisfactory in the long run. "Tell me what to do" is the child talking. "Leave me alone to do what I want" is also the child talking.

Back to green tea. If you paid attention at the time, you know the Church "clarified" that green tea is against the Word of Wisdom in 2019. First in an August 2019 article in the New Era, a magazine targeted to the youth of the church, then ratified in an official statement dated August 15, 2019. In the modern Church the Word of Wisdom, as defined, is talked about as a commandment and obedience is a requirement for a temple recommend. In short, if you ask a Church official, the answer is drinking green tea is forbidden.

I'm proposing a three-part process for analyzing a suggested commandment, characterized as identification, taxonomy, and philosophy. For the green tea case, here's what it might look like:

IDENTIFICATION Who says so? The New Era? The Church newsroom? A general authority? A scripture? God? A revelation?

Implicit is the question of whether it matters to you. Are there sources you recognize as authoritative, and others that are just advice or counsel? Do you look for a cross-check, something like consistency or repeat mention, or an explainable logic? Can one reference in one authoritative source be enough? Are there sources you will take at their word? Or do you require verification from a higher authority? Or from your own spiritual witness or answer to prayer? The green tea example raises the additional questions of how we get new commandments? If you can't find it in Leviticus, is it really a commandment?

TAXONOMY What kind of commandment are we talking about? Big or small? Mortal or venial? Cultural? Constitutive? Relational?

Implicit is the idea that commandments are not all the same. That's not always obvious in the middle of a Sunday School lesson, but it must be true. Even the Church's instructions treat some but not all matters as serious enough to talk about with the bishop, and some so serious that a Membership Council is mandatory. The temple recommend questions describe some issues in absolute terms, and others in striving terms. It seems that some failings call for remorse, and others boil down to "don't do it again." The green tea example can be puzzling in this regard. If I now recognize green tea as part of the Word of Wisdom that I intend to keep, but it wasn't stated or wasn't clear the last time I sat for a temple recommend interview, should I feel any kind of remorse or is it enough to stop drinking green tea? The answer may be influenced by how I view the Word of Wisdom—as a health code, a matter of simple obedience, a token of membership, or a set of recommendations.

PHILOSOPHY Why do I care? Is it about my prior commitments, e.g., a commitment to obey? Is it guilt or anticipated guilt if I don't? Am I worried about consequences? About getting caught? Is my concern narrowly on scoring a temple recommend? Is it about being right with God?

Implicit is a recognition that commandments are not "just because." We care about commandments in different ways and for different reasons. You may care for reasons different than mine. Why we care matters. Putting this in green tea terms, if I think green tea is a commandment only in the sense that the Church made it part of the temple recommend interview, and if I am not concerned about a temple recommend but I am concerned about being right with God, I may be able to dispatch the green tea question with little concern. On the other hand, if I have all those same attitudes, and I *also* care about commandments as a matter of fitting in with the community, I may come to a different conclusion.

It is worth repeating that the end goal here is not obedience. Nor is it free-form to do whatever you want. The end goal is to be able to say, even if only to yourself, "I do this because" and "I don't do that because." It is to fill in the "because." This is not an overnight task. It might be the work of a lifetime. But it is a necessary task for survival on the inside of the edge, where you have given up both childish rote obedience and reflexive rejection. Where "because I said so" is no longer enough.

IDENTIFICATION

It takes less than a shower-length amount of introspection to conclude my mother is the source of most of the commandments I recognize as such. She didn't use all the same labels, but I certainly know it when I see it, label or no. Another few minutes of introspection reminds me that more than 50 years ago, during my teen years, I determined she was not always right, but not always wrong. Doing what she said was not sufficient. Nor was doing the opposite. In effect, that early realization is the seed of this whole chapter.

I suspect that I am not alone, that many of us learn from a parent, or a Sunday School teacher, or a camp counselor. In other words, the first "commandments" we know are rules taught to us by some adult. And by now most of us have separated or individuated from that adult in a way that puts those rules in question. Because that's what children and teenagers do as they grow up.

There are other sources, of course. Frequently, next to mind is scripture. When some church authority wants to tell you what to do, they are likely to cite scripture. But that's complicated. There are the ten commandments (Exodus 20:1–17). And traditionally 613 commandments in the Law of Moses (the Talmud). Jesus fulfilled the Law of Moses (Matthew 5:17; 3 Nephi 12:17) but did not destroy the law. Not one jot or one tittle will pass from the law until heaven and earth pass (Matthew 5:18; 3 Nephi 12:18). There are two great commandments, to love God and to love your neighbor. But the two great commandments are not in substitution for or replacement for all the rest; rather, they are a basis for ("on these two commandments hang") all the law and the prophets (Matthew 22:40). If that were not confusing already, experience tells us churches emphasize some, soft-pedal others, and ignore many.

For Mormons the temple recommend interview questions can be the functional list of commandments. Probably no Church leader would agree or would say outright that 15 or so questions cover the field and there is nothing else to think about. But an observer in a sociological field study of the Mormons might find that list compelling.

Taking a somewhat different direction, commandments can be sourced from observation, trial-and-error, scientific discovery, logic. From the great books. From the stories and experiences of wise elders and sharp analysts. In practice this happens all the time. Even words taken directly from the Bible are often supported by explanations that rely on logic or common sense.

Finally—or sometimes firstly in a typical Mormon tally of sources—is the Holy Ghost.

> The Holy Ghost usually communicates with us quietly. His influence is often referred to as a "still small voice" . . . The Holy Ghost speaks with a voice that you feel more than you hear . . .[1]

We don't need to argue terminology here, but some people might call this conscience. The Church often uses "Light of Christ," explained as "the divine energy, power, or influence that proceeds from God through Christ and gives life and light to all things."[2] Other terms include *sensus divinitatis* or sense of divinity (John Calvin in the 16th century), and "an innate sense of God" (Karl Rahner, 20th century Roman Catholic theologian). By one name or another, the idea is that there is an inborn or gifted understanding of right and wrong and of God's will.

The guidance of the Holy Ghost can be a final arbiter of commandment—a powerful final authority. However, it is not uncommon to question or doubt the influence of the Holy Ghost. There may be times when it feels like the heavens are closed and there is no guidance. There may be times when the influence is experienced as a nudge or as encouragement without detail, or when guidance is ambiguous or hard to read. It may come to feel like the guidance is both dependent on righteousness and always in line with what the Church teaches. In fact, the Church teaches this circular logic—that obedience first is the key to true guidance, and that guidance con-

---

1. *Gospel Principles*, Chapter 21: The Gift of the Holy Ghost, p. 123 (The Church of Jesus Christ of Latter-day Saints, 1978).
2. *Gospel Topics*, Light of Christ (The Church of Jesus Christ of Latter-day Saints).

trary to the principles taught at church is misunderstood or misdirected. From the same Church reference:

> [T]he Holy Ghost will come to us only when we are faithful and desire help from this heavenly messenger. To be worthy to have the help of the Holy Ghost, we must seek earnestly to obey the commandments of God. We must keep our thoughts and actions pure.

So what are commandments? Given the preceding paragraphs, I can confidently say "it's complicated." Proceeding from complicated, there are two likely directions. One direction is to find or choose a source to rely on, one that feels good or works for you. You are more likely to take that direction if you are looking for external validation that you've got the list, that you're thinking about everything you should be thinking about, that your goal will be satisfied whether it be salvation or happiness. If that's the direction you take, you could reasonably choose The Church of Jesus Christ of Latter-day Saints as your source, but many other teachers and churches and books would be happy to provide you a list. The other direction is to conclude there is no sure, confident, indisputable, externally motivated catalog of commandments, and instead work with a continually shifting and uncertain and perhaps loosely defined set of issues to think about, likely prioritizing the issues that are right in front of you. Some of us need a feeling of certainty. Some of us are better at living in uncertainty. But my guess is that the inside of the edge considerations that bring a reader to this book will pair with an inability to settle on a single external source, and whether we like it or not, most of us will find ourselves in the uncertain and loosely defined category.

However you get to it, the necessary answer is a personal one. What counts for you? What do you respond to? What have you made important in your life? There are any number of supposed-to answers; the bottom line is that no supposed-to counts unless it matters to you.

TAXONOMY

When a preacher gets going on a motivational sermon, the commandment in question is always the most important thing in the world, and the wages of sin on that count are dire. But we all know commandments and sins come in varying sizes and weights. There are damn-you-to-hell sins—what a Catholic might call mortal sins. There are feel-bad sins that are mostly a problem only if you think they are. There are constitutive commandments, i.e., rules that define the group or relate to commitments or promises made. There are relationship commandments—actions and omissions that may or may not have weight in isolation or as a pure hypothetical but become a real problem when they injure a relationship or damage a community.

The idea that commandments and sins come in varying sizes and weights is not heretical. I find the idea well accepted as a theoretical matter. However, when put to the question, I have found church leaders reluctant to talk about practical examples or real world application. As a result, most of the work is left for us to do, individually and in conversations like these.

When I have the conversation with myself, here's the way my mind goes. I offer this in lieu of the real conversation I'd like to have, as an example and illustration, certainly not a definitive guide or rule book.

> There are sins I think of as **DAMN ME TO HELL** sins. They've got words swirling around like "better I were dead" and "never, not once" and "millstone around the neck." They scare me. The truth is that most of these mortal sins are pretty far from my everyday life and from anything that tempts me. But not everything is distant or unimaginable for me individually, and I know people who know people with life experience that includes everything on the list. These are not fan-

tastical issues; they are real life. I need to think hard about judgment and recidivism and repentance and atonement. Also, I'd like to spend a few minutes on the question whether some of the damn-me-to-hell sins are in that category as a kind of bogeyman, a scary story of my childhood, and don't really belong in my adult version.

There are a lot of commandments that seem **WEIGHTED** or **SITUATIONAL**—important but in varying degrees and sometimes in conflict with other commandments or virtues. Whether or not church leaders want to talk this way, it seems to me that most of my day-to-day life is full of conflicts and tensions of this sort—choosing the lesser of two evils, or giving up one good thing because another is more important. It seems to me that much of the world's great literature wrestles with these issues.

Among the weighted or situational commandments, the ones that increasingly occupy my attention involve behaviors and attitudes that affect individual people I care about, or threaten a relationship, or might damage people collectively or the community as a whole. I'm seeing that these **RELATIONAL** matters are where I want to spend my time and attention. I notice the relational aspect adds concerns that are sometimes lost in a standard church curriculum. Breaking a promise can damage a relationship. But so can scrupulous attention to rules in preference to human needs or charity. And when I tire of talks about worthiness that focus on obedience or purity, I can still understand adultery as a violation of the marital relationship and that's powerful for me.

Shifting my attention to lesser matters, I notice a whole lot of seemingly **ARBITRARY RULES**, and I need to give some attention to the topic of **GUILT**. With regard to arbitrary(?) rules, I want to be careful not to dump them too quickly. Some of the rules may be the product of long experience and represent an important kind of wisdom; probably not as a damn-me-to-hell warning, but good advice for the general or most common case. A seemingly arbitrary rule might actually be a relational commandment. Also, there's a whole class of rules that define community and could define me as in or out. I want to be intentional about such boundary-defining rules.

About **GUILT**, I feel it all the time about all sorts of things. My mother did her job well. I feel guilt about big sins and I also feel guilt about breaking a clearly arbitrary rule set by a control freak. It's an ongoing project, figuring out what to do with guilt. My mother did her job too well, to the point that guilt is not a reliable indicator for me.

Finally (for today), some people suggest I should lump everything into a **RELATIONSHIP WITH GOD** bucket, and in effect work on the first great commandment as motivating all the rest. It sounds good, but the fact is I don't find the concept of a relationship with God very useful. Not to say it's wrong. Yes, I can shovel almost everything into that big concept. But then it's not analytically useful. It proves too much; it smooths over distinctions; I end up in a scrupulous do it all, every time, without fail, panic.

Furthermore, long ago I came to believe that the best way to show I love God is to love my neighbor. I know that is not everybody's take on the two greatest commandments, but it works for me, and, notably for this larger thought process, it has the effect of turning me back to the **RELATIONAL** matters described above.

So did you enjoy that peek into my train of thought? If we could sit and discuss in person, this could be five hours of conversation. There are many more questions than answers. We might not resolve anything. And this is the work we all need to do.

Your categories and questions may be longer, or shorter. This is not an exercise in perfection or absolutes. The point is not to get it right or reach a kind of certainty or sure thing, but to do something useful for your own understanding of commandments and examination of conscience. Once you acknowledge that commandments and sins are not all the same, some sort of taxonomy is inevitable. Differences mean labels and categories. For a long time, maybe forever, the resulting thought process is likely to generate more questions than answers.

PHILOSOPHY

The third set of questions can have four-syllable names, but come down to the simple question "why do I care?"

There are two extreme replies to why-do-I-care? One is I don't—don't care. The other is that I care only about avoiding guilt.

Insiders accuse outsiders and questioners of hedonism. There is a sense in which anything less than or different than saluting church rules with a "yes, sir" looks like doing anything you want, when you want. It is likely the accusations will never go away. However, my personal experience and my interactions with people on the edge looking in is that there is almost always a serious ongoing desire to do right. Many questions about what that is, but genuine concern. Furthermore, many rules (commandments, instructions) have to do with how to live and love and cooperate with other people. That is a vitally important consideration in life generally, and a necessary part of staying engaged with any community. Commandments simply do not disappear.

Outsiders accuse insiders of being guilt-ridden or thoughtlessly duty-bound. In my experience it's not really true. I do find many traditional insiders getting along on routine that can look thoughtless. However, when pressed, in Sunday School or giving a talk or in private conversation, most people have something more to say than "I do what I'm told." The difference for folks living on the inside of the edge is that being on the edge is associated with wanting more than rote obedience, with talking about commandments as though there is something to debate rather than take them as a given, and with a higher likelihood of concluding on different behavior than prescribed by the Church.

Moving beyond simple hedonism and scrupulosity, on my own journey I have considered and wrestled with all of the following approaches.

TRANSACTIONAL THEORY expects rewards and punishments linked to behavior. Blessings for good deeds. Punishment for sin. Exaltation in the Celestial Kingdom for putting it all together and enduring to the end. It's really hard to ignore transactional theory—it is preached all the time and is a natural, nearly inevitable, thought for the majority of us who live in a market economy that promotes the idea of private property. I can't get it completely out of my head. However, transactional theory is often problematic for folk living on the inside of the edge. Sometimes the problem is that both blessings and punishments seem to come indiscriminately to both the worthy and the unworthy. For many of us, lived experience is so loosely correlated with behavior that transactional theory is not believable, not trustworthy. Sometimes the problem is that the New Testament and Book of Mormon image of Christ and the atonement and a loving God—a careful Christology and soteriology—promises a kind of universal salvation that does not fit comfortably with a transactional model of commandments and sin.

CONSEQUENTIAL THEORY treats commandments as distilled if-then statements, albeit with cultural and historical overlays and necessary but confusing simplifications that make for a lifetime of study. More like predictions than rewards. Rather than thinking of Y as a blessing for doing X, as in a transactional theory, thinking of Y as a more-or-less likely natural consequence of doing X.

HAPPINESS THEORY considers commandments like a psychiatrist's or internist's prescription. Something like "In the long run, on balance, this will make you happy." Or healthy. Or functional. Or fully realized. Or the opposite, that failing on certain commandments will act like a cancer, perhaps starting small but ultimately destructive or deadly.

BEST-SELF THEORY is loosely analogous with happiness theory but arguably more robust. (And not incidentally generally more satisfying to me.) Best-self theory postulates that somewhere there is a knowledge of one's best self—what I am capable of, what it is like to be whole, what the transcendent me looks like. The knowledge might be conceptualized as residing in God or the Holy Ghost, or in my parents, or in the church, or in myself. In this view, scripture and church teachings, lessons from parents, the guidance of the Holy Ghost, the promptings of conscience, guilt and shame, and the principles and logic that come from all variety of study, are all pointing toward my best self. Of course the messages have in many cases been generalized and homogenized and may be subject to transmission errors, so I have to study the texts and meditate on their meaning for me in the search for my best self.

RELATIONAL THEORY considers a relationship with God and with other human beings to be the goal or the ultimate good, and views commandments in terms of what will enhance or detract from robust, loving, supportive, lasting relationships. Personally, I believe there is treasure in terms of profound truths to be found in relational theory, but I know I am a work in progress and haven't grasped them yet.

The point of outlining multiple theories and approaches is not to propose a right way or wrong way. Rather, it is to illustrate the philosophy exercise and to break up simple binaries. To show that there is more than one way to think about why we care. The goal here is not obedience or compliance. The goal is to answer for yourself what are commandments, what is their nature, and why do you care. This might be the work of a lifetime rather than a flash of inspiration. But it is a necessary task for survival on the inside of the edge, where you are no longer taking orders but also are not leaving.

REPENTANCE

A deep doctrinal discussion of repentance and atonement and forgiveness is a different book. Instead, for this book the repentance topic is about those traditional members and church leaders who will call you to repentance.

If you work out commandments for yourself, instead of taking the whatever they say strict obedience route, there is a high likelihood you will end up with a different practice than standard Church expectations. In five syllable words, you will add to your heterodoxy some amount of heteropraxy. If your own evaluation includes a significant weighting on community, on appearances, or on shibboleths, your heteropraxy may be subtle or hidden and may escape notice. For the rest of us, someone will notice and someone will criticize. At one level this is just life on the inside of the edge. Get used to it.

In progressive Mormon circles it has become commonplace that everybody is a cafeteria Mormon. For your own peace of mind, this can be a useful mantra. Whatever choices you make, however you have decided to live on the inside of the edge, chances are you are not alone, and not one-in-a-million, but more like one-in-two or -five or -ten. However, "we are all sinners" is not a useful phrase for purposes of backing off the critic. There is a reason for Jesus' discussion of the mote and the beam (Matthew 7:1–5). Jesus wasn't describing the rare or exceptional case. Your critic has reasons for what they do and they're perfectly satisfied that they're right; the same critic is sure you don't have justification for what they see as your failings.

There is a second level of concern about sin and repentance. From Primary days we are taught the awfulness of intentional sin. Repeated sinning and repeated repenting is frowned on. Scripture can be quoted for infinite forgiveness, for seventy-times-seven forgiveness, for three times, and for one ("if he doeth it again, he shall not be forgiven" in D&C 42:26). A law-and-order disciplinarian-type church leader is likely to cite the latter over the former. With this baggage, the idea of intentionally repeatedly "sinning" may be intolerable. From the outside the consciousness and intentional nature of your choices may be a never-ending reason for criticism. Such external criticism may turn out to be too much and finally a reason for leaving. Or it may lead to a mixed bag of toughened skin and reduced exposure, i.e., avoiding formal interviews, making concessions for appearances, evading or avoiding or even lying.

The most lasting answer to external criticism, the necessary answer for your own sanity and long-term well-being, is to do the real work of identifying, labeling, and rationalizing commandments and sins. Do it for real. Make it good enough that you have fully satisfactory answers in your own mind to external challenges to your heteropraxy.

However, I confess that notwithstanding all those brave words, because of decades of parent-to-child instruction in commandments and sin, and despite decades more of thinking for myself, I don't believe I will ever be free of my mother's stern disapproval.

SEX

This is not a chastity lesson. That's a different book. Instead, for those of us working in survival mode, this chapter argues that with respect to the wide range of possible questions about sex:

> The Church is not very helpful, and that's not likely to change any time soon.

> and

> When you do your own work you are unlikely to end up believing the Church was right all along about everything. At the same time, if you are serious about the exercise, you are unlikely to end up thinking that anything goes and nothing matters.

THE CHURCH IS NOT VERY HELPFUL

The ideas in this chapter have their genesis in multiple experiences as a bishop that inform the following hypothetical:

> Imagine a young man sitting in the bishop's office. He says: "I am gay. I hope to find a partner and expect that with that partner I will have a sexual relationship. That partner will be a man. So I'm not going to follow the Church's rule. I already know that. All bets are off. None of the rules work, nothing that I learned in Primary and in the YM/YW program applies. But I've been dating a man and the relationship is too physical. It doesn't feel right. What should I do?"

Unfortunately, in this situation the bishop is likely to answer "don't, just don't." That is the sense in which the Church is not very helpful. "Don't, just don't" is a failure to minister to a member in need.

The problem is that the Church position on sex and marriage is simple and limited. Quoting from the Proclamation on the Family:

> We further declare that God has commanded that the sacred powers of procreation are to be employed only between man and woman, lawfully wedded as husband and wife.

If you ask questions beyond that simple statement about anything sexual or with sexual overtones, you are likely to get a "no" or "if you have to ask, don't."

There is so much more to talk about. I can imagine (in a different book) a chapter on masturbation, another on pornography, a third on R-rated movies. Chapters on clothing modesty. A whole book on differences of opinion and practice between spouses, including on oral sex. Another on what to teach your children. And several volumes on sexual practice, preference, and desire, outside the world of strict monogamous heterosexuality. There are a host of difficult marriage and non-marriage situations, and as many or more regarding reproductive rights and opportunities and technologies.

There are messages and talks and speculation and letters on all these subjects in the Church world. But for anything official or authoritative or with a Church imprimatur, you will be hard-pressed to find anything more interesting than mainstream conservative religious views, which usually amount to "no"—no to all of that. For the most part, The Church of Jesus Christ of Latter-day Saints fits comfortably within mainstream conservative churches and traditions. Cross-religion (Jewish, Muslim, LDS-Christian, Protestant-Christian, Catholic-Christian) qualitative studies show religion promoting marital fidelity and modesty in dress (more often for women, but also sometimes for men), and affecting discussions and practices around contraception and family planning. Within the general ambit of Augustine's influence on Christian thought, Mormonism is arguably even on the liberal end, actively celebrating sex between a lawfully wedded husband and wife.

Church scripture—the Book of Mormon in particular—includes passages that can be seen as hostile to women, including for example treating rape as taking away the virtue of the victim (see Moroni 9:9). However, despite dismay over these passages, they do not make Mormonism an exception or a standout within a Christian tradition that has treated women as temptress and an occasion of sin. That turned Jezebel, a Phoenician princess who married King Ahab of Samaria into a jezebel—an impudent, shameless, morally unrestrained woman. That forbade women from teaching and praying based on the writings of Paul. By contrast, Mormonism can be seen as improving on the general case by, for example, teaching of Eve as the hero of the Garden of Eden story.

Positioning the Church within mainstream conservative Christianity is not to say it's all good or you are supposed to like it or even accept it. Rather, it is to say this sort of teaching and these attitudes are not likely to change quickly if at all, and that reacting or objecting is more like taking on religion than distinctively taking on Mormonism.

As noted, the Church is not likely to change attitudes or teachings about sex. One reason is that there is little peer pressure to change. The Church is comfortably mainstream among conservative churches and traditions. Another reason to have low expectations in matters of sex is that the Church in practice leaves itself little room for nuance or tailored solutions.

- With respect to age, the Church treats six-year-old children and sixteen-year-old teenagers and twenty-six-year-old adults the same. There are doctrinal tools to differentiate. For example, we could easily imagine a soteriology—a doctrine of salvation—that distinguishes before baptism and before temple covenants. However, at least in matters of sex and sexuality the Church insists on worthiness before baptism and worthiness before entering the temple, which pushes the assignment of responsibility and obligation to earliest times and collapses the age categories.
- As a culture we are very weak at ordering and prioritizing. We have a vague sense that more recent statements should take priority over old statements, but the Church almost never clarifies that an old statement was wrong or has been superseded. We have a vague sense that a decades-old statement that has not been repeated or reinforced might be a dead letter. But we're never sure, and we are sufficiently practiced with proof-texting scripture that we also proof-text Church statements and talks by leaders of a different age. For analogous reasons, the list of sins never shrinks. We only add. Nobody ever says "that used to be considered wrong, but we know better now."
- The institution and the culture treat sexual matters as absolutes, as checklist items rather than matters of

development and learning. The checklist expectation is that you just obey, 100%, always. It's a world where the general expectation is that you never confess sexual sin because you never transgress. It's a world that often ignores and denies even the existence of sex and sexual feelings outside marriage. As one of my male friends exclaimed to me, "the best shorthand for what the Church taught me is no erection before marriage."

- By long practice the Church talks about ideals and strict binaries. In less-than-ideal situations or minority circumstances, we tend to bracket any discussion for consideration in the next life. In effect we exclude or ignore less common situations in the present. We have little practice with complexity.
- Finally, the Church's conservative and unchanging approach to matters of sex is locked in place by our demand for authoritative answers. As a group we are accustomed to bright lines and declarative sentences. We are not practiced at hearing suggestions as suggestions. We are not ready to hear alternatives as possibilities, even if they were offered in those terms. In effect we demand revolutionary change or no change. We make no allowance for gradual change or nuance.

To highlight the last point about not being ready for anything less than authority and command, I recall a young person talking with me (as a bishop) about masturbation. This was surprisingly common, even without invitation or direct questioning. On that occasion the narrative stopped after about 3 minutes, while I was still listening with questions in my mind. What does this mean for this individual? How is it a problem? What do they want to do about it? After a full minute of silence, the confession came: "I don't know what comes next. Before getting this far, every bishop before you has already started telling me what to do." That's a problem. As long as that is what we ask for and expect of the Church, we will not improve the dialogue.

POLYGAMY

The Church of Jesus Christ of Latter-day Saints, among all the branches of the Restoration, is defined by polygamy. The Church would like us to think it was all over before the end of the 19th century, but that's simply not true. We're now going to spend 1,000 words on polygamy because it can't be ignored by anybody choosing affiliation with the twenty-first century Church.

Plural marriages continued well into the 20th century. The Second Manifesto in 1904 recognized that marriages had continued post-Manifesto, and even after the Second Manifesto established marriages were not dissolved. Plural marriage principles continue to the present day, when a man sealed to one woman can be sealed to a second woman in a subsequent marriage, after his first wife dies, thus solemnizing a plural relationship with the promise that the man and both women will be together in the hereafter. There are publicly acclaimed plural relationships of this sort by prominent Church leaders. This is not hidden or secret.

Beyond practice and principle, the long shadow—what Carol Lynn Pearson calls the Ghost of Eternal Polygamy—lives on in the beliefs and expectations of many members. Polygamy has not been disavowed or rejected. The Principle has not ended; only the practice of two or more wives at the same time. Many Mormon men grow up understanding and believing that they may have more than one wife, possibly in this life (seriatim for the time being), and more confidently in the next. Many Mormon women grow up understanding and believing that their husband-to-be will expect multiple wives, that they are expected to accept and even celebrate the possibility, and that their eventual role is bearing and mothering children forever. These expectations and beliefs can be profoundly damaging to a first marriage marital relationship; divorce or death compounds the complexities. Former unhappy marriages might not be dissolved. Divorced and widowed women become unavailable or uninteresting to Mormon men by the fact that they are already sealed to their first husband and not available to be sealed to a next husband. Subsequent marriages create unanswerable questions for children and spouses about who belongs to whom, about what "family" means.

The rules and requirements of polygamy are confusing and unclear. It is reasonably clear that nineteenth century Mormons believed plural marriage was a commandment of God and that obedience would bring great blessings.[1] However, the practice can be understood as *permitted* when the prophet directs, or as *required* when the prophet directs, or as a *decision by the man and first wife* together, or as a *decision by the man alone* in practical effect (see "law of Sarah"). Some nineteenth century leaders taught that plural marriage—meaning at least two wives—was a requirement for exaltation in the Celestial Kingdom. However, the modern Church says there is no such requirement for exaltation, or that speculation about the matter is misplaced.[2] Many people read "the new and everlasting covenant" in Doctrine & Covenants Section 132 to mean plural marriage, but the modern Church teaches that the phrase encompasses "the fulness of the gospel of Jesus Christ, including all ordinances and covenants necessary for the salvation of mankind."[3] In these several ways, it is easy and even common for two people considering marriage to have different views about the importance, practice, and continuing relevance of plural marriage: as permitted

---

1. "Plural Marriage in the Church of Jesus Christ of Latter-day Saints," one of the Topics in the Gospel Library (The Church of Jesus Christ of Latter-day Saints).
2. *Doctrine and Covenants and Church History Seminary Teacher Manual*, Lesson 140 (The Church of Jesus Christ of Latter-day Saints).
3. Elder Marcus B. Nash, "The New and Everlasting Covenant," *Ensign*, December 2015.

or required, as a decision by a couple or by men only, as a continuing practice, or replaced by marriage and sealing in the temple. A man and woman in a modern monogamous heteronormative marriage can be of two minds about plural marriage in any number of ways, making for a built-in rift in the marriage.

Polygamy is an inescapable aspect of modern Mormon practice. When the Church says one man-one woman, there is an implied asterisk. When a husband and wife make their marriage vows, there are usually unstated assumptions about plural marriage. Women and men have to wonder whether the picture of eternity painted by the Church is something they even want, casting a shadow over the importance of family. For some, the ghost of polygamy colors their intimate relationships as they don't trust or feel walled off from their partner.[4] For others, the history of polygamy puts an asterisk on every sex-related teaching, as though we're trying to prove too much.[5]

To many observers it seems obvious that polygamy is a problem, one the Church should disavow. Such a move seems highly unlikely. In the present, plural marriage (seriatim for the time being) is recognized in our temples, and top church leaders have been sealed to a second woman after the death of their first wife. With respect to the past, the Church has shown a great reluctance to disagree with or disavow any past leaders. The common perception is that we never apologize, we were never wrong, we only move forward. Many

---

4. See "How Do I Love Thee?" a chapter in Carol Lynn Pearson's *The Ghost of Eternal Polygamy*. "When my husband told me . . . that he fully intended to be obedient to God in all things, including plural marriage, I felt a terrible rift being born between us. . . . Since then the rift is ever there. A part of me is walled off, wondering how I can be with a man who looks forward to this future, knowing it pains me terribly, but feeling my suffering isn't his problem or concern."

5. Is the law of chastity absolute? Or is it fluid, changing with the times and circumstances? Are the Church's strict rules based on eternal principles? Or are the strict rules a reaction to anti-Mormon sentiment over polygamy, including portrayals of Mormon men as libertines? Is present-day hyper-vigilance intended to show how much we've put that all behind us?

church leaders count polygamous families among their ancestors. To disavow polygamy might feel like declaring oneself illegitimate. Official Declaration 1 was carefully worded to not disavow polygamy but simply declare an "intention to submit to those laws [forbidding plural marriages]." We know plural marriages did not end but continued in Canada and Mexico where they were legal for a time, and that polygamy continued clandestinely in the United States (until as late as 1925 by some reports). Despite a century or more of reinterpretation, it would be challenging to reconcile scripture, including Doctrine & Covenants 132, in the context of a total dismissal of polygamy.

For all these reasons, I think it highly unlikely the principle of polygamy will be disavowed in my lifetime. Furthermore, I don't see a path to incremental change. I think any significant change would be revolutionary or revelatory, which is not a strong foundation for hope or expectation of change. The natural conclusion is that polygamy is something you have to deal with if you intend to stay in contact with the Church. It's not going away.

BUILD YOUR OWN

If the Church's teachings in matters of sex and sexuality are inadequate, and the Church is not likely to change or move forward during our adult lifetimes, the only way forward for people living on the inside of the edge is to determine our own sexual ethics.

Since this is not a chastity lesson, the exercise here is not to propose a set of rules but to think about the parameters and considerations to do it yourself. Here are some things to think about:

PERSONAL AUTONOMY There is something important in the idea of individuals, every individual, controlling and being responsible for their body and their mind and their feelings. How this works in edge cases and extraordinary circumstances might be the subject of a shelf of books. But it seems right to give serious weight to a principle of personal autonomy.

Personal autonomy is important in both directions. I am responsible for my body and mind and feelings. For me to deny my sexuality, or to think sex is all there is of me, either way, would deny my self-hood and make it impossible for me to be autonomous. I am not responsible for your body and mind and feelings, but to act like I am, or to deny that you have them and to deny your personal autonomy in exercising and experiencing them, would be to treat you as an object rather than a person.

CONSENT There could be a lengthy discussion about "no means no" versus "yes means yes." There might be nuanced (or obvious and highly objectionable) questions about impaired judgment, and about priming and grooming and victim blaming. But the base case of non-consensual sex being negative, bad, sinful, criminal, is not controversial.

AGE Notwithstanding the Church's reluctance to define or acknowledge age differences, it is natural to think that what's appropriate at 6 is different from what's appropriate at 16, and different again at age 26. If we're doing the work for ourselves, we are likely to take on age as a relevant and distinguishing factor.

MARRIAGE Weddings matter. Long-term commitment matters. Marriage is a deep kind of consent, not to sex any time any place (we are still autonomous actors) but to the general idea of an ongoing intimate sexual relationship. Covenants that induce and encourage reliance are powerful. Whether as an absolute or a preference, whether the Mormon version of "for time and all eternity" or the more secular "for better for worse, for richer for poorer, in sickness and in health," marriage matters.

CHILDREN Jesus said, "Let the little children come to me, and do not stop them, for it is to such as these that the kingdom of heaven belongs" (Matthew 19:14 NRSV). Bringing a child into the world; adopting a child; taking responsibility for a child. Abortion. Physical, sexual, emotional abuse. This is all serious business. Nobody should be casual about children. Any system of sexual ethics must take children into account. Furthermore, I would make the case that *everybody* involved must take children into account. Sometimes we see attempts to rationalize that "it's women's work and women's responsibility" or (at another extreme) "without men there would be no children, so men bear all the responsibility and obligation." These strike me as selfish and self-serving, and usually inconsistent and illogical. There may be various ways to allocate or share responsibility, in principle and in practice, but there is nothing ethical about totally excluding someone from awareness of and accountability for children.

CONNECTION A strict Augustinian will talk about sex only for purposes of procreation. Seventeen centuries later, many of us moderns also think about sexual intimacy as strengthening emotional connection and commitment, as developing and maintaining love and belonging. There is an important value to human beings in connection and relationship, in knowing and being known. This cuts both ways. It means there are benefits to physical sexual intimacy in addition to procreation. It also means that there can be non-physical connections formed—by intimate conversation for example—that might correctly be considered in the context of "sexual" activity.

CONSEQUENCES For many of us, talking about sex sooner or later turns to concerns about appetite and desire and virtue and vice and impulse control. A mature approach may strive for balance, or may focus on mid-term and long-term consequences, but only the most libertine will start with an anything-goes ethic. And those libertines who also pay attention to personal autonomy and consent and commitment and age and children and relationship will end up taking account of consequences. One way or another, almost everybody who is serious about this exercise ends up settling into a consequential set of principles.

It shouldn't be shocking that a man or woman in an opposite-sex committed marriage might end up with a sexual ethic for themselves that looks just like the Church's teachings. This exercise never was about proving the Church wrong.

On the other hand, it would be somewhat surprising if a well-developed sexual ethic under these several principles ended up with a flat "no" in all the other cases and situations and circumstances of life.

COMMUNICATION

Pick up any marital advice manual or sexual ethics guide and you will read about communication. Good communication with a partner is obvious and regular good advice. We can also tie back to the several principles above. Respecting personal autonomy cannot be done without communicating. Making assumptions and demands is to treat the other as an object. Communicating is to treat the other as a person. Consent requires communication. All sorts of failures occur when people make assumptions, or project on the other that what I want is what you want. Pregnancy and birth control and miscarriage and adoption and education and religious affiliation and more are shared obligations, opportunities, decisions. Connections depend on communication, verbal and non-verbal. Sharing means talking.

This section could be finished in the one paragraph above, except for polygamy. Because this is a book for Mormons, we do have to reference this peculiar communication issue, almost unique to The Church of Jesus Christ of Latter-day Saints. Polygamy is in the bones and sinews of the Church. It's not going away any time soon. And it has the potential of damaging relationships from inception.

If we can't change the history, and can't change the present reality of polygamy in the Church, we are left with making choices for ourselves in our own lives. We can reject outright the principle and the practice of polygamy. We can think about polygamy as a possible principle for others, but not for me. We can find a nuanced position that rejects polygamy in life but is open to the possibility in the hereafter.

I'm not about to dictate any particular approach to polygamy, i.e., that my way is the only way or that you are misguided or stupid if you think differently than I do. I am reasonably confident it isn't necessary to agree with the Church about polygamy, past or present. I'm not even sure it is necessary for spouses to agree with each other. This can be complicated, and good people make all sorts of choices and compromises (and good people change over time). However, when it comes to marriage or long-term commitment or children, it seems like a good idea to talk about polygamy with your spouse/fiancé/significant other. Doubts and misunderstandings, whether real or imagined, can be corrosive. Communication is an important corrective.

SUMMING UP

For purposes of survival on the inside of the edge:

- Settle into the idea that, on matters of sex and sexuality, the Church is not all wrong but also not all right. One important corollary is that you are probably not going to find yourself perfectly in sync with the Church or always approved or validated.
- Resign yourself to the idea that the Church will not change on a time scale that matters for your life and may never speak to matters that are of intense interest to you.

- Work out your own system of sexual ethics. Don't be surprised if it parallels the Church in some respects and differs in others.
- Communicate with your spouse or sexual partner. Don't shy away from the difficult subjects, including that within the Mormon context the shadow of polygamy is forever.

CONTROL

Sooner or later the Church will try to control you.

That's slightly hyperbolic. Not everybody, not always. It's just that this is a flash point for me personally, so I feel the pain, I make plans as though it's going to happen around every corner, and I have structured my relationship with the institutional church to minimize the possibility of control.

From the Church side of things, we are likely to hear "no, we don't do that" and "not us!" I think that's because the word control conjures images of prison guards or dictators and almost nobody wants to think of themselves that way. But think of control in terms of paternalism, like a father trying to manage a rebellious teenager, and the shoe fits. It's the parent-child relationship all over again.

Control might be a pointed and shaming talk from the pulpit. It might be directly telling you what to do. Attempts at control might come with threats. A precipitous release from a calling. Refusing or pulling or just threatening your temple recommend. Informal church discipline—a restriction on receiving an ordinance or exercising priesthood, or a restriction on giving a talk, a lesson, or a public prayer. A "stop or I'll hold a Membership Council." A scheduled Membership Council.

Maybe it will never happen, but you know it could. Something you write or say comes to the bishop's attention. Somebody complains about you. Your neighbor reads a Facebook post that expresses doubt or criticism, and turns you in. Living on the inside of the edge means living in anticipation of a summons. The bishop or stake president calls you to his office for a problem about which he is going to try to exercise control.

There are many reasons to be summoned to the office, some of them positive, some of them innocent. However, knowing how the Church works in general, when you don't know the reason it is common to feel afraid. Fight or flight is a normal reaction. Pay attention to how you feel. Assuming you don't take the flight option, it might turn out to be useful to play it back to the bishop. Sometimes bishops don't think about how they caused a fight-or-flight reaction, and that such feelings can happen even without the slightest sense of guilt.

One special reason for a flight response is that many of the control issues affecting sincere folk on the inside of the edge are peculiar to being an active member of The Church of Jesus Christ of Latter-day Saints. They are about making you a good member with respect to matters that would never come up for criticism in the outside world. If you're sleeping with your best friend's husband or wife, there may well be serious trouble but it's a different kind of trouble and could come up in any religious or not-religious community. The issues most likely to bring a reader of this book to this chapter are heterodox or apostate statements or actions—something that would warrant a shrug at best outside the Church. It could be big and dramatic, but it could also be as small as a mildly critical comment in Sunday School, or an unidentified Starbucks cup in your hand. Something that would draw no notice in the secular world but draws criticism inside the Church.

From the loyal committed church member's and church leader's point of view, telling you what to do might be just asking you to do what you should have been doing all along. It's even possible that they are right. However much I recognize they might be right, however much I believe they believe they have good intentions, I want to run (always) or fight (sometimes). I don't like being told what to do even when they are right.

The fight-or-flight reaction is sure to make you think about leaving for good. In fact, it might be the proverbial last straw. Leaving is always on the table. However, this book is about survival, and survival in these cases is about sticking it out at least one more time.

If you do have a talk with the bishop, chances are it won't go well. This is not a part of the church experience where there is a neat win-win solution; much more likely this is a coping and managing and minimize-the-cost kind of church experience.

So what about coping? Minimizing the cost? I propose here a three-part strategy:

- Differentiate
- Shrink the cost
- Take the offensive

DIFFERENTIATE

There's a whole chapter on differentiation. But it gets further emphasis here because control situations are where the test comes, where the rubber meets the road. The bishop or stake president is a man with authority accustomed to being listened to and obeyed. He has been the child in the patriarchal structure for years, and now he's the parent, the father figure. He assumes power. He assumes you will come when called. He assumes you will take direction. He assumes you will be pleased and satisfied by praise and will be respectful even if hurt by criticism. On your side, if you have any significant experience as a church member, you will be drawn toward the conventional role of subject or child or penitent. You are likely to accord great respect to the office even if not always the person. You are likely to answer the call and take direction.

Regarding the bishop-as-father-figure, I don't know any exceptions. I've known self-aware bishops and stake presidents who know they're doing it, who know they are exercising authority and acting as a parent. But I don't know any (including myself, back in the day) who manage to set aside the position. Even with the best of intentions, it is almost impossible to avoid the mantle of authority because the examples of our lives make it so, because the leaders above the leaders tell us so, and because we members in the pews constantly remind our leaders that's what we want. It is what we all expect, and bishops and stake presidents step up to our expectations.

There are bullies in leadership positions. They insist on having their way and do not tolerate backtalk. If you have to deal with a bully, my best advice is buckle up and ride it out. I have been involved in individual cases where something could be done at a church administrative level. But most stake presidents are strongly inclined to support and sustain the bishops they called, even if they might have private regrets on occasion, and most men who call stake presidents will support them in their calling for their full term. However, in my experience, true bullies are unusual and a majority of bishops and stake presidents don't want confrontation and don't like being a disciplinarian. Their problem is less about being a bully, and more about making something happen. Most bishops and stake presidents believe in gentleness, kindness, and love unfeigned (referring to D&C 121:41 and 42) but are less attuned to the virtues of patience and long suffering. They feel called and obliged to be men of action even if it's not their natural inclination.

In short, if you ask for or allow a parent-child conversation, that's what you get. And the only way a parent-child conversation goes well is for you to agree, to do what you're told. Bless you if that works for you, but for me it's a recipe for a short path to the exit. The alternative, where there is still hope remaining, is to differentiate into an adult-to-adult conversation. That conversation might end up confrontational instead of pleasant or cheerful. Personally, I'd like to avoid confrontation but when there's no other choice I would choose confrontation over surrender.

Differentiation does not dictate the outcome. It doesn't even dictate whether you take a meeting. You may well take the call and agree to meet and in the end at least appear to take direction. However, if you do agree to meet, the survival goal is to take the meeting not as a penitent asking what did I do wrong and what am I supposed to do now, but as a knowing conscious decision to remain engaged, including to take a meeting with the bishop when he calls. Not just because he called, but because you decide that taking the meeting is the right thing for you at this stage in your journey. Alternatively, if you decide to take a different road—to decline the meeting or leave the church or take the meeting but agree to disagree—differentiation means you take that road knowingly, as a conscious decision, and not as an autonomic fight-or-flight reaction.

I would be remiss if I didn't acknowledge that gender comes into play here. The bishop or stake president is always a man and always steeped in patriarchy. If you present or interact as a man, you have a challenging conversation ahead. If you present or interact as a woman, you can easily think the challenge is insurmountable. These are not absolutes—I've known some bishops and some stake presidents who are consciously even-handed with men and women, and I've known a few women who are already primed for take-no-prisoners battle. But stereotypes are types for a reason, and men wielding authority is a constant in the Church. A differentiated person seeking an adult-to-adult conversation will take these types into account. A man might take a meeting that a woman refuses. A woman might insist on someone else being present, on never taking a meeting alone. These are rational choices. We can wish the world were different, but this chapter and this book are about the real world, the unreformed church, the way it is.

SHRINK THE COST

Perhaps the most common form of control is the implied "or else." It's a play on unnamed fear—the power of a father telling a child to behave. It is seldom necessary to spell out the punishment; just knowing a possibility exists is enough. Nor is it necessary for the church leader to understand or intend to engender fear. The bishop can be fully conversant with and intent on persuasion, long-suffering, gentleness and meekness, and still exercise control through fear. Because the fear is in us: we make it, we live with it.

One way to deal with fear is to face it, name it, and shrink it. Most of the actual "or else" is a form of withholding—ultimately withholding or withdrawing membership, but with many intermediate steps. At a first step, the bishop can withhold approval. We want to be liked and approved of and welcomed. The more we buy into the parent-child model of church and member, the more we want and need approval. Face it. Name it. Be adult about it. Sooner or later, most people living on the inside of the edge have to give up on approval and allow that acceptance and, occasionally, respect, may be as good as it gets.

Another kind of withholding is to withdraw a calling or a temple recommend. You could argue that all church service is voluntary and to not be asked or to be released early would be a boon. However, a church calling can be an important part of identity, a source of pride, a marker of community, a reason for continued activity. Threatening a release "if you don't shape up" can be a meaningful threat. However, if you face it, name it, count the costs and benefits, it is possible to take on some of that outsider point of view. Maybe a break would be a good thing, after all.

Withdrawing or denying a temple recommend is another complicated threat. It's the subject of a separate chapter, *The Temple Recommend*. There's no doubt that controlling the temple recommend is meaningful within the institutional church and the cultural church. At the same time, we make it so. We give the recommend its power. And we can take it back. It's not easy and it's not perfect, but I am part of a world of active church members who do not have a temple recommend, who refuse the interview, who have a recommend but refuse to go, who sit outside the temple while their children are married. It can be done. It's not light and easy, but it can be done. Face it. Name it. Count the cost.

Informal church discipline can include several kinds of restrictions, including a restriction on taking the sacrament or giving a prayer. These may be important markers in a repentance process, but they can also be threatened as a form of punishment and control, including by freighting them with an "until you change." Let's acknowledge that even for a person who avoids public prayer whenever possible, being told no can hurt, and having to decline publicly hurts more. However, there is a rational argument that withholding the sacrament or an opportunity to speak or pray hurts the church and the community more than the individual at the same time that it acts as an invitation to leave. Here's where differentiation and minimizing the cost and taking the offensive merge. Where an adult in the room might say "Really?! And what do you expect to accomplish? Who are you hurting? Do you hear yourself?!"

Finally, there is the category of formal church discipline, now called Membership Councils. This topic has its own chapter in the Working with the Institution section; I note here simply that there are ways to minimize the cost of excommunication. It's incredibly difficult and I weep for friends who continue to be constructively engaged with the church after feeling forced to resign or being formally rejected and denied the sacraments. But through the tears I see examples. It can be done.

TAKE THE OFFENSIVE

Take the offensive is different than being offensive. This is not about angering or antagonizing the bishop. It's more about taking charge, or at least sharing in control of the situation. For a personal example, I walk a very fine line with respect to being controlled (for therapists in the audience, yes, let's talk about my mother). I feel well differentiated after years of real on-the-couch therapy, and I am not actively looking for an exit. But I have a hair trigger about matters of control. As a result, my "taking the offensive" manifests as avoiding meetings, refusing worthiness interviews, and when I do have a conversation, warning off commands or direction in advance with some version of "if you try, I will walk—the conversation will end." My taking the offensive is to spend my energy protecting myself. Others might be more creative and more constructive, but I opt for self-preservation first.

You cannot do much about the man you're meeting with, but you can prepare yourself for battle. In the words of 1 Peter 1:13, you can "gird up the loins of your mind" (KJV) or "prepare your minds for action" (Wayment). You can reinforce your differentiation work. The church is not you, you are not the church. You have a self-determined life that does not depend on the approval of any church leader. You can preview the worst case and minimize the costs. After all, you're on the edge already. You can step off if necessary. Permanently, or for a sabbatical period, or for the remainder of this leader's tenure. You can even build up a little anger. Somebody ratted on you and that's not right, not the way a community should work.

Then you enter the room in control of your own actions and reactions. At a minimum, you can act as an adult in the room, recognizing the parent-child dynamic and refusing to play. That shift alone virtually guarantees a better outcome for your own physical, emotional, and spiritual wellbeing, no matter how contentious the meeting and without regard to immediate stated outcome. At a more assertive level, you can say no to a meeting. You can make clear your position. You can threaten to walk out. You can walk out. You can resign. You can make noise about what happened. You can go to the press.

Obviously, not all tactics apply to all situations. The point is not to go to war, but rather to recognize that the tools are in your hands. You are not a passive observer in the drama playing out.

Finally, once you can protect yourself, if you have personal fortitude and energy remaining to work the system, go a step further and call on your bishop or stake president to be his best self. Give him room and opportunity to be a pastor, to love and support, to be helpful. Sometimes that looks like a second chance, or a pre-meeting, or a "think about it and let's talk again." Sometimes that looks like dropping a stereotype. People change. Some people do rise to an occasion, some people live up to high expectations. If you've got the personal wherewithal, set high expectations and ask for them to be met.

ANGER

If you are angry about the Church or the Mormon culture or the church people, there's no sense denying it. Denial is generally a bad idea anyway. But talk to your therapist. This chapter is not about denial or cure or treatment.

There are lots of reasons to be angry in connection with the Church. Individual leaders abusing you or hurting your friends. Policies that damage loved ones. Misunderstandings. Offenses intended and unintended. Lies and deception. Feeling pressed to take a position or teach a doctrine that doesn't feel true. Discovering that you have been gaslighted. Watching poor decisions drive people away. Occasionally you can do something about the reasons, the root causes. If you can do something, go for it. Make a difference. More often there is no fix, no repair. And you're still angry.

I am going to argue here for Stoicism, a Stoic approach to anger management. In the very simplest terms, this means do not act out of anger. Period. Full stop. Ever. This is not a philosophical argument (although it could be) or a scripturally based truth argument or a modern psychology textbook argument. This is simple pragmatism.

TEMPORARY INSANITY

Anger is not a minor or side issue. It is one of the seven deadly sins. The New Testament Jesus said "anyone who is angry with a sibling will be in danger of the judgment, and whoever says to his brother or sister, 'Raqa,' will be brought to the council, and whoever says 'fool' will be sent to a fiery hell." Matthew 5:22 (Wayment). As a child I read these New Testament lines and worried that the feeling alone would condemn me. I took on the task of not feeling anger. It didn't work. As an adult it is reasonably clear that anger is not condemned because of the experience or feeling—something that happens to everybody I know. Rather, anger is condemned because of actions that stem from it. Actions bring judgment—the fiery hell of Matthew 5:22. From anger there can explode cursing, hate, slander, threats, even assaults and murder. Anger is a cousin to hostility, intolerance, revenge, and wrath. A distinctively Mormon example is condemnation of "evil speaking of the Lord's anointed" which (in my opinion) is best thought of as anger turned to cursing, slander, and threats.

I believe anger can be and often is (also) damaging to the individual. So much so that it is tempting to discuss the problem and potential damage here. But that would be a different book and a different set of skills and knowledge than I have. Here I will just reiterate "talk to your therapist." Another path would be to make a modest prescription regarding anger. To speak about moderation and tolerance and counting to ten. To argue against letting anger turn into cursing, hate, slander, and threats. But that would also miss the point.

Instead, my position is that we should not act out of anger at all, in any way. My argument is essentially Seneca's argument, stemming from his observation that anger is a form of temporary insanity. Lucius Annaeus Seneca (Seneca the Younger) wrote one of the earliest treatises on the subject, *On Anger*, in the first century A.D. Seneca observed that, whether justified or not, anger is abrupt, intense, and disproportionate, and that abruptness, that intensity, that disproportionate irrational extreme, marks anger as a form of insanity. Whether or not you buy Seneca's argument, the key observation for us in the twenty-first century is that church members and church leaders seem to believe it. Members and leaders generally do not have the skills or knowledge to deal with anger. When they see anger, they react as though it is temporary insanity. They simply do not know what to do with anger, so they make it your failing, your error, your insanity. And they write you off.

STOICISM

Distinguishing between feelings and actions is a necessary predicate to pitching Stoicism as a response to anger. In casual conversation in the twentieth and twenty-first centuries, Stoicism may be described as repressing feelings or enduring patiently or being immune or inured to feeling. Simon and Garfunkel's Rock, in other words[1]:

> I touch no one and no one touches me
> I am a rock I am an island
> And a rock feels no pain
> And an island never cries

However, this characterization dates to the sixteenth century and is not fair to Stoicism as a philosophy or ethic of life. Instead, Stoicism is better captured by the ideas of fortitude and self-control and reasoned behavior over destructive emotions.

Stoicism is not a prescription that dulls against the feeling of anger; Stoicism does not direct us toward Simon and Garfunkel's rock that feels no pain. Stoicism acknowledges that anger happens, argues that anger is destructive, and dictates not acting out of anger. The Stoic argument is that anger is always negative, always destructive, always a temporary insanity, and never a good basis for action.

---

1. Simon and Garfunkel, "I Am a Rock" (1965).

In the Stoic understanding there is no such thing as moderate anger or righteous anger or justified anger that can be taken as a legitimate basis for action. The Stoic argument is for a reasoned, controlled, ethical person to eschew anger and look instead for positive or constructive emotions and principles to motivate action.

To not act out of anger does not mean no action at all. Rather, the Stoic ideal would be to act or not act in a reasoned way in response to positive emotions. A sense of indignation at witnessing injustice is a positive emotion. A desire to make the world a better place is a positive emotion. Jesus cleared out the temple with good reason, as explained in all four canonical gospels. The temple example is not one of a weak shrinking violet, but neither is it one of red-faced rage. Clearing out the temple is presented as a reasoned way to improve the situation, not as action out of anger.

Although taking forceful action can be an appropriate response, sometimes reason leads to non-action, and that can be the most difficult response of all. We might call it resignation or surrender or serenity, but by any name it amounts to recognizing things we cannot change and sitting with them, not doing anything. Anger makes us want to act, to do something, anything. But putting aside anger and exercising reason and control may mean to let it be. Not lash out. Not fight. Not run. Just sit. Accept what cannot be changed. As in the serenity prayer, "Father, give us courage to change what must be altered, serenity to accept what cannot be helped, and the insight to know the one from the other." In this context it can be useful to remember that along with the autonomic fight-or-flight response to danger, we also have a steady-the-ark sort of righting reflex. In ordinary circumstances the righting reflex tries to correct the orientation of the body, but in stressed situations the righting reflex tries to correct the orientation of whatever is askew around us. Fight or flight or righting can be reactions to danger and can be the immediate impulse when we feel anger. Stoicism is to put it all on hold while reason prevails. Don't fight. Don't run. Don't right.

Stoicism isn't easy and doesn't come naturally for most of us. But Stoicism is the way to go for people who want to live on the inside of the edge. The alternative—angry outbursts, lashing out, threats and challenges—will be ignored or isolated or expelled.

APPLICATION TO THE CHURCH

Although anger is a matter of general concern, and Stoicism arguably a form of all-purpose wisdom, there are a few characteristic or more-common-than-usual issues in connection with the Church. For survival purposes it can be useful to map these characteristics and prepare for them in advance.

CHOOSE TO BE OFFENDED?

Church leaders tend to emphasize offense or being offended as a cause for anger. It seems that this is part of a logic that goes like this:

> **STATEMENT 1** Anger is an understandable response to someone being vindictive or malicious or hateful, or attacking, hurting, or abusing you.

> **STATEMENT 2** Attacks of that sort can happen, but they are rare. The Church as an institution and church leaders in general are not out to get you, are not vindictive or malicious.

> **CONCLUSION** Therefore (i.e. because harm is not intended) if you feel anger related to the Church or church leaders it is most likely all in your head. It is most likely you choosing to be offended.

There are two obvious problems with this logic chain. One is the factual assertion in Statement 2, the "in general not out to get you." This may be factually incorrect. More importantly, there is a systematic mismatch between the perceptions of leaders and the perceptions of members. The second is that Statement 1 does not describe the universe of anger-causing situations. Statement 1 implies attacks are the only times anger is an understandable response, and that is simply not correct.

With respect to leaders out to get you, there are many more reports of vindictive church leaders than leaders who admit to being vindictive. I am not aware of statistics or even studies. "Rare" or "generally not" are more like assertions of faith than statements of fact. An even more certain problem is that there is no standard definition of a leader on the attack, and there can be a mismatch between leader and member. To a leader it may seem perfectly reasonable to demand change or request compliance. We can easily imagine the thinking: "It's for their own good." "It's God's will." "They knew the rules." To the individual any demand or request or suggestion, any rejection instead of affirmation, anything short of unconditional love and support, can feel like an attack.

With respect to reasons for anger, someone out to get you would qualify. However, the stories about offense and being offended—about being angered—include many more circumstances and events than a straightforward attack. We get angry about harm to our friends. We get angry about mismanagement and avoidable problems and failure to pay attention. We get angry about gaslighting and being lied to and finding out that our trust was misplaced—that what was promised has not been and never will be delivered. We get angry about unfairness and hypocrisy and exaggerations that cause harm. The list goes on and on. A lot of it is real. Very little of it has to do with direct attacks by vindictive leaders.

EXPECTATIONS

The Church's description of itself, including phrases like "one and only" and "Kingdom of God on earth" can seduce us into unrealistically high expectations for the institution. If we are led by a prophet of God, why were we left in the path of the hurricane? How is it that programs don't work? Was polygamy—which we had to stop but not completely—right or wrong? Why am I broke when I pay my tithing religiously? Who thought *that* man would make a good bishop?

A rational, reflective view of most institutions around us would accept that this is the work of men (and sometimes a few women) who have feet of clay. Who have mixed motives, unsteady energy, and cloudy vision. It is too easy and too common to expect more of the Church, and to expect it yesterday.

The Church could do more to help us see and build expectations around a human-led trial-and-error bumbling-forward institution. But failure to do more is also one of the very human failings of the institution. The practical result is that we individual members have to do most of the work, learning to accept the failings even while the Church denies them.

PASSIVE AGGRESSION

There are several possible responses to situations that make us angry. A common typology mentions passive aggression, open aggression, and assertiveness. The kinds of advice often dispensed by church leaders sound a lot like passive aggression. The kinds of advice often dispensed by outside experts, and the Stoics, sound a lot like assertiveness. The difference is worth thinking about.

Assertiveness begins with self-confidence, to move forward into talking and listening and looking for help. Assertiveness gives credit for good intentions and apologies, makes space for patience and forgiveness, communicates feelings, and measures other people's feelings. Assertiveness works in relational and relationship terms, seeking an outcome that furthers community. Assertiveness sounds like an adult-to-adult approach to solving problems and encouraging constructive change. It fits the model of living on the inside of the edge.

However, church leaders often try to suggest a passive aggressive approach. In passive aggressive mode you don't admit you are angry and don't confront anybody. You pretend everything is fine. In a negative sense you become silent, back into a shell, sulk, procrastinate. In a more positive-sounding sense, you buck up, put on a smile, make the best of your lot, look outward to make life better for others. Church leaders are not likely to call it passive aggressive, but "buck up" and "put on a smile" and "lose your life in service" are commonplace.

If you differentiate and practice Stoicism and make your own decisions about how to respond in an angering position, you are likely to be assertive. Assertive is not church style. Assertiveness is countercultural. Assertiveness is not likely to make everybody happy.

SUMMING UP

The preceding *Application to the Church* discussion may leave you thinking that dealing with anger with the Church while on the inside is hopeless, or at least more work than you are willing to take on. Remaining on the inside while angry is a strong choice to take.

On the other hand, acting out of anger is likely to damage relationships, to hurt yourself, and to break your relationship with the Church. Acting out of anger is not the path of survival. The Stoic route is your better option. Feel the anger, but take a reasoned and constructive approach to action, including to allow for periods of surrender and non-action. Be assertive but pick your spots. Manage your urges to make loud noises and break things and turn that energy toward making a difference.

WORKING WITH THE INSTITUTION

MAGICAL THINKING

PROLOGUE

This chapter is not really about prayer or miracles. This chapter is about certainty and the danger of certainty broken. However, there is a risk that 150 words from now you will start thinking I'm dissing on priesthood, prayer, and miracles and worry that you're reading the words of a faithless ne'er-do-well. That may be a fair description in some people's minds, but let me address the concerns by providing a disclaimer, a testimony as it were. I'm a fan of prayer. I pray every day. I have issues with the priesthood, but they are not the dismissive kind of issues. Rather, my concerns are about power and influence maintained by virtue of the priesthood, and about too much exclusivity. I believe in miracles, and the course of my life has been altered by powerful spiritual experiences. If we explored in detail, it is quite likely that my prayers are not like your prayers and the miracles I recognize are not all the same ones you recognize. We are individuals, after all. But my life of the spirit is real and affirming and rich. I hope yours is too.

STAR WARS

For many Mormon boys born after about 1965 the Star Wars Force is the Priesthood in action. If we just listen to Yoda and practice diligently, we can exercise the Force. We can heal the sick, see the future, swing the light saber, harness fire, levitate objects.

Maybe some of that list is metaphorical, but the idea that the Force really is the Priesthood runs through a generation or two of Mormon boys introduced to the Aaronic Priesthood in their eleventh year.

"Priesthood equals the Force" is a form of magical thinking. Magical thinking could also be termed mechanical thinking or mechanistic, like a lever you push to get a predictable outcome. Some levers are obvious, some are hidden. The idea is not that you see all the gears and levers working, but that you have confidence the gears will turn, the levers will move, the results will be achieved. Certainty, confidence, predictability, one-to-one correlation, these are all characteristics of magical thinking.

Turning back to the magic reference, think about a stage magician. If they are good at their job, two seemingly contradictory facts are true at the same time. Their performance is mysterious, surprising, exciting, even awe inspiring. And their performance is predictable, mechanical. Push the hidden lever here and a rabbit pops out there. You can't see or understand how it happens, but after a show or two you are confident the rabbit will pop out every time. It's the "every time" that makes this an apt example. Magical thinking is an outgrowth of a desire for certainty, for the sure thing, for control of our circumstances and destination. We want to grab hold of the lever that will make the blessings pop out.

For a religious example, perhaps the first to mind is the answer-to-prayer prescription of D&C 9. If you have a question, study it, ask if it is right, and if it is right your "bosom shall burn" but if it is not right you will have a stupor of thought that will cause you to forget.

This sounds mechanical. As a proof text there is no limit, no qualification. It doesn't seem to matter whether the question is important. It doesn't seem to matter how the question is phrased (almost every question can be put in a positive or a negative form). It doesn't seem to matter what your priors are—i.e., what you already know, what the probability is, for and against, or what you want the answer to be. It sounds easy to implement, predictable, confident, certain. That certainty is magical thinking.

The problem—the crux of this chapter—is that real life intervenes. Sometimes the feelings are ambiguous. Sometimes it "worked" yesterday but there's nothing today. Sometimes an answer doesn't come, even about the most important decisions. Sometimes all logic and prior learning says turn right, and the question, "Should I turn right?" results in a warm happy feeling, but the question "Should I turn left?" *also* results in an indistinguishably warm happy feeling. If we have bought into the magical thinking, if we were sure, confident, relying on and even dependent on predictable answers, when they don't come on command it can feel like the floor has dropped away. Dashed confidence is painful. Losing control can be devastating; maybe doubly so when it entails recognizing that the sense of control was an illusion all along.

My first adult understanding of the dilemma was in consultation with 20-something dating couples who enquired about getting married. A dozen times I had a couple come to me with some variation on "his prayer says yes, but mine says no. How can that happen?! What do we do??" (Mormon culture is still patriarchal enough that the man would often argue his answer controls. Mormon women of that age, in my experience, were not standing for it. I declined to arbitrate, but those are stories for another time.) The difference—his answer is different from my answer—was difficult with respect to the marriage proposal itself. But it was also challenging for a sense of self, confidence in the way the world works, and more than twenty years of a belief system about God, about prayer, about religion.

Sometimes the reactions were as bad as "if I can't count on answers, what good is the Church or religion anyway?"

EVERYDAY MORMONISM

There are lots of examples of magical thinking in Mormon practice and experience. Have you ever had any of these thoughts?

- I know better than to take D&C 9:8 strictly literally. If I pray about something important, I can hope for an answer, but it might not come every time. But if I *fast* and pray then an answer is sure to come.
- If I call my home teacher for a blessing, I'll probably feel comforted and will hopefully heal in full and faster than otherwise. But if I get a blessing from an *apostle* I will walk again.
- If I give to charity, I will feel good about myself and make the world a better place. If instead I give a full honest tithe to the Church, the windows of heaven will open, and I will get back more money than the 10% I gave.
- Sitting in a temple recommend interview, I'm sure the bishop can read my mind or at least my intentions. If I lie, he'll know it. On the other hand, if he signs the recommend it's because it is supposed to happen, notwithstanding anything I say or believe.
- An angel, or my grandfather, or Satan, or the bishop, is watching me and knows every move, every sin, every good deed.
- We are holding family prayer, reading scriptures together, meeting in Family Home Evening, attending church regularly with the whole family, I'm staying faithful to my spouse, and keeping the checklist com-

mandments, all in full confidence that as a result my children will be with me forever.
- The Atonement will wash away all my sins. If I only confess and don't repeat, they're gone.

Taking the 500-foot view, this is all about a transactional gospel. If I do good, if I follow the rules, I will be blessed. If I sin, I will be punished. The "will be" in those sentences is the linkage, the mechanic, the magic. It's the sure thing we all want.

One common characteristic is if-then certainty. That's the danger to watch for. There is plenty of room in our conversations and our daily walk for faith, for miracles, for inspiration. We can be open to answers to prayer. Many of us have numinous experiences which register as God, or other kinds of elevated experience. We can talk about miracles. We can live in the midst of the spiritual. Alternatively, we can be skeptical or agnostic. Not confident any of this really happens. All sorts of experience and belief are possible without challenging our presence in the Church or interest in religion generally. But certainty—or more precisely certainty dashed—is a problem. Certainty dashed can be destructive.

Another common characteristic is that most of us have been there. Most of us say "yes" to one or more, or even all, of the examples above. A lot of what we learn in Primary is magical thinking. A lot of what we learn watching Star Wars is magical thinking. A lot of what we wish for, how we want the universe to work, is magical thinking.

WHAT TO DO ABOUT IT

The problem is that most of us have some form of magical thinking, and, with the rare exception of unicorns who float through life always at the top of the charts, real life fails us. The prayer isn't answered. Or the answer we thought was right is proven wrong. We give a blessing, and someone dies. We seek counsel from the highest and wisest authority we know, and it disappoints. We do something sinful or criminal or forbidden, and we get away with it. For all our best efforts, children leave. The prophet says something we just can't accept. We see someone in the temple we know is going to hell.

Life is not certain, and it beats us down. When the magic breaks, it is disturbingly common to give it all up. To leave the Church and even to leave religion and God altogether. People really want the sure thing and when they lose that thread, they hurt and they leave.

There seem to be only a few options for dealing with dashed certainty. One option, of course, is to leave. That's on the table. To leave and give up on the project of religion altogether. Or to leave in search of a new and different certainty somewhere else. Another option—advocated in this book—is to grow up, to move into an adult version of life where there are no sure things, where we are not in control and nobody else is either, where every step is risky, where the path is rocky. Where decision making is a wisdom practice that takes time and study and effort and ends in measured risk taking.

The rocky path never turns into a sure thing, but it can be joyful, exhilarating, even life affirming. This is how I take the verse in Philippians 2:12, to work out my salvation with fear and trembling.

ESPECIALLY-FOR-MORMONS RABBIT HOLES

It is likely you have some magical thinking deep inside you. You picked it up when you were five years old and never got rid of it. It is highly likely the Church will not be helpful in the project of moving beyond but will persist in transactional gospel messaging that keeps people in a magical-thinking frame of mind. You'll have to do most of the work on your own. In that process, there are several especially-for-Mormons rabbit holes to be aware of and process in advance, if possible.

"WHETHER BY MINE OWN VOICE OR BY THE VOICE OF MY SERVANTS" (D&C 1:38)

Along with Wilford Woodruff's discourse at the dedication of the Salt Lake Temple ("The Lord will never permit me or any other man who stands as President of this Church to lead you astray." See Official Declaration 1), D&C 1:38 is often cited for the proposition that the words of the prophet are a sure thing. Guaranteed. No need to look further. Even to say that it is wrong to look beyond or listen to anyone else.

There are reasoned, thoughtful analyses of these phrases in scripture. If you're looking for hermeneutics or line-by-line parsing that shows the lines don't mean what people casually quote them to mean, the arguments are available. D&C 1:38 does not actually say every word the prophet says is the word of God. It says the word of God can come through a prophet. In the context of near destruction of the Church over polygamy and a declaration that reverses former teaching, there is a good argument that "never lead astray" refers to the Church as a whole, not to individuals in their private lives. But this book is not a doctrinal text, and for present purposes it is enough that such arguments exist. What's important is that belief in the inerrancy of the prophet is common and is a kind of magical thinking. If you have a touch of this thinking, even if it's way in the back of your mind from seminary lessons 20 years ago, you are at risk of breaking.

Survival is about naming the problem, facing the problem, and making your own way on your own two feet. Inerrancy and infallibility are problems. Name them, face them, make your own decisions.

THE COVENANT PATH

President Nelson has made the *covenant path* a focus by including and emphasizing the covenant path in his first public address and repeating it many times since.

The covenant path is often described as a series of ordinances and sacraments—baptism and confirmation, sacrament, priesthood ordination, temple endowment, and temple sealing. The ordinances are described as required gates on the road to heaven. Often it is implied or inferred that the ordinances are more than just required but are *sufficient* to get to heaven. Not meaning to detract from the value and significance of ordinances, and of covenant making and keeping, when the series of ordinances is described as necessary *and* sufficient the path represents magical thinking. The if-then (do these things and you get to heaven), the mechanical nature, the certainty—these point to magical thinking.

Another way the covenant path is described is gaining a temple recommend, participating in the several temple ordinances including making covenants there, and keeping those covenants, i.e., enduring to the end. These steps are presented as necessary, and often implied or inferred as sufficient. Again, because necessary and sufficient implies certainty, this version of the covenant path also represents magical thinking.

The Church encourages the idea of certainty. In 2009, in his talk *The Power of Covenants*, Elder Christofferson said "[S]acred ordinances are performed in temples. . . . If we are faithful to the covenants made there, we become inheritors not only of the celestial kingdom but of exaltation, the highest glory within the heavenly kingdom, and we obtain all the divine possibilities God can give." Many of us thrill to the confident future promised. We want the if-then nature of covenant keeping = exaltation. It is one of the signal claims, an essential attractor, to The Church of Jesus Christ of Latter-day Saints. (To be sure, other churches, other religions, make different claims with an if-then character.)

As noted above, this is not a doctrinal text and we are not going to settle the certainty claims here, for or against. What we are here to discuss is that for some of us questions arise, we lose confidence, we are not sure the covenant keeping = exaltation equation always holds.

When there is a breakdown in confidence about the covenant path, or in the terms of this chapter, when there is a breach in the magic, there is work to do. One direction—as repeated by many leaders—is to get back in the boat. Squash the uncertainty and seek renewal—renewal of covenants, renewal of confidence. Another direction is to leave because the Church has failed you. The third, the subject of this book, is to take on the essential chaos of the universe, the absence of the sure thing, and go forward making your own meaning for life.

In considering your options, I recommend the words of President Nelson in that first public address, shortly after he was set apart as the President of the Church. Speaking about the covenant path, he said:

> [K]eeping those covenants will open the door to every spiritual blessing and privilege available to men, women, and children everywhere . . .
>
> The ordinances of the temple and the covenants you make there are key to strengthening your life, your marriage and family, and your ability to resist the attacks of the adversary. Your worship in the temple and your service there for your ancestors will bless you with increased personal revelation and peace and will fortify your commitment to stay on the covenant path.

President Nelson's promises—*open the door, strengthen, resist attacks, personal revelation, peace*—are wonderful promises. But they are not the sure thing, the guaranteed seat at the right hand of God. These opening, strengthening, resisting promises are the kind of ideas on which you can build an adult version of the covenant path.

D&C 132:20 "COMMIT NO MURDER"

Several single adults came to me when I was serving as bishop to tell me there were private discussion groups—including some gay and some straight members—talking about D&C 132:20 and speculating that if they could just pair up, get married in the temple, and not commit murder, they would score the sure thing:

> Then shall they be gods, because they have no end; therefore shall they be from everlasting to everlasting, because they continue; then shall they be above all, because all things are subject unto them.

I found that troubling, because I didn't and don't believe it myself, but more because I feared that kind of talk would lead people to make unfortunate short-sighted choices about marriage. I counseled against placing confidence in that scripture. I talked about the context of plural marriage. I talked about qualifiers in the scripture itself ("sealed by the Holy Spirit of promise" and "abide in my covenant") and other scripture and teachings that counsel wisdom and faith and salvation in Jesus Christ, and more. I recognized the lure of the sure thing and I feared it.

Now suppose you got married with a thought in the back of your mind that sealing in the temple pretty much guarantees your ascension. And now your marriage hits a rough spot, or is coming apart, or came apart. If you bought into the sure thing in the first place, if that magical thinking was part of your worldview, the breaking can be a crisis for your marriage first of all, but also for your faith, for your path in life, for your self-confidence and self-worth.

I believe the magical thinking was wrong in the first place, and my global recommendation would be that we dispense with all such teaching and get real about life and the hereafter. But that does not answer the pain in the moment. For the pain, I offer sympathy and recognition. For the path forward, I offer the suggestion that you first dispense with the magical thinking. Set that stumbling block aside and proceed with the real-life work of forming and managing relationships with real people.

THE HOLY SPIRIT OF PROMISE
(OR MAYBE SECOND ANOINTING?)

In Section 76 of the Doctrine & Covenants we read about a vision of "them who shall come forth in the resurrection of the just" who are described this way (verses 50–53, paraphrased):

> They who received the testimony of Jesus and believed
>   on his name and were baptized,
> who were washed and cleansed from all sin by keeping
>   the commandments,
> who overcome by faith,
> and are sealed by the Holy Spirit of promise.

It's an appealing picture with the flavor of a sure thing. Sometimes we refer to this as one's calling and election made sure (see also 2 Peter 1:3–10 "if ye do these things, ye shall never fall"). Many of us want to be one of those people. But the bar is high to begin with, and then there's the Holy Spirit of promise to look out for. In his *Mormon Doctrine*, Bruce R. McConkie explained it this way:

> [A]n act which is sealed by the Holy Spirit of Promise is one which is ratified by the Holy Ghost; it is one which is approved by the Lord; and the person who has taken the obligation upon himself is justified by the Spirit in the thing he has done. The ratifying seal of approval is put upon an act only if those entering the contract are worthy as a result of personal righteousness to receive divine approbation. They are 'sealed by the Holy Spirit of Promise, which the Father sheds forth upon all those who are *just* and *true*.' (D&C 76:53.) If they are not just and true and worthy the ratifying seal is withheld.

So add to the list being *just* and *true* and *worthy*, and probably add *enduring to the end* to boot.

Some explanations describe the Holy Spirit of Promise as an assurance felt by the individual, not something conferred or declared by another. That subjective nature probably saves the idea from the mechanical one-for-one linkage that makes for magical thinking. Most people who call for the assurance of the Holy Spirit of promise are never sure. Hopeful, but not sure.

Some explanations suggest that through an ordinance referred to as the Second Anointing there can be an objective event in time that seals the promise[1]:

> Godhood was therefore the meaning of this higher ordinance, or second anointing, for the previously revealed promises in Doctrine and Covenants 132:19–26 implicitly referred not to those who had been sealed in celestial marriage but to those who had been sealed and ordained 'kings and priests,' 'queens and priestesses' to God. . . . [I]t is not known to what degree the conferral of godhood by the second anointing was held to be conditional or unconditional. Most of the earliest nineteenth-century comments explicitly dealing with the second anointing clearly imply that the ordinance was then held to be unconditional. . . . The unconditional promise of exaltation in the highest degree of the celestial kingdom as gods and goddesses inherent in this priesthood sealing ordinance of Elijah was weighty indeed . . .

About the second anointing, first I would observe that it's not a likely concern for typical readers of this book and perhaps I should stop there. If you are in line for a second anointing, you probably won't listen to me anyway. But I would observe that confidence in

---

1. David John Buerger, "The Fulness of the Priesthood: The Second Anointing in Latter-day Saint Theology and Practice," *Dialogue: A Journal of Mormon Thought* 16(1) (1983): 21, 36–37.

an absolute unconditional depends on confidence in everything that went before. Confidence about the restoration of the Priesthood and confidence about its efficacy and confidence about Joseph Smith getting this aspect right and confidence about reliable transmission to the twenty-first century. That's a lot of if-then sure things, a lot of magical thinking.

EYESIGHT

I got glasses when I was five years old. I hated them. They made me feel different and failed or broken. Three or four years later we were in Salt Lake City for a General Conference weekend. I looked forward to my grandfather introducing me to David O. McKay, the president of the Church. Grandpa came through. I remember meeting President McKay on the balcony of the tabernacle at Temple Square. I didn't tell anybody, but I came to that meeting believing that shaking the hand of the prophet would fix my eyes and I would not need glasses. I knew the stories from the Gospels and I wanted it to be so. I did shake the hand of the prophet. My eyesight did not change.

I believe magical thinking is at the core of many issues with the institutional church. We think bishops are oracles and can read minds. We think callings come from God in a flash of revelation without the intervention of human minds or hands. We expect men called as Prophets, Seers and Revelators to not only tell the truth but tell it in advance, to anticipate trouble, to lead the way. My eight-year-old self believed the prophet's touch would be like Jesus's touch and I would see clearly and without aid.

Magical thinking perpetuates and strengthens the parent-child relationship that we've just spent 100 pages working our way out of. Magical thinking sets us up for disillusion and disappointment. Magical thinking—when it doesn't come through—can damage our relationship and trust in God. When the magic breaks, when the certainty fails, the loss can be devastating. That loss is one of the most common reasons cited by people who leave the church. For purposes of survival, inside the edge or outside the edge, magical thinking is a stumbling block we have to surmount or bypass or dismiss. Life is complicated and hard. There is no magical way out.

TALKING WITH THE BISHOP

DON'T.

When I want to describe this chapter in a provocative way I give it that one word—**DON'T**. The longer version is somewhat more reasoned and a little less provocative:

> Think carefully about what you want, what you reasonably expect, and what you give up, before talking with the bishop.

—and—

> When you do talk with the bishop, make it an adult-to-adult conversation, and don't ask for something he can't give or can't know, or ask him to be someone he can't be.

Although this book is not a memoir, for this chapter it is relevant that I have been a bishop. In that role I saw two things. One was that members too often have an oracle view of bishops, i.e., they come to the oracle-bishop to receive God's word. The second was that bishops are tempted and too often succumb to an oracular view of themselves, i.e., if it comes to mind while I sit in this seat, it must be the will and mind of the Lord.

I loved my ward members; the more I knew the more I loved, and I tried to do right by them. My friends and family members who have served or are currently serving as bishop tell me the same. (We all know horror stories, but the horror stories I know are all second and third hand. Nobody has admitted to me that he was a bad bishop.) Notwithstanding my desire and sincere effort to do right while serving as a bishop, I tallied four or five times per year that felt inspired or directed. With hindsight, it seemed that I was right about half the time. As a result, my starting point expectation is that God-to-bishop-to-member direction can happen—it's not a zero—but such direction is not frequent or dependable or predictable enough to make it the foundation for talking with the bishop, either for the member or for the bishop. I was not an oracle. I should not ever have thought I was an oracle. I would not ever advise someone else or myself to talk with a bishop as an oracle.

SNOWMOBILES In February my current bishop and I went snowmobiling into the Uinta mountains. We had a good time and even gave service to a couple of novice riders from California, so I can tell a spiritual experience story if called upon. However, the fact is that my snowmobile ride had nothing to do with the Church. My current bishop is a friend and neighbor. We talk motorcycles and snowmobiles and road and snow conditions. Similar age, male, some common experiences. We have an easy camaraderie. But it's not about the Church.

I'm privileged that way. For many of us, most of the time the bishop is formidable and distant. No matter how friendly and outgoing a personality, he's like the Principal or the Judge—the authority figure you don't want to spend much time with. Most of us don't get to talk with the bishop in an easy conversation about snow conditions. And it must be the case that familiarity on any front, even about motorcycles, makes everything else easier or more relaxed or conducted with a presumption of good will. Queue up discussions about old boy's networks, private clubs, men looking out for each other. I could worry myself about taking advantage of a relationship pretty much limited to middle-aged men. But that's not this book. For this book, my approach to the snowmobile conversation is enjoy it if you've got it, but don't mix snowmobiles and church. That kind of relationship is not and cannot be defining of our relationship with the Church because it applies to too few and in a highly discriminatory way.

SMALL TALK My current bishop, and in fact the most recent three or four bishops that come quickly to mind, are friendly outgoing people who say hello to lots of people, who smile a lot, who are quick with praise and congratulations, who enjoy a quick conversation in the hall. Not everybody is like that. But if your bishop is one of the friendly types, don't shun him. Say hello. Smile. There is no upside to making the bishop an enemy or an alien. Be human.

THE OFFICE Now to the serious stuff. When do you talk with the bishop as Bishop. In his office. With a straight face. For real. Here's where the short answer is *don't* and the long answer is *think carefully about what you want*.

Don't talk with the bishop if it feels like you are walking into the conversation as a child seeking a parent's advice or permission. Don't talk with the bishop if it feels like you're about to get a scolding from dad. Stop and do the differentiation work first. Don't talk with the bishop if he's a bully. Wait until you are strong enough to push back, and he knows it. Or wait until he is released. Your life in the church is much longer than any one bishop.

The following six general cases all assume you are ready to approach the conversation as an adult talking with an adult, with eyes open and mutual respect. These are six general cases where you might choose to talk with the bishop:

1. You need a temple recommend.
2. You feel a need to confess something 'serious.'
3. You need help: financial, physical, psychological. You need money or assistance of some sort.
4. You want to unload—tell him all your gripes and complaints about the Church.
5. You have a complaint about a person in the ward. Something affecting you directly or affecting someone you are close to and feel responsible for. Anything from teasing to false doctrine to abuse.
6. You want the straight scoop. What does that scripture mean? May I drink [fill in a desired beverage]? Can I baptize my child?

TEMPLE RECOMMEND

If you want a temple recommend you must meet with the bishop or a counselor. If you follow the advice of the next chapter on the Temple Recommend Interview, manage the process, and make it a yes-yes-yes-no kind of interview, there's a fair chance it will be simple, straightforward, and quick. That's what the bishop expects. That's what most bishops want most of the time. On the other hand, if it's complicated or you make it complicated, you will end up in a conversation with the bishop.

Previewing the next chapter, some people want answers. They want to know what a question means. They want to know what happens if the true answer is half yes and half no. But in real life there are no pat answers. There is no cheat sheet. No secret or confidential answer guide. There's not even a yes-yes-yes-no multiple-choice grading sheet. There are only a handful of official interpretations.

"Tithing means 10% of increase." "Hot drinks means coffee and tea." "Garments should not be removed for activities that can reasonably be done while wearing the garment." There is no passing grade. No suggestion that 80% is good enough. Or that 80% is *not* good enough.

Since there is no cheat sheet, if you do manage to have a conversation and do get an answer from a bishop about anything interesting, you are getting the bishop's opinion. If the bishop explains what "increase" means, he's making it up. If the bishop answers your question about garments during sex (one of the notorious questions people ask) with anything other than "seek the guidance of the Holy Spirit" he's making it up.

Let's acknowledge that the bishop "making it up" might be inspired. It might be Truth. It might be exactly what you need to hear at the moment. But there are several limitations on that possibility. One limitation is that unless you take as an operating principle that everything the bishop says is God's word to you in a literal plain meaning sense, there is still interpretive work ahead of you. However you do it—whether by a spiritual feeling, or logic, or watching for micro-gestures that suggest the difference between opinion and inspiration—you've got work to do.

Another limitation follows from the fact that there is no cheat sheet with standardized answers. Significant real-life experience with leader roulette suggests there is no guarantee the next answer will be the same. In fact, the likelihood of getting the same answer twice in a row is inversely correlated with the difficulty of the question. Temple recommends take two interviews. Leaders change. There is a new bishop coming in less than five years. Sometimes you can choose and sometimes you take the next available slot, but (for renewals) there are three people in the bishopric and three people in the stake presidency you might meet with. If you are in the regular temple recommend business on a two-year cycle, you get one, two, or at most three interviews with any one person. What are you going to do with disparate answers, anyway?

In short, if you want a temple recommend, the strong recommendation is to make a self-assessment in advance and if you judge yourself ready, go in for a yes-yes-yes-no kind of interview. Save the deep conversations for another time and place. Take control of the situation as much as possible, choosing who to talk to, choosing what to talk about, choosing the tone of the meeting.

CONFESSION

Confession is a complex subject; let's break it down.

Confession is made to God and to persons who were harmed. And sometimes to other people, including sometimes the bishop. There is an important utility to confession to God and to the person harmed. That's a whole other book. These comments are not about that sort of confession.

There is purpose for confession to other people, other than to God and the person harmed. At least four purposes can be discerned.

First is to seek absolution—a formal release from guilt, obligation, or punishment. There are Christian traditions—generally the older ones, Roman Catholic, Eastern Catholic, Eastern Orthodox—that offer absolution as a Sacrament, where the priest, acting on behalf of Christ, concludes with "I absolve you from your sins in the name of the Father, and of the Son, and of the Holy Spirit. Amen" (Roman Catholic). In most Protestant traditions absolution is seen as an extension of baptism, or part of the ongoing life of the church, or is disregarded or disapproved. Culturally, Mormonism is in the latter camp, not using or speaking of absolution except in disapproval (typically an anti-Catholic conversation). The world of Mormonism is not quite so simple, however. D&C 132:46 includes the phrase "whosesoever sins you remit on earth shall be remitted eternally in the heavens." And there is evidence that sins were expressly forgiven in the Nauvoo era School of Prophets. Notwithstanding these references, it is not clear in Mormon theology that any human being in the modern era has the power to remit sins, but it does seem that if or to the extent there exists such a power, it resides with the Prophet-President, and possibly the Apostles, and is not delegated to stake presidents and bishops.[1] In short, absolution is not something we seek from a bishop. It's not on the menu.

Second is to seek counseling. To work out the relative significance, the long-term effects, the causes. This is a kind of confession that happens in 12-step programs. And with counselors, i.e., therapists and psychologists. And with close friends and advisors and trusted confidants. It can be incredibly valuable. And it can in theory happen with a Mormon bishop. The problem with Mormon bishops on this score is that many bishops think of themselves—are instructed and trained to think of themselves—as judges, as a "judge in Israel." A judge is not a counselor. There are men serving as a bishop who understand the difference and can adopt a counselor role. But it is difficult to tell from the outside. And it is all too easy to trip a counselor-type bishop into a judging role.

In a sense, the too-common failure of Mormon bishops to act as counselor is the reason for the "Don't" at the head of this chapter. If you can ascertain that your bishop is that special kind who can and will separate out the role, ask for it and celebrate it. But be careful. New bishops are more likely to be judgmental. Give them time to season. Most bishops have little experience with an adult-to-adult conversation while in their official role. You might have to ease your bishop into a listening and counseling role. Furthermore, as roles have been clarified and reinforced (in 2019) the elder's quorum president and the Relief Society president may be better positioned for the counselor role. They do not have the explicit judge-in-Israel assignment, and they do have a responsibility toward adult members that more closely follows the idea of counselor than judge.

---

1. Kimball, Edward L. (1996) "Confession in LDS Doctrine and Practice," *BYU Studies Quarterly* : Vol. 36 : Iss. 2 , pages 19–21.

Third is to seek the help of the Church in the repentance process. I have heard numerous fear-based comments about church discipline (now called Membership Councils). For many of us external discipline is something to avoid at all costs. However, at times a person might feel a genuine need or desire to work through a disciplinary process, and find it beneficial. It happens often enough that we need to allow for the possibility. The process of being separated from some kinds of participation, even having one's membership withdrawn, can facilitate a repentance process for some. If that is what you need, do ask for it. Do it intentionally, consciously, telling the bishop what you need and why. This is an important, albeit limited, exception to the "Don't" about talking with a bishop.

Fourth, the Church tells us that serious sins—sins that may call for membership to be restricted or withdrawn—must be confessed to the bishop. The requirement, the command form, the "must confess," is clear. But let's stop to think about where the command form comes from. In a church offering absolution there is a clear logic to telling member-penitents to confess their serious sins. There might be terms or conditions on the absolution, but the end result looks like a reward for the benefit of the individual. In a church focused on protecting and preserving the institution, dealing with members' serious sins, some of which might be notorious, has an understandable purpose. But it seems to be more for the benefit of the institution, not the individual. In a church acting in the parent role, telling the member-children to confess is what parents do. It's a form of control and training, for the purpose of turning children into responsible adults.

For a life on the inside of the edge, having differentiated yourself, having carefully considered what the church is to you, and now trying to approach the church on an adult-to-adult level, is there still a place for confession of serious sins in the Church, considering that the Church does not hold out absolution as a prize? As discussed above, if your bishop is ready and able to be a counselor, you may want to take advantage of that opportunity. If you need the church discipline process for your own work to be effective, you should ask for it. On the other hand, if you're thinking about confession simply because it was commanded, or out of fear—because you're afraid of compounding the severity of the sin, or afraid of being found out and dealt with more harshly than if you turned yourself in—you might want to review your differentiation work and review what the church is to you, before you take the irrevocable step of confessing a serious sin.

It is fair to note that the preceding paragraphs have the effect of discouraging confession where it is commanded and are perhaps the most controversial statement in this chapter from the standpoint of orthodox Mormon practice. In other words, don't bother asking a church representative or your bishop for a second opinion about confessing serious sins. You already know the answer.

One last note about confession, related to privacy or confidentiality. In general people expect confessions to be private and confidential. Roman Catholic practices—well staged in movies and mysteries—make us think that way. Unfortunately, confession to a Mormon bishop is not a reliable forum in terms of privacy and confidentiality. In my experience there is little-to-no training on confidences, including how confidences should be treated in a legal setting. There is a general expectation that the bishop will not talk to the public, and a good counselor-type bishop will often hold confidences quite strictly, but a judge-in-Israel-type bishop may take actions based on what is confessed including in a Membership Council, may consult with the stake president in a difficult or important matter, and may subtly or explicitly coerce further telling. Unless you know the individual and have utter confidence in his discretion, when you do talk with your bishop assume your story will be repeated. In too many cases this caution alone is a good and sufficient reason for the "Don't" of this chapter.

FINANCIAL ASSISTANCE

The church welfare program provides physical support—money and food—to many people in need. The system is complicated by four realities:

1. The bishop holds the checkbook. Needs may be identified to or by the elders quorum president and the Relief Society president, but sooner or later there is a bishop in the mix.
2. Church funds are usually a last resort rather than first. You are likely to be asked to use family support first, then government welfare, before church resources come into play. You are likely to give up a lot of personal financial information in the process.
3. Some bishops apply a worthiness test to church welfare. The current General Handbook says "Assistance can be given regardless of whether the member regularly attends Church meetings or follows Church standards." (GH 22.5.1.1) However, there are old patterns and instructions to apply a worthiness test, and some bishops will withhold assistance from members who do not attend regularly, or will instruct members to pay tithing first before receiving assistance.
4. Bishops sometimes attach obligations and expectations. Bishops have near unlimited unreviewable discretion to attach strings to assistance, and culturally the Church includes a lot of workfare believers (workfare is a welfare system that requires those receiving benefits to perform some work or to participate in job training).

In short, if you need financial assistance from the Church, you will have to talk with the bishop. It may be demeaning, and bring into question everything you have ever done *vis a vis* the Church, and impose requirements you didn't choose or ask for. The bottom line is that living on the inside of the edge is difficult by itself and adding in financial assistance from the Church may be impossible. A hard truth.

My real life experience is not as harsh as the preceding paragraphs sound. A majority of the bishops I have known personally see church welfare and financial assistance as a way to help. They do not take a hard line on assistance. They ask "what can I do?" rather than "what have you done?" But a minority of bishops I have known personally use church assistance as a wedge to strongly encourage full activity. They ask "what will you do in return?" or "not until you come back to church."

Do you know who you are talking to? In other words, this is where Don't might turn into Have To, but count the cost, assess the risk, measure your need, before jumping in.

TELL ALL

Many people who are in or have been through a faith crisis have a compulsive need to tell people all about it, all about what they have learned and what their new world looks like. It is a convert's zeal. The bishop is often the first or favorite audience.

This is one of the places where "Don't do it" is strongest.

Think it through. If your best friend happens to be the bishop and you're out for a walk, maybe you can talk with him as a friend. But as a capital-B Bishop, what do you expect to get out of the conversation?

Are you planning or hoping to run him away from the Church? First of all, that's not likely. Second, trying to run him out is almost the definition of apostasy. Tread lightly!

Are you hoping for answers? You are likely to be disappointed. Whether the questions are about history, or scripture interpretation, or racism, or mistakes church leaders have made, or spiritual experiences that differ from what we were taught to expect, or an understanding of God that's not like the temple portrays, or almost anything we can put into words, by the time a desperate urge to tell all comes to a head, most of us have read and studied and discussed and tested enough to know there aren't answers of the "it didn't happen" or "he didn't say that" or "you're mistaken" sort. Instead, sometimes there are no good answers, and when there are useful responses they tend to be in the form of added information or an alternate approach or a different way to process. If those responses are useful, they are useful in a thoughtful discussion mode, not a heated debate mode.

If you find yourself approaching your bishop as an oracle, in effect looking for direct answers from God, take another look at the Magical Thinking chapter. Apart from the idea of a direct line from God, your bishop doesn't have a separate answer sheet, a secret volume of history, an explanation you haven't seen. Your bishop may be a wise man fully equipped for a conversation about your concerns. If so, consider engaging on a discussion basis as opposed to asking for answers. But recognize that is probably not the bishop's specialty and certainly not his calling, not the reason he has that role. Count to ten before asking for something that may not be available.

Are you hoping for validation? Stop and think about that. Do you really need the bishop to tell you that what bothers you is real? He might be someone whose opinion you respect. But just as with answers, it isn't likely he has any more knowledge about questions than the other wise people in the ward. In fact, reports from many who have tried a Tell All suggest the median or average bishop will not understand you in the first place.

Or do you just want dad to tell you it will all be OK? Sorry, that's a biting way of saying that if you're slipping back into parent-child mode, give yourself some space to think twice.

On the other side, there's a cost. By having the Tell All conversation you give the bishop all kinds of ammunition to judge you. To withhold a temple recommend. To give or take callings. To hold a Membership Council. To give you orders that you may or may not be able to follow.

Frankly, I have given bishops a lot of information about myself. But I'm not asking for anything. I don't do interviews. I'm not looking for a calling. I'm not a temple recommend holder. I don't need or ask for answers. My sharing is essentially peer-to-peer, in the nature of "You have a radical element in your ward; we'll all be better off in a community sense if you know who I am; I will help where I can if you ask; I'm not looking to make trouble; I'm not asking for anything." If you get to that sort of calm place, go for it. However, it might be relevant that it took me between 10 and 20 years to reach that point. If you do an equal amount of work, you will know for yourself what works and what doesn't.

COMMUNITY PROBLEMS

A Mormon ward is a small town sort of place. People love each other. And annoy each other. When it is bad, people tease and abuse. And sometimes teach false doctrine.

The original meaning and sense of "judge in Israel" is the mediator for these kinds of problems. This is a legitimate and genuine role for the bishop, although most bishops I know hate it and would rather you forget this part of their job. If there is no better answer, appeals do go to the bishop.

But most of the time the better approach is to talk to the offender directly. All the dynamics of difficult conversations come into play. We sometimes criticize church leaders for paying too little attention to D&C 121:41–43. We should probably spend equal or more time taking the lesson to heart ourselves:

> No power or influence can or ought to be maintained by
> virtue of the priesthood, only by persuasion, by long-

suffering, by gentleness and meekness, and by love unfeigned; by kindness, and pure knowledge . . . reproving betimes with sharpness . . . and then showing forth afterwards an increase of love . . . that he may know that thy faithfulness is stronger than the cords of death.

If you are going to be part of the community, be all in. Take part in the dynamics of a communitarian organization. Talk with your neighbor. Practice kindness and meekness. Argue with your neighbor. Love your neighbor.

It sometimes happens that the bishop must intervene. For myself, I consider that a failure. It reinforces a hierarchical system that generally frustrates and annoys me. Usually, it's not the end of the world, but it is another point for the general principle of not talking with the bishop.

THE STRAIGHT SCOOP

Occasionally the bishop really is the wise old man in the ward. You want to know what a particular scripture verse means. You want to parse the Word of Wisdom in a gray area. You want to know what the rule book says. You want permission for something.

If you have a convenient casual opportunity for this sort of conversation, maybe it can work. However, there are several reasons to hesitate.

- Bishops are almost always incredibly busy. Adding to their load is not a kindness.
- Bishops are almost never the only source. Your elders quorum president or Relief Society president or other wise man or wise woman almost always can do just as well or better.
- In this internet enabled world, with tremendous resources available at the touch of a button, including

the Church Library app, the General Handbook online, volumes of Church history, and much more, you can usually find answers for yourself. Most importantly, your bishop does not have another source of answers you can't find on your own. Inspiration, maybe. But you are entitled to the same for yourself, and you'll need your own inspiration or judgment just to interpret your bishop's answers if he shares them.

As with every section of this chapter, there are exceptions. The largest area of exception, where you do end up talking with the bishop, is in areas where he exercises sole discretion. For example, in most cases the bishop makes unreviewable judgment calls about administration of the Sacrament and other ordinances that happen at the ward level. There are guidelines in the General Handbook and some people are inclined to read the guidelines and make their own decisions. If that's you, do not go to the bishop to ask a question you really don't want answered. But if you want to know your bishop's judgment or opinion or practice in an area where the bishop has genuine responsibility, you have to ask.

SUMMING UP

If you know you are on the edge, which already makes you an outsider in some senses, and you still want to be part of the community, start with the presumption that you will never have a real conversation with your bishop.

If you want a temple recommend, go in for a yes-yes-yes-no report.

If you need to work a repentance process, manage your own process. Ask the bishop for help in specific ways when and if you need it, but don't view the process as turning yourself in for whatever he dictates.

If you need assistance, whether financial or with people issues, try everything else first (which is what most bishops will tell you anyway) and seek out the bishop cautiously and as a last resort.

If you're tempted to spill all your doubts and questions and angst on the bishop, don't. Fight the temptation. Find someone else.

But if your bishop is both a friend and the most knowledgeable person around, and you can get him out of his office for a long walk and a friendly chat, count yourself very lucky indeed and enjoy the conversation.

THE TEMPLE RECOMMEND

Anyone with a year or more of teenage or adult experience in the Church will understand the significance of the temple recommend. There is no avoiding the issue. Church programming is designed to encourage everybody to go to the temple and for that purpose to attend a regular temple recommend interview. The process starts in the year you turn twelve and continues for the rest of your life in the Church. One of the meanings of "covenant path"—common twenty-first century terminology—is going to the temple. Bishops keep lists. Executive Secretaries make calls. Some will respect a "no thank you, please take me off the list." More will keep calling.

Equally important is the cultural sense that the temple recommend is the sign of full membership, full fellowship. The in-crowd, the people with the more responsible, more visible callings, the faithful, have temple recommends. The temple recommend is the hall pass; with a current recommend in hand, most times there are no further questions asked. Current temple recommend holders move around the Church and in and out of temples and chapels and callings as a matter of right.

The opposite is true as well. Because of the cultural placement and social realities, a teen or an adult without a temple recommend who comes to church is thought of as working on it, or in a repentance process, or struggling with a bad habit. There is no place in the social hierarchy for active but without a recommend. The member without a recommend is always suspect, always examined, always doubted.

Finally, there's the temple marriage and sealing process, where temple weddings are encouraged (although no longer required) and attendance by anybody—family, friends, loved ones—requires a temple recommend. The family pressures to be there, to be part of the family, can be enormous.

For many this adds up to a near equivalency of temple recommend and activity. For some, not having a recommend is tantamount to leaving the Church altogether. In short, choosing to live on the inside of the edge is also choosing to deal with the temple recommend.

YOU ARE NOT ALONE

To be the one fourteen-year-old in the Church group not doing proxy baptisms is untenable. You might as well drop out. But that's a problem for another book. By the time high school graduation and missions come around, life maps diverge. Some get married. Some go away to college. Some drop out of the Church completely. Many leave home, far enough away to make their own life and build their own reputation. This all allows some amount of room for individual choice, for a whole range of relationships to the Church.

Looking around at the adults in the chapel on Sunday morning, I know—from experience and local counts—that typically fewer than half of the adults present on Sunday have a current temple recommend. Surely that number varies dramatically from place to place, but it is safe to say there are a lot of never-recommend and endowed-but-no-recommend adults in the pews every Sunday. Add in the folks who "know" that if they were fully disclosing they wouldn't have a recommend, and the number of members feeling they are second class citizens is a good part of every congregation.

It doesn't really matter what the overall numbers are. The fact is that if you are sitting in Church on Sunday morning feeling uneasy about your temple recommend status, you are not alone.

APPROACHES TO THE INTERVIEW

So long as you stay on the inside you will deal with the temple recommend and the temple recommend interview. That is not equivalent to saying you must have a temple recommend. Although it is not simple and there are costs, one obvious option for living on the inside of the edge is activity without a recommend. The message here is not that you must or should have a temple recommend. The lesson here is about having a strategy, an approach. In a differentiated adult-to-adult relationship with the Church, you take control. You figure it out. You manage the process.

NO INTERVIEW

Some people decide or choose or feel compelled to avoid the temple recommend interview altogether and accept the consequences. (This is where I live.)

Reasons differ. Maybe you had a bad experience with a church leader in an earlier interview. Maybe you object to one or more of the questions or the process or the exercise of control and avoid the interview on principle. Maybe it brings on an anxiety attack just thinking about walking in and sitting down.

If this is where you find yourself, write the script. An explanation will often be answered by an attempt to fix you. If you'd rather be left alone, consider a short version of no. For example, try "I don't do interviews." Not an explanation, not a psychotherapy session. Simply no interviews.

RETURNING

It happens that someone who has lived the no-interview life for a time wants to change. Which means talking to the bishop (see *Talking to the Bishop*). Recognize that this will be seen as a form of repentance even if you have no actual problem to confess. Not doing worthiness interviews is a Church sin, in terms of practice and culture. Coming back to interviews is repentance. As a result, it would be wise to take a no-judgment-conversation with the bishop first, rather than jumping into a temple recommend interview. Manage complexity in a conversation before going to the temple recommend interview. Prepare the bishop and yourself for a simple yes-yes-no-no interview.

SPILL IT ALL

Sometimes people on the edge imagine a temple recommend interview as an hour-long disclosure and maybe debate—the full monty interview.

Before you go in for a full monty interview, re-read the *Talking with the Bishop* chapter.

And now think about it again. From multiple conversations I gather several motives for the spill-all temple recommend interview:

- Perhaps it's a "take me as I am" test. I'm going to tell all and hope to pass. If it works I get the best of all worlds for myself—a temple recommend just as I am, known and respected.
- A version of "take me as I am" is to ask for inspiration. Viewing the bishop as an oracle, if he says I pass it's as good as God saying I pass.

- Or maybe it's a protest move. I'm going to present the bishop with what I think are reasonable complaints or issues and maybe he will add my name to the mounting numbers of people affected by something the Church is wrong about.
- Sometimes the full disclosure can be a deflection of responsibility. Everything that comes of this is to the bishop's credit or else the bishop's fault. It's not about me but about the system.
- Or perhaps it's a radical respect for the system. I am supposed to go to the interview, I am supposed to answer truthfully. Let the chips fall where they will.

For an opinion, I wouldn't recommend a full-disclosure interview for anybody and I wouldn't take one myself. In part this is the fundamental conceit of this book. Surviving on the inside of the edge is a matter of making your own way, choosing your own path. Not chasing external validation. Furthermore, the odds are against you. Debriefs about actual full monty interviews are far more often disappointing and alienating than joyful and welcoming. If that's not enough, consider the bishop's situation. The hour-long full disclosure interviews are grueling and usually finish with no good answer.

Suppose he says yes. That doesn't mean Truth has happened. That doesn't govern church policy or principle. Whether you think of the bishop as just a man, or as a speaker for God, the very most you get is that you, individually, in this time and place and circumstance, get one of two signatures on a recommend. It might say you're OK. It could just as easily say you need this. Or it might mean your bishop wants everybody in the temple short of creating a danger to themselves and others. It is not really a validation or approval of the essential you, and it is not strongly predictive of the Church generally or the next bishop or the next interview. It is a small temporary win.

Suppose he says no. That does mean that in his view something needs to change. But it doesn't tell you whether the bishop is the voice of God, or a thoughtful man, or a man in a bad mood, or a bad bounce in leader roulette. It does mean you don't get a recommend and that's disappointing and maybe even angering. But it doesn't judge you as a person, beyond the fact that you individually, in this time and place and circumstance, don't get a recommend. It might say you need to change. It could just as easily mean you're not lucky today.

Furthermore, we have a two interview system. If you determine to do a full disclosure interview with your bishop, what are you going to do in the second interview? Do you lay it all out for the bishop and stick with yes/no answers at the stake level? Do you take advice from the bishop on the second interview?

In short, the results of a full disclosure interview are seldom satisfying. Seldom as good as managing the system for yourself. My recommendation is that you decide in advance whether you want a recommend and are 'worthy' of a recommend, and then make it happen.

YES/NO

The most common approach for middle-way Mormons, for people on the inside of the edge who want a temple recommend, is to work through the questions personally, individually, perhaps in conversation or consultation with others (including even the bishop sometimes) who have given thought to the questions and the process. Work through the questions, judge yourself, and based on that judgment either decline the interview (judging negatively) or go in with yes/no answers.

Make no mistake. Yes/no isn't easy. You have to decide what standard to use, you have to judge yourself, and you have to evaluate the questions.

First, decide what standard you are going to use:

- What you think your bishop thinks? What if your stake president and your bishop are not aligned?
- What you think the General Authorities—the anonymous person or committee who wrote the questions—thinks?
- What your friends or your parents or your junior primary teacher or your internet group thinks?
- Your own intuition and study and prayer and life experience?

The standard you use is further complicated by the several questions, different wording, and different levels of certainty. For some of the questions—about tithing and about the Word of Wisdom, for two easy examples—you may be fairly certain what your bishop thinks or what the Church means. For other questions—the question about supporting or promoting contrary teachings, practices, or doctrine, for example—you might not know what your bishop thinks, or you might be aware of a variety of opinions among church leaders. You may feel differently or end up using a different standard for different questions. At least you are likely to think about it.

Second, how do you assess yourself? What if you recognize in yourself ambivalence—not a straight yes, not a straight no. The questions do not lend themselves to nuance. Is a 60/40 assessment a "yes" or a "no"? Are you a fair judge of yourself? Are you harder on yourself than others? Or do you alibi for yourself? How much credit do you give yourself for effort? Or good intentions?

Third, what do you think about the questions? Do you dismiss or short-change a question because you think it is wrong or irrelevant or uncomfortable? Or because it is new? Do you think of some questions as absolutes, while others can be satisfied with "I'm trying" or "usually"?

Most church leaders have their own answers to these questions, for themselves, and maybe for you if you ask. Most church leaders who have answers are confident they are right. But there is not a rule book that answers these questions for bishops, and there is significant variation in practice. Your current bishop's version may not be the same as the next bishop or the last bishop. The current bishop's version may not be the same as either of his counselors or any of the stake presidency. In fact, with six men to choose among, it is highly likely that they do NOT all have the same answer. It's an interesting phenomenon, the combination of significant variation, few discussions, and high confidence individual by individual. One more reason to question the value of asking.

There is also the possibility of lawyering the questions. For most people most of the time there is an obvious meaning and an obvious yes or no for each question. However, there is no authoritative resource explaining what they mean, and someone thinking like a lawyer can take them apart word by word, study the history, question the intent, and find all sorts of nuance and interpretations. Take the first question, as an example:

> Do you have faith in and a testimony of God, the Eternal Father; His Son, Jesus Christ; and the Holy Ghost?

Lawyering this question could include these ideas:

- What is "faith in"? Does it mean believing, or hoping, or knowing, that they exist? Or does "faith in" mean a confidence that they can do what they say they can?
- This sounds like a creedal statement. Is there a Church creed with detailed explanation? Does any creed that includes a Father, Son, and Holy Ghost formulation satisfy the question? Does "testimony" imply a Mormon testimony? Or just some version of a tripartite God?

- Are the details important? Or is this basically asking whether one is a theist? What if I don't care about the details, but I think you care?
- While there has long been a general expectation that temple goers be believers, the earliest version of this first question was added to the temple recommend interview in 1985. Does the fact that temple recommends were issued before 1985 without ever asking this question mean it can be treated as a nice-to-have rather than strict requirement? Can it be read for the general proposition of "believer" rather than any particular formulation?

You may not be comfortable with these sorts of questions. "Lawyering" is a curse word in many circles. But it might be useful to know that the same kinds of questions can be asked about every one of the temple recommend questions. Your bishop might have strong opinions about some or all of these questions-about-questions, but he doesn't know the answers and he doesn't have a guidebook to turn to for in-depth explanation. The General Handbook (at 26.3) says "The priesthood leader may explain basic gospel principles. He may also help members understand the temple recommend questions if needed. However, he should not present his personal beliefs, preferences, or interpretations as Church doctrine or policy." There is a lot of lawyering room in that statement for the bishop to express his opinion (which he may not view as opinion), but there are not any answers.

Most people living on the inside of the edge who choose to sit for a temple recommend choose to keep it simple and deliver yes and no answers. Most advice to people living on the inside of the edge is in accord. Keep it simple. Simple makes the interview itself straightforward. However, preparation for simple can be a lot of work. If you respect the system, studying out the questions, thinking about your life, and measuring yourself can be a serious and deep examination. Religious traditions of all sorts for centuries have pushed for this kind of work, both in private contemplation and supportive conversation. Mormon traditional practice is not set up for the supportive conversation, but you can make it happen. Find a good friend. Ask them to tell you when you sound crazy, whether you are operating at the alibiing and rationalizing extreme, or at the self-flagellation scrupulous extreme. Ask them for a reality check.

LIE

We all know the possibility, even likelihood, that it happens. Some people decide they need a temple recommend for their job, for their family relations, to attend a wedding, to maintain a calling they value. Or just to avoid sticking out. They go into the interview and lie.

The Yes/No approach and the Lie approach look the same in the interview. The difference is in the mind or spirit or conscience. The Yes/No approach includes a sincere albeit nuanced belief in the rightness of the answers. The Lie approach does not include that sincerity.

The magical version of Mormonism says the bishop will catch the lies and deny the recommend. Real world experience says bishops are not that good or not that inspired. Bishops do in fact yank recommends when it is not warranted and do in fact sign recommends when the answers are lies.

Some doctrinal expositions say the individual will soil the temple and condemn themselves by entering unworthily. Whether or not you absorbed that sort of doctrine, the decision to lie one's way through the interview typically includes dismissing any such concerns. And this is not the book for lecturing on the point.

To be sure, I believe the Lie approach is like a cancer. A quiet-for-a-long-time killer. I believe that believing oneself a liar is bad for the soul. Something to avoid. Not in a lightning-strike-from-heaven or gaping-gates-of-hell sense. But in a corrosive sense.

I know people who lie to attend their daughter's wedding. It is not my place to judge and this is not that sort of book. But for the long-term welfare of the individual, when I get preachy I think words like "exigent circumstances" and "don't do it again." For your own soul.

SUMMING UP

Act, don't be acted upon.

If you decide not to hold a temple recommend, two things follow:

- Count the cost. That doesn't mean you can't complain, but don't let it destroy you. Life in the Church without a recommend is both doable and common.
- Script a way to say "no thank you" so you don't have to debate your decision.

If you decide to hold a temple recommend, two things follow:

- Manage the interview. Figure out how you can answer with a yes-yes-yes-no pattern. Do your preparation and ask your questions outside the interview room.
- Pay attention to your self-esteem, your conscience, your soul. Find a principled way to manage the interview so that you feel good about yourself.

CALLINGS

Living on the inside of the edge means you're going to get the call. Literally—the call from the Executive Secretary asking you to come talk with the bishop. It's part of the deal, on the inside.

FIRST THINGS

It is increasingly common to ask, what is this about? Custom and practice is for the Executive Secretary to say nothing more than time and day to make an appointment. And it is true that the Handbook (at 30.1.1) says "A person who is being considered for a calling is not notified until the calling is issued." But neither custom nor the Handbook prevents the Executive Secretary from distinguishing between tithing settlement and disciplinary action and a calling sort of meeting. He may not know the calling anyway, and if he does know he will probably feel restrained from giving any detail. But just to say "this is about a calling"—just that much—is both a courtesy and a grown-up way to manage things.

It used to be common for a bishopric member to talk with a husband before extending a call to his wife. It was also common to be hurt by that practice. My wife Linda writes "My husband and I had moved to New England and were settling happily into a vibrant ward of other young adults. One day the bishop—who was a friend—caught me in a hallway and said, 'I've talked to your husband about this, and I want to call you to be. . .' Honestly, I can't remember what he called me to be. He lost me at 'I've talked to your husband . . .' It felt like a gut punch and did not mesh at all with how I knew God felt about me in particular and women in general."[1] That event happened 40 years ago. She still cries at the memory.

A preview conversation with either spouse should not happen. If it does, the natural and easy script is "talk with my wife." (And maybe "don't do that again.") The modern counsel (GH 30.2) is that the "The leader may invite the spouse of a married person to be present and give support when the calling is extended."

THE CALLING

Once you are in the room, knowing this is about a calling, what are your options?

Here's a list of bad options:

- Go adversarial. Attack.
  This is not advisable and generally inconsistent with a decision to stay on the inside. If you really are in attack mode, it would be better to just refuse the meeting.

- Declare that you will not accept any calling.
  When this is how you feel, better say it. Accepting a calling because you are too shy or too scared to say anything causes more trouble for everyone, both in the short term and the long term. However, there is more than one way to signal that you are not up for a calling

---

1. Linda Hoffman Kimball, "Navigating Spiritual Wounds," *Segullah*, July 27, 2021.

and almost all options are preferred to making the big announcement just as a calling is being extended.

- Launch into a big discussion about your issues with the Church.
If there ever is a right time and place for the big discussion (probably not; re-read the *Talking with the Bishop* chapter), it is not at the table when a calling is being issued. Just saying no is a much better option.

- Treat it as a call from God and give an automatic yes.
In other words, the magic calling approach. It is practiced by many members. But that's not how the system really works, and you know better. Even by the Handbook, leaders are supposed to seek the guidance of the Spirit *and* consider worthiness, personal or family circumstances, benefit to the people who will be served, benefit to the member (the person being called), benefit to the member's family, ability to fulfill family and employment responsibilities, and the effect of the calling on the marriage and family (GH 30.1.1). There is no way the bishop or the entire bishopric or the entire stake presidency know all of that without your help.

The better way is to approach the conversation as an adult-to-adult conversation. Not order taking or order giving. If you let yourself walk into a meeting with the attitude of a child summoned by their parent, you didn't get the message; that is not a good survival strategy. What you want is an adult talking with an adult seeking understanding and sharing information. All with a bias toward saying yes.

ADULT-TO-ADULT CONVERSATION

The bishop has some amount of information, including almost always knowing more than you do about what else is going on in the ward. But the bishop doesn't know you like you do. And if you are living on the edge it is a near certainty that what he doesn't know is significant in the sense that it makes a difference with respect to callings you might be able or willing to do.

The bishop has a big responsibility to staff the ward and to do so while considering worthiness, personal and family circumstances, benefits to at least three different constituencies, and the effect of callings on the individuals, the families, and the marriages. It is common courtesy, and mature adult behavior on your part, to recognize and make allowance for all the challenges he faces. To top it off, he has to deal with you—adding significantly to the challenge.

At the same time, you hold at least two key cards. One is a whole lot of information about yourself, your situation, your family, your interests and abilities, and the status of your relationship to the institutional church. The second card is that you can always say no.

Personally, I hold a third card I think of as measured understanding. I can't formally hand it over, but I can recommend measured understanding when it works. To explain, there is one line of my patriarchal blessing that has stayed with me for 47 years. Excerpted and slightly paraphrased, it says that the Lord's gift to me is a *"measured understanding of that which is greater and that which is lesser that I may be about the Lord's business to the greatest effect."* For me this is the ultimate play; in the final analysis it is my judgment that counts, with or without a formal calling. We talk about a diversity of gifts, and maybe not everybody can claim this one. But if you can get a glimpse of how you can be about the Lord's business to the greatest effect, you should pay attention.

INFORMATION GATHERING

By the time you get into a meeting where a calling will be extended, the bishop has already taken account of what he knows about you and your situation, what he knows about the needs in the ward and the other members with their knowledge, abilities, and personal and family situations. He has taken account of suggestions made by his counselors and often an organization leader. And he has prayed about the calling and has some level of confidence this is a good thing, or else he wouldn't start the conversation.

Unless you are unusually close with the bishop, you don't know what he knows. That is, you don't know all the same things he knows. You don't know what he thinks he knows about you. You don't know all the things he is taking into account. You don't know how his prayers are answered, or not. You don't know what other changes are in the works. You don't know his expectations for you. Does he imagine you will do what he would do in the calling? Or does he imagine you will follow your own idiosyncratic approach?

In an adult-to-adult conversation all of this information is fair game. To make this a productive discussion, if you have any response other than a quick no or an easy yes, ask questions. Discuss.

On the flip side, suppose there are callings you would quickly accept, callings you would reject out of hand, and other callings in between? Suppose there are callings you would accept if the need is great or the inspiration is profound? But not just as a fill-in until somebody better comes along. Suppose you would accept a calling to do it your way, but say no to a calling to do things his way?

Suppose there are changed circumstances in your life? Suppose a faith crisis has happened since you last talked with the bishop? Suppose there's another baby coming or a big change in working hours? If it is relevant to the calling under discussion, give him information.

If this kind of discussion puts you off or frightens you (perfectly understandable), pretty quickly your choices devolve to saying no to everything or saying yes to everything. Or putting the bishop into a guessing game about what you might do or say. None of those seem like good options. Choosing among false negatives, false positives, and guessing games, when I'm unwilling to have an open conversation with the bishop, I tend to choose false negatives as the least bad option. That is, saying no to everything. You may choose differently, but there is no cost-free choice in this situation.

BIAS TOWARD YES

Implicit in choosing to be inside instead of outside is that you want to be part of the community. Perhaps gingerly and with clear boundaries, but still part of the community. A local Mormon ward community is one in which almost everybody helps and nobody is paid. Choosing to be inside is almost the same as choosing to serve. That doesn't mean saying yes every time to any calling. That doesn't mean breaching your own boundaries. But it does suggest a thumb on the yes side of the scale.

Furthermore, if you have even a modicum of empathy for the bishop's position and responsibilities you will also bias toward yes. It's a big job. Everybody who says yes and pitches in makes it easier.

PRIDE AND PRESTIGE VS DISCERNMENT

If you spend any time watching the Church you see there are always some people—almost always men—on the fast track. They hold leadership callings from teenage years onward. They are the Assistant to the President in the mission. They are an elder's quorum president in their 20s, a bishop in their 30s. When you read the background of new General Authorities, often their personal journey through the hierarchy looks like this.

However, for most members—including almost all women, and a majority of men—we wake up in middle-age realizing our church careers are going nowhere. We teach, we sing, we serve as counselors. We visit the poor and the fatherless and succor the weary and try to be disciples and all the good things, but we're not making it up the church ladder.

LIVING ON THE INSIDE OF THE EDGE

If you find yourself on the edge, you are very likely in the latter group, the not-fast-trackers. Some reach the edge *because* they're disappointed that church-as-career hasn't worked out. Many more reach the edge of their own accord but with a realization that edgy people don't get the cool callings and don't have a bright future in the leadership circles.

At one level this is just a suck-it-up-life-isn't-fair situation. There are some strategies to get back on track if that is important to you. The best one (in my opinion) is to move to an area where members are spread out and leadership experience is rare, hang on to your temple recommend, and make yourself known. Most other strategies look like putting on the mask of the loyal follower. If those latter strategies appeal to you, you might be reading the wrong book.

Among the people I know who are not on the fast track and who choose to live on the inside of the edge, those who are happiest with their situation do two things:

- Find a way to release the ego-satisfaction of certain church callings and settle into serving individuals one at a time.
- Seek out their own vocation-type calling, i.e., find the thing they are most suitable for or directed toward or enthusiastic about.

Although Mormons use the word discernment as in distinguishing spirits, discernment as an epistemological religious practice is not a common usage. But in the non-Mormon Christian world people talk about discernment as a way to understand one's calling, and it is an important subject. A Google search for books on discernment brings up "best books on discernment," meaning there are so many they can be ranked. From the dictionary, the general idea is a practice and an ability that leads to sharp perceptions, that goes past outward appearance and makes nuanced judgments. In a Christian setting, that same practice of discernment is often described as discovering God's will. Discernment applied to finding a vocation ends up not with direction from an institution or a leader, but with self-awareness, a divine intuition, an awakening to the real, a confidence about what God would have you do. People who find that kind of a calling tend not to worry or care about prestigious church titles.

MEMBERSHIP COUNCILS

Your Stake President holds all the cards. Church discipline has the appearance of a legal system, but the reality is that stake presidents are nearly unreviewable judge, jury, and prosecutor. Most of the interesting or difficult questions you might imagine boil down to what does your stake president think.

HISTORY

Membership Councils have taken the place of what we used to call Disciplinary Councils, and before that Church Courts. The result of a Membership Council can be a bishop's or stake president's decision to withdraw a person's membership or to impose formal membership restrictions. These terms are in place of what we used to call excommunication and disfellowshipment. With all these terms floating around, the topic is generically "church discipline."

Church membership restrictions are ecclesiastical, not civil or criminal. For periods of time in the nineteenth century—in Nauvoo, at Winter Quarters, in the provisional State of Deseret and in the Utah Territory—the Church functioned as a theocracy or theodemocracy (a Joseph Smith coinage) exercising governmental power in its area of influence. The twenty-first century Church does not have and does not exercise classic forms of state control and punishment. However, out of those periods we have scripture and historical remnants that give the impression of state control and state punishment. Enough so that we sometimes talk confusingly of the church punishing people, both as something we fear and something we want depending on whether we are perpetrator or victim.

Within the history of the Church there are also periods where public shaming has occurred. Members were expected to confess serious sin in public. Church discipline resulted in social and economic isolation, in small communities where it really mattered. The twenty-first century church does little public shaming and for the most part opts for confidential rather than public discipline. However, the fear of shaming persists and can still happen in smaller communities where Church membership dominates. People who are employed by the Church in any role—from janitor to church education to general authority—can lose their job over membership restrictions. And people who are employed by or otherwise economically dependent on church members, including service providers, content creators and distributors, and anybody who trades on reputation and relationship in the community, can be affected economically and socially by church discipline.

Although there is a book or at least a long-form article to be written about the pros and cons and future of church discipline, for purposes of this book church discipline is not going away any time soon, so it's a feature or bug of the current system we learn to deal with. Learning to deal with it takes three phases:

- **UNDERSTANDING** The system is not all that it seems.
- **CONSEQUENCES** For some of us some of the time the consequences are not quite as bad as we fear.

- **MANAGEMENT** To some degree we can learn to manage the process. In important ways this refers us back to the *Control* chapter in the Working with Ourselves section.

UNDERSTANDING

STAKE PRESIDENT

The single most important reveal about Membership Councils specifically and church discipline generally is that stake presidents run the show.

- Bishops do hold Membership Councils in some circumstances and manage a fair amount of informal discipline and limitations on members, but bishops take direction from their stake president ("A bishop counsels with the stake president about specific situations. He must receive approval from the stake president before holding a membership council." GH 32.5.2) and refer most of the serious cases to a Stake Membership Council. This is required if a man or woman who has been endowed will likely have his or her membership withdrawn (by practice and by the GH at 32.5.1).
- It is widely believed that stake presidents receive instruction or advice from their Area Presidency and other senior church leaders. Some of this is by the book. See GH 32.6.3 regarding matters that require extra sensitivity and guidance, which include apostasy and embezzling church funds, and questions related to "persons who identify as transgender" (GH 32.6.3.2). Some of this is rumored, especially when it appears there is a systematic approach or pattern to a series of

membership removals (excommunications). However, whatever happens behind the scenes, it is all in the form of suggestion and advice. The stake president is still the one holding the Membership Council. I have known a stake president to be released for not following advice, but the equivalent of the Area Presidency at the time did not step in and hold their own disciplinary hearing.

- There is a Membership Council and instructions about holding Membership Councils. However, the stake president or bishop decides who is present, starting with his counselors (by default), and the purpose of the Council is to advise the stake president (or bishop), who has final responsibility for the decision (GH 32.10.3, bullet point 9). The Council does not control or decide the outcome.
- There is an appeal possible in some circumstances. However, reported experience is that appeals are not considered for matters of procedure or General Handbook instructions, but only considered for matters of new information or fundamental fairness. And are seldom successful.
- This chapter does not focus on removal of restrictions or readmission to the church, but in fact there are certain matters for which First Presidency approval is required. (GH 32.16.1, bullet point 9). These include murder and incest and other serious matters, and most relevant to this chapter, apostasy.

In short—after five longish bullet points to explain possible exceptions—the bottom line is that the stake president (or mission president in mission branches and districts) holds most of the cards and runs the show—most of the time, in most circumstances. Advice and recommendations from all directions, including the General Handbook, is relevant and reviewable. But all the advice and recommendations funnel into the stake president and his decisions are very nearly unreviewable. If you don't like what your bishop is doing, an appeal to the stake president can be productive. If you don't like what your stake president is doing, tough. While there is a formal appeal process from the stake president, in most cases it is a paper tiger.

REPENTANCE VS PROTECTION

The church discipline system has a dual character. On the one hand, it is supposed to make us better, to help the individual through a repentance process to become a new person. On the other hand, it is supposed to protect the church—the institution and the community—by removing or expelling people who would cause harm. There is a good argument that mixing the two purposes was a bad idea from the beginning and needs to be reformed. However, for so long as we live in the present system, bishops and stake presidents can and will mix the concepts and the rhetoric, in both directions. In other words, they can impose limitations intended as control and punishment and eviction while saying it's for your own good. And they can exercise patience and kindness while your actions continue to harm others.

Whatever language the stake president or bishop uses, it is vitally important that inside-of-the-edge people understand what's up, what is the purpose of a disciplinary meeting. Broadly speaking we can distinguish four categories (with made-up names simply to be memorable):

- **VICTIMLESS SINS** Private behavior and choices where you generally acknowledge problems with such behavior and choices.
- **SINS WITH VICTIMS** Behavior and choices that are hurting other individuals, in your family or your com-

munity. Where you generally acknowledge problems with such behavior and choices.
- **FUNDAMENTAL DISAGREEMENT** Behavior and choices that your church leader thinks are wrong and damaging, but you don't agree there is a problem in the first place.
- **PRIOR DECISION** Situations where withdrawing your membership is decided already.

In the *victimless sin* category, it would be surprising to hold a Membership Council in the first place. These are generally counseling and assistance situations, unless they escalate to a fundamental disagreement where the bishop thinks it's a big deal and you don't. For people living on the inside of the edge, the expectation is that if you are in general agreement and want help you go to the bishop, but if you think or know there is a fundamental disagreement you don't bring it up.

The *sins with victims* category is or should be the core of a church disciplinary system. These are cases where there is likely to be a difference of opinion about who is harmed and how, misunderstandings of facts, legal system-like questions about punishment, rehabilitation, and restorative justice, and religious questions about sin and repentance and contrition. If you are involved in this kind of case, you may not like it and may feel harmed by the system. However, while an outside observer might question whether the matter should be adjudicated in the law or the church or both, the same outside observer is likely to think it should be taken up somewhere.

For purposes of this book and questions about living on the inside of the edge, the *fundamental disagreement* and *prior decision* categories are what you came here to read about. If you marry someone of the same sex, you think it's a right and proper and holy thing to do. Under current standards, your bishop and stake president likely think otherwise. If you preach or publish about how sinful or misguided current church leaders are, you probably think it's important, i.e., right and proper and necessary. Your bishop and stake president likely think otherwise. At a somewhat less dramatic level, if you smoke marijuana recreationally you might (or might not) feel a touch of guilt, but if it's a regular practice you have probably worked out a good and right feeling about the practice. Chances are your bishop and stake president don't agree with you.

When your bishop or stake president sees but doesn't agree, there are (broadly speaking) three possible outcomes:

1. You change. Call it repentance. Call it a concession. Call it a cost/benefit analysis. The result is that you make the big move.
2. You reach détente. A don't-ask-don't-tell stand-off. An agreement to disagree. An agreed withholding of a temple recommend but otherwise full participation. If your bishop or stake president is open to negotiation, there are all sorts of middle-way positions possible.
3. You leave or resign and/or your membership is formally limited or withdrawn, in one step or through an escalation process.

An important exception to these three possible outcomes is the *prior decision* situation. "You change or you go" is a too-common starting point for a church leader placed in a position of authority. Church culture is strongly hierarchical and leaders believe they should be listened to and obeyed; the Church is not big on discussion and compromise. In practical effect a *prior decision* means the stake president has made up his mind before he even sees you, and opens with a belief that no option 2 is possible. He thinks you either give in or go. He might be wrong about that. There might be a middle ground. But recognizing that he has already made a decision is important in how you manage the process.

APOSTASY

People living on the edge often have a heightened interest in the charge of apostasy. For the typical centrist member, apostasy is sometimes in the news but almost never a personal concern. But for someone on the edge with recognized differences and issues with the institutional church, apostasy looms as a danger, a fear, a possibility. The basic definition of apostasy seems to set a high bar, but the danger persists.

> Repeatedly acting in clear and deliberate public opposition to the Church, its doctrine, its policies, or its leaders. (GH 32.6.3.2, first bullet)

"Repeatedly" and "clear and deliberate" and "public" are followed by "persisting" and "showing a pattern" and "continuing" and "formally joining" (in following sentences in the description of apostasy). This sense of continuation and repetition and formality makes it unlikely anyone will slip or trip into apostasy as defined. Maybe heterodoxy or even heresy, but apostasy as defined requires repeated clear and deliberate action.

On the other hand, the definition is full of undefined and sometimes controversial terms. To begin with, what does "opposition" mean? I expect there is wide agreement that a direct public challenge, i.e., arguing in public that the church or a doctrine or policy or leader is wrong, is opposition. Publicly criticizing church leaders seems to be a particularly sensitive form of opposition. But what about arguing for or voting for or campaigning for a law or candidate or practice the church opposes? That is, not taking on the church directly, but arguing a contrary position in a different forum. In recent conversations this includes same-sex marriage, abortion, recreational marijuana, certain religious freedom issues, and even property taxes and income taxes on churches. Suppose you believe a same-sex couple will be excommunicated if they get married; is it opposition to perform the wedding, in a civil service without any reference to any particular church? For another example in a public service setting, is it opposition for a church member on the city council to vote against a zoning variance that would permit a Mormon temple to be built within city limits?

For an answer, see above regarding the stake president. The answer to how "opposition" is defined is not found in a book or hinted at in General Conference or the teachings of any of the General Authorities. "Opposition" means what your stake president thinks it means.

Similarly, what are the doctrines, what are the policies, who are the leaders? Is there a list of doctrines? What about policies? The words "doctrines" and "policies" were just added in 2020. Has anyone worked out what they mean? Are all doctrines and policies equally important? Which leaders count? Your local Relief Society president, or only the prophets and apostles, or whoever is holding the Membership Council?

For an answer, see above regarding the stake president. You can find endless arguments about policy and doctrine, and whether "leaders" means only prophets and apostles, or also means your bishop or Relief Society president, but the answer is the same. Doctrines and policies and leaders mean what your stake president thinks they mean. In particular, "leaders" almost always includes your stake president.

My opinion, based on years of observation inside and outside church disciplinary councils, is that the definitions seldom matter at all. The reason is that most cases in the realm of apostasy are decided based on defying an order. "Opposition to leaders" is the entry point. If the bishop or stake president tells you to do something, or to refrain from doing something, or to not do it again, whatever the original offense, if you do it again you may now be acting in opposition. A similar self-referential or recursive process can be found in following sentences in the Handbook, which include the phrase "after being corrected by the bishop or stake president." To be charged with a direct act of apostasy can mire a Membership Council in debates about these several terms, and different people will have different opinions about "opposition" and "policy." However, an indirect act of apostasy, i.e., doing what you were told not to do, refusing to follow orders, can be a trivial case for a Membership Council and for the stake president holding the hearing. The stake president said don't and you did it anyway. Case closed.

CONSEQUENCES

Without question, the church disciplinary system can be painful and even devastating. I am going to argue here that it's not quite as bad as it looks, but that is arguing from a low bar. Not as bad as it looks is still painful and even devastating. Having set a very modest expectation, the reason for talking about consequences at all is that there is a lot of fear around church discipline, and it helps manage emotions to take a clear-eyed look at what can happen and what it might cost.

First of all, let's acknowledge and set aside the *victimless sins* and *sins with victims* categories. You know something needs to change. You might not like it, and you and your bishop might have different levels of concern and different ideas about process, but you can usually agree that it's good for you and good for the community.

Next, consider the too-common situation where your livelihood is threatened by church discipline. This is a truly difficult place to be, and church discipline can loom large in your life plans. It's a reason for people living on the inside of the edge to find other kinds of employment. However, realistically in the way these matters are administered, formal church discipline is like the edge of the cliff, and the temple recommend like a fence well away from the edge. If you are not able to maintain a temple recommend with a reasonably straightforward approach to the interview process, you have jumped the fence and your employment is at risk already. Formal church discipline might be the last straw, but you've been dancing on the cliff edge for some time.

Consequences with respect to church activity—speaking, prayers, temple recommend, etc.—are no small thing. However, if you're really on the edge to begin with, these are generally mixed experiences. Some costs, but also some benefits. Cue here the jokes about getting a 10% raise when you are told you can't pay tithing. And a lot of these costs are ones you make up. It's a loss because you want it. If you didn't want it you wouldn't feel the loss. This can be something of a salve. Not a cure, but something to soften the blow.

A somewhat complicated category of loss is the ordinances you have enjoyed. If you value your baptism, if you want to take the sacrament, if membership is important to you, taking them away hurts. Some part of the pain is self-generated. You only hurt because you care. But another harm is the specter of permanence. There is a common argument from church leaders that baptism is canceled, that ordinations are of no consequence, that everything you were taught to value and to strive for is gone, eliminated, removed. The message is that you are consigned to the lowest order of heaven unless and until you return to the Church's good graces. This is deeply meaningful and hurtful. A friend showed me a letter she received from a local church leader saying she was no longer considered "born in the covenant." In her family of birth this amounted to, and was described by them as, being disowned.

The doctrine of permanence or cancellation is not clear. Personally, I don't believe it—I don't believe the effect of covenants and sacraments and ordinances is canceled. However, "not clear" is the limited offer I can make in the realm of not quite as bad as it looks. On the side of cancellation, people typically argue from D&C 128:8 that by the power of the priesthood "whatsoever you bind on earth shall be bound in heaven, and whatsoever you loose on earth shall be loosed in heaven." The "loosed in heaven" phrase, used as an assertion of power and authority in the priesthood, gives a sense of cancellation. Arguing to the contrary, on the side of continuation, D&C 128:8 has to do with proxy ordinances, and logic and common sense tells us it's complicated. Can we really bind a deceased person to a baptism they did not and would not choose? Can the power of the priesthood force into place a marriage that the couple never chose and would not want? These rhetorical questions may be unanswerable but demonstrate that it's not a simple matter, that the Priesthood declaring something doesn't necessarily make it so. For living persons there is the further argument that the effect of a baptism or confirmation or ordination or sealing is between the individual(s) involved and God. In other words, the Church and the Priesthood can be viewed as facilitators, while the power and ongoing effect happens in the heart and soul of the individual and in their relationship with God.

Finally, with respect to cancellation or continuation of past ordinances, the Church's record keeping system evidences at least ambivalence; I would argue that it comes down on the side of continuation rather than cancellation. GH 32.14.4 describes what happens when an individual is readmitted, after having their membership withdrawn (being excommunicated). The process requires a new Membership Council and a new baptism and confirmation. However, after the new baptism and confirmation, and after restoration of blessings for someone who was previously endowed, a new membership record is created that shows the *dates of the original baptism and other ordinances*, and the record makes no reference to the loss of Church membership.

Perhaps the most lasting and consequential effect of the church disciplinary system is loss of connection with the Church, loss of status, and loss of self-respect. People I know who have been excommunicated haven't come back. People I know who have been excommunicated and did return feel like permanent second-class citizens in the Church. They assume they are forever closed off from higher callings. They believe their opinions voiced in Sunday School are accorded lower status because of their history. People I know who have been harshly treated even if not excommunicated talk about it 30 years later as a permanent psychic scar. I was genuinely surprised when I was called as a bishop, when the stake president's recommendation was approved. I believed there was a permanent black mark in the file related to issues from my mission days (and then I went on to feel like a failure as a bishop in half-a-dozen ways). I don't have a satisfactory answer. I'm sorry.

The trauma persists, the scars are real, even when the bishops and stake presidents involved are kind and thoughtful and caring. It might be conceivable to build a better system, but that's a different book. For our purposes, in the survival game, perhaps the only small comfort is that when we add up all the people who have been subject to church discipline, and all the people who also have reason to feel second-class—female, LGBTQ, single, divorced, poor, poorly educated, no temple recommend, no mission, etc.—that is a large majority of active church members. None of us are alone.

MANAGEMENT

For management of the Membership Council or church disciplinary process, the basic principles are the same as discussed in the *Control* chapter in the Working with Yourself section of this book. Take the offensive. Be an adult in the room. Decide what you want. Work with the stake president. Take account of everything your stake president says, everything you know about him, everything that matters or moves him. When it comes to serious matters in a Membership Council context, your stake president is the key to the whole process and outcome.

> **SIDEBAR** In limited cases for some privileged people there is sometimes a way to play the system. The Church is sufficiently hierarchical that if you can find

an obviously senior church authority to speak for you—someone your stake president will respect as senior—that can make a difference. It's not in the book, but it works. Having grown up with an Apostle-then-President for a grandfather, I'm sure I have enjoyed such privilege in the past. I remember thinking it was available to everybody. It's not. Don't count on it.

Being an adult in the room means learning the system and preparing your case. Being an adult in the room means not looking for or expecting a fair adversarial system, but recognizing that the stake president is effectively prosecutor, judge, and jury, with a very limited avenue for appeal. Being an adult in the room also means preparing yourself. Take stock of where you are, what you care about, what lines you cannot cross, what you are willing and able to change, and what you are not. Decide whether you are willing to remain part of the system. You have choices, including to refuse a meeting, to speak or not speak to a Membership Council, or to resign in advance of a Membership Council.

Finally, for those few who have the personal fortitude and energy to work on the system at the same time they are subject to discipline, call on your bishop or stake president to be his best self. Give him room and opportunity to be a pastor, to love and support, to be helpful. That might mean negotiating over process (who is in the room, for example). It might even mean negotiating the result. After internalizing how much power the stake president has, you might well conclude that arguing as if before a judge is less effective than negotiating for common ground and win-win propositions.

WORKING WITH THE CULTURE

CHURCH VS GOSPEL

You've heard the arguments. "That's church, not gospel," meaning, the part of the church you're complaining about is not the gospel of Christ and can be taken relatively lightly as a man-made artifact. "That's culture, not the church," meaning, even if you are bothered by culture, don't dismiss the church. "That's policy, not doctrine," meaning, the teaching or practice you are picking at is time-bound and is likely to change.

From a different point of view, consider Eugene England's essay "Why the Church is As True As the Gospel" (Sunstone 1999), arguing there are good reasons to be part of the human-made church and in the pews on Sunday. And the earlier "The Gospel and the Church" (Ronald Poelman, October 1984 General Conference) which *as revised* argues that understanding the proper relationship between the gospel and the church will lead to "the realization of gospel goals through happy, fulfilling participation in the Church."

Welcome to the dance. These distinctions and comparisons are performative (chosen to have an effect) rather than constative (descriptive, can be true or false). They are advocacy, arguments to convince you to stay or to obey. They are not Truth, not in the way we usually think of abstract propositions, nor are they particularly useful for a person trying to live on the inside of the edge.

On the decomposition side—distinguishing and diminishing the importance of culture and policy—one reason the distinction doesn't work is that the Church or church or culture or teaching or practice we live with and deal with, that we are on the edge of and trying to stay engaged with, is all of the above. Making fine logical distinctions doesn't change real life experience. When a hand is raised in Sunday School, you get gospel or church or folklore or policy or doctrine without distinction and often without awareness. Definitions shift for the convenience of the speaker. There is no essential or fundamental line between culture and church or policy and principle.

On the synthesis side—the church equated to the gospel—the argument proves too much. Church-equals-gospel ends up meaning everything is part of the whole. Every lesson, every requirement, every obnoxious teenager and abusive leader, every temple recommend question and difficult lesson manual and anything else you find disagreeable is part of the gospel. Maybe that works for some people, but for anybody working to survive on the inside of the edge, the implied all-or-nothing position is not survivable.

POLICY IS NOT DOCTRINE

The strong case for distinguishing policy from doctrine or church from gospel comes up in explaining history and change over time. If you engage at all, you are likely to hear the following sorts of arguments:

> Q: How is it that for more than a century, boys were ordained to the Aaronic Priesthood only on their twelfth birthday or later, and now they can be ordained when they are 11?
>
> A: Church policy, not doctrine.

Q: Does that mean girls can be ordained?

A: No, that's not policy, that's doctrine.

Q: How is it that for more than a century men of black African descent could not be ordained to any kind of priesthood, but since 1978 they can be?

A: Policy, not doctrine.

Q: How do you know?

A: Because it changed. In 1970 we described it as doctrine, with an explanation. Since the change in 1978, from that point on we have called it policy and disavowed all former explanations.

Policy tends to be time- and place-sensitive. The gospel is supposed to be eternal, always and forever the same. That might work if we stuck to a narrow definition of gospel such as the saving acts of God due to the work of Jesus in Gethsemane or on the cross, and Jesus' resurrection from the dead bringing reconciliation between humans and God. This is the sort of definition I find by an on-line search in basic Christian (not Mormon) sources. We might cite Paul's first letter to the Corinthians: "That Christ died for our sins . . . that he was buried, and that he rose again the third day." Or 3 Nephi 27: "This is the gospel . . . that I came into the world to do the will of my Father . . . that I might be lifted up upon the cross . . . that I might draw all men unto me." But we don't. We keep wanting to include church practices and teachings in the "gospel."

The cross and resurrection can feel very limiting. We want to expand. We want to preach the lasting and eternal importance of temple practices and covenants; we want to include priesthood authority and keys as something permanent; we want to describe ordinances and sacraments, including baptism and marriage and sealing as eternal principles. We fear that anything we don't describe as a lasting part of the gospel might drop into the human-made category, including that what is made by humans can change and is susceptible to exceptions. On the other hand, whenever we describe something as a lasting part of the gospel and then it changes, we engage in an embarrassing revision of history.

Very quickly it becomes apparent that distinctions between church and gospel, and between policy and doctrine, are artificial and instrumental, i.e., made up with an end in mind. If it's important to the speaker, it's gospel. On the other hand, if you're looking for an exception or want to feel good about cafeteria style Mormonism, you tend to describe lots of things as policy or practice, where others would call them doctrine.

From the institutional point of view, the distinctions hardly matter. Apostasy as defined by the Church includes "clear and deliberate public opposition to the **CHURCH**, its **DOCTRINE**, its **POLICIES**, or its **LEADERS**" (GH 32.6.3.2, emphasis added). Furthermore, the practical effect of church discipline practices is that these terms mean whatever your Stake President thinks they mean.

The bottom line is that there is very little utility to distinguishing between policy and doctrine or arguing that an observance is only a practice and shouldn't be taken seriously.

CHURCH EQUALS GOSPEL

The Church teaches that the Church and the gospel are essentially the same thing. Gospel goals are achieved through Church participation. Faith in Christ is confidence in the Restoration and the divine calling of Joseph Smith. Supporting and devoting resources to the Church is building the Kingdom of God.

Equating the Church to the gospel is not a small thing. It is radically different from mainstream Christianity and even the main threads of restoration theology. For many Christians the *gospel* is Jesus on the cross and reconciliation between humans and God, and *churches* are meeting places, congregations, a set of teachings and sacraments, a place to practice, a hierarchy of leaders and decision makers. In that kind of understanding, equating gospel and church would be a category error. The common understanding of the restorationist movement reinforces this view. As a broad generalization, the idea of restoration is to correct faults or deficiencies in the church by appealing to the primitive church for a model.[1] The Sixth Article of Faith positions Joseph Smith's church in just this way: "We believe in the same organization that existed in the Primitive Church, namely, apostles, prophets, pastors, teachers, evangelists, and so forth." For most restorationist movements the primitive church referenced is a hierarchy of leaders and decision makers, a meeting place, a congregation. By contrast, for the modern Church of Jesus Christ of Latter-day Saints the primitive church referenced is all that but merged into the gospel as the Kingdom of God on earth.

Modern Mormons are likely to turn to the Church's definition of itself. When we talk about The Restoration (the Joseph Smith restoration) we refer to an apostasy that removed the fullness of the gospel from the earth, and describe a restoration of the fullness of the gospel in the nineteenth century. Standard Mormon doctrine is that "The fulness of the gospel has been restored, and the true Church of Jesus Christ is on the earth again."[2] In practical effect there is no difference between the institutional earth-bound church and the gospel and the Kingdom of God. They are one and the same. The Church of Jesus Christ of Latter-day Saints is "the only true and living church upon the face of the whole earth." The capstone covenant

---

1. Douglas Allen Foster and Anthony L. Dunnavant, *The Encyclopedia of the Stone-Campbell Movement: Christian Church (Disciples of Christ), Christian Churches/Churches of Christ, Churches of Christ* (Wm. B. Eerdmans Publishing, 2004).

2. "Restoration of the Gospel" entry in *True To The Faith, A Gospel Reference* (The Church of Jesus Christ of Latter-day Saints, 2004). Note that "fulness" was the common spelling in the nineteenth century and "fulness of the gospel" appears that way in several places in the Book of Mormon and Doctrine & Covenants. "Fullness" has been the more common and now standard spelling since early in the twentieth century.

in temples, the Law of Consecration, is a covenant to support the Church as equivalent to the Kingdom of God on earth.

> The law of consecration is that we consecrate our time, our talents, and our money and property to the cause of the Church; such are to be available to the extent they are needed to further the Lord's interests on earth.[3]

Some of us—people on the edge perhaps more than others—might question whether certain outlying or peculiar aspects of the Mormon experience belong as part of the gospel. This will forever be an open question for individuals, but there is a good argument the Church itself does not allow for exceptions. Ronald Poelman's 1984 "Gospel and the Church" talk is ancient history, but the changes to the original illustrate what many people think is the official church view. In the original Elder Poelman made several distinctions between the gospel and the church. Following the conference the talk was rewritten, re-taped from the pulpit in the Tabernacle, and spliced into the conference tape for distribution, thereby becoming the official version. The differences in text are revealing. The original included a suggestion that failure to distinguish between the gospel and the church could lead to confusion and misplaced priorities. The revised final official version says that understanding the proper relationship between the gospel and the church will lead to "the realization of gospel goals through happy, fulfilling participation in the Church." The original suggested that as we increase in knowledge, acceptance, and application of gospel principles, we become less dependent on church programs and our lives become gospel centered. The revised final official version replaces "less dependent on Church programs" with "more effectively utilize the Church."

---

3. Elder Bruce R. McConkie, "Obedience, Consecration, and Sacrifice," April 1975 General Conference.

The close identification of Church with gospel, and of church participation with gospel goals, can be problematic for people working to live on the inside of the edge. As discussed above in *What is the Church*, survival entails defining the church for ourselves; not accepting somebody else's definition, much less accepting an all-in-one church-equals-gospel definition. Survival entails making adult decisions about interviews, managing the temple recommend process, interrogating the bishop about callings. Accepting a church-equals-gospel position makes all those decisions a foregone conclusion. It is theoretically possible for you to reach the same conclusions on your own. But taking them on as decided for you, as if there is one category, one activity, one thought—ALL IN—is a recipe for disaster in a life on the edge.

WHAT TO DO ABOUT IT

You may choose to argue distinctions between church and gospel, between policies and doctrine. That's a personal decision. The analysis above suggests you should treat it like you would a sport or a hobby or an academic exercise. Something you volunteer for, where you might keep score but when the game is over, or you get up from your study desk, life goes on mostly independent of anything you discovered.

Likely, hopefully, you are interested in learning the gospel, developing faith in Jesus Christ, working out the meaning of salvation, finding God. The analysis above suggests you need to be about that business largely on your own. The institutional Church provides some tools and some learnings, but the idea that the Church equals gospel is so deeply ingrained that Church teachings may be confusing and may even require some unlearning. You will have to separate twenty-first century custom from nineteenth century teachings from first century writings. You will have to confront the one-true-church doctrine and consider whether The Church of Jesus Christ of Latter-day Saints is the one true church, whether there is "One Lord, One Faith, One Baptism" (Ephesians 4:5) as many Christians will recite, or whether there are many paths or some form of universal gospel.

However, for readers of this book the question is not where to find a new hobby. Nor is it how to find God, important as that is. For readers of this book the question is about surviving on the inside of the edge. For that purpose, I suggest there is no deep meaning or importance to the church vs gospel distinction or alignment. The lines that look important from a distance are like lines in the sand—easily disturbed and quick to wash away. Instead, I suggest the metaphor of a dance. Step lightly in and around "church" and "culture" and "gospel" and "doctrine" and "teaching" and "practice" and so on. Recognize that the Church or church we engage with is all of that and more—gospel, institution, hierarchy, culture, folklore, policy, doctrine, nineteenth century teachings and twenty-first century teachings. Take in all of these arguments as an observer with a light touch. Don't let any of the decompositions or syntheses become determinative. Use them all to find and make sense and make room. Rest on the words of the modern hymn *Lord of the Dance*:

> I danced on a Friday
> When the sky turned black
> It's hard to dance
> With the devil on your back.
> They buried my body
> And they thought I'd gone,
> But I am the Dance,
> And I still go on.
>
> Dance, then, wherever you may be,
> I am the Lord of the Dance, said he,
> And I'll lead you all, wherever you may be,
> And I'll lead you all in the Dance, said he.

SHIBBOLETHS

A shibboleth is like a group password or a token of belonging. The word comes from chapter 12 in the book of Judges, where the Gileadites and Ephraimites could tell each other apart by pronunciation of "shibboleth" because the Ephraimites had no "sh" sound in their language. As a result, the most common modern use refers to distinctive words or phrases. However, shibboleth can refer to any custom, principle, practice, or belief that distinguishes insiders from outsiders.

Shibboleths are important because you can't choose them. You can choose what to do about them, you can choose not to care, but you can't make them go away or be irrelevant. Shibboleths tend to be meaningful to the inside group, almost meaningless to outsiders, and of intense interest and attention for people living at the edge.

The Mormon community has a lot of special vocabulary, including common words with special meanings. Anybody wanting to move within the Mormon world needs to know that wards are congregations, not voting districts; Primary is a noun, not an adjective; stakes are ecclesiastical units, not tent pegs; and Seminary is a high school-age supplemental religious education, not a graduate level preparation for the ministry. To be fair, this book makes no concession to specialized Mormon language, and if you have managed to read this far, you likely have the vocabulary down pat. What is more interesting for this discussion is the common language cues, customs, and practices that serve as shibboleths, as markers or tokens of an insider.

There are a lot of shibboleths in Mormon culture, but three examples should suffice to make the important points.

The way you **PRAY AND BEAR TESTIMONY** indicates insider status. In English-speaking units, insiders use King James English as public prayer language, for example "we ask thee" and "thy Son" just as in the Sacrament prayers. "You" and "your" stand out enough to say the speaker is not of the tribe. Similarly, insider prayers are addressed to "Heavenly Father" (with small variations). Never to Jesus Christ or Lord or Heavenly Parents (or any other form that would imply a feminine). An insider testimony almost always uses "I know" phrases. Depending on the speaker's age, an insider testimony (older version) is likely to include "the Church is true" and "the Book of Mormon is the word of God" or (younger version) likely to follow the so-called Testimony Glove formula.[1]

- I know that God is our Heavenly Father and He loves us.
- I know that His Son, Jesus Christ, is our Savior and Redeemer.
- I know that Joseph Smith is a prophet of God. He restored the gospel of Jesus Christ to the earth and translated the Book of Mormon by the power of God.
- I know that The Church of Jesus Christ of Latter-day Saints is the Lord's Church on the earth today.
- I know that this Church is led by a living prophet who receives revelation.

---

1. "Testimony Glove," *Friend*, October 2008: 23.

There have been talks suggesting prayer language is mandatory and discouraging some of the variations noted. The Friend magazine article recommending the Testimony Glove refers to "essential parts to a testimony." However, the fact that some leader or periodical suggested a particular formulation is required does not make it a shibboleth. Instead, shibboleths arise as people persist in using the phrases. Endless repetition makes shibboleths. After hearing prayers one way for years, an insider doesn't need to think or analyze when you slip in a "you" instead of a "thee." After hearing testimonies one way for years, an insider recognizes an outsider instantly upon hearing "I believe" instead of "I know." On the other hand, an outsider to the culture probably won't pick up on the differences and if they do hear they don't care.

You can choose to use "you" in addressing God. You can choose to deliver a completely non-traditional testimony. Nobody will stop you. Alternatively, you can decide to treat public prayers and public testimonies as a culturally sensitive performance and use all the traditional words and phrases. You can decide you don't care what others think and choose not to pay attention. However, you cannot turn off the instantaneous recognition that you are or are not one of us. That recognition and label is completely out of your control.

COFFEE works as a shibboleth. An insider would never be seen drinking coffee. An insider might say it's about obeying a commandment. Or qualifying for a temple recommend. Or because they have internalized the Word of Wisdom as the right way to live. An insider might even say they don't like the taste. But allowing for and not detracting from any of those explanations, an insider will know with absolute certainty that being seen drinking a cup of coffee would mark them as a renegade or heretic or unbeliever—an outsider. At the same time, a true outsider, someone who has no connection or history with the Church, would hardly notice a cup of coffee. It carries a clear message to the in-group. It means almost nothing to outsiders. It is fraught with meaning for someone on the edge.

You can make your own decisions about the commandment or obedience aspect of drinking coffee. You can make your own decisions about answering the temple recommend questions. You can make your own decision whether you care. But you cannot make your own decision about what other people will think. About the labels they will apply. You cannot make coffee meaningless in the culture. In that way, appearances do matter.

CLOTHING works as a shibboleth. Garments (another special-use word) are themselves a shibboleth—a very strong marker when noticed. However, garments are worn under other clothing and often hidden. As a result, the practical mark of the insider, the shibboleth, is outer clothing that would cover garments, which usually means sleeves, covering the middle, and a long-enough skirt or slacks to cover garment legs. Clothing styles change from place to place and are influenced by climate, but even in temperate climates a sleeveless top is of little note in the outside world but scandalous in the Mormon world.

You can make your own decisions about wearing garments. You can make your own decision whether you care. However, if you do not wear garments or do not wear clothing that would cover garments, you cannot decide what other people think about you. You cannot make clothing meaningless. In many climates you cannot even choose to fit in, because any choice you make will stand out as odd to someone—to insiders, or to outsiders.

WHAT TO DO ABOUT IT

Some of what we are calling shibboleths have additional meanings and importance. For example, some of the markers have that significance because they have been made part of the temple recommend process, and some of the prayer language, for example, gets emphasized over the pulpit. However, for many of us, much of the time, shibboleths feel like a prime example of appearance over substance.

As such they can be enormously frustrating. The outside world doesn't care. In many cases you don't really care. But the culture cares and will not go away and will judge you every step of the way. If you are annoyed and would prefer not to think about this subject, you are not alone.

If you are intent on passing as a completely traditional dyed-in-the-wool insider, you will need to pay attention to all the markers of belonging. We have only discussed three here; the real list may seem endless. Don't get a tattoo or a second ear piercing. Wear a white shirt, long tie, and dark suit to church (men), or a skirt or dress (women). Avoid using the word "Mormon." Practice using the phrase "member in good standing." Put up #givethanks posts on Facebook at the right time of year. Learn the names of at least 15 men and two or three women in the leadership of the Church. Memorize meeting schedules. Insiders are assumed to know these things. And for all that effort, people who really know you won't be fooled. They will just think you have the role down pat.

If you are a little more relaxed about how you are seen and labeled, you might be able to treat shibboleths as an opportunity. Down-play their substantive importance in your mind and focus instead on the signaling function. It is possible to be playful about shibboleths. By paying attention to a handful of class markers you can choose to pass as a mainstream insider. Or you can take the markers in a different direction—bare a shoulder and order a latte and scandalize your neighbor. If the temple recommend is important to your place in the society, work the system for the temple recommend. If you are staying in to be a voice for change, or to make space for the marginalized, use the shibboleths in whatever way gains you the right kind of credibility. If you want to signal committed-but-interesting, maybe you wear a suit and tie, and a pink shirt. If you are staying because it is home, or because you feel called to stay and you really don't care what people think, use the shibboleths to make yourself comfortable in the group. Maybe that's a pink shirt, no tie, and rainbow socks, and a custom crafted testimony in your own words.

Life on the edge can be a fearful slog. Paying attention to the shibboleths can be part of that fear. Or life on the edge can be an adventure. Playing the culture as you choose is adventurous. Since you can't have a world without markers, and you will be judged no matter what you do, my recommendation is to play it your way. Use the system rather than let it use you.

ORTHODOXY

We police orthodoxy.

As a general matter the institutional church does not police orthodoxy. The belief questions in the temple recommend interview might trip you up. Joining another church and advocating for that other church in (Mormon) Church meetings is likely to get you into hot water. And the various forms of apostasy (see the *Membership Councils* chapter) are a form of heterodoxy subject to discipline. However, if you are reasonably quiet about your beliefs you can have a long and uncontested relationship with the institution. We don't generally have Inquisitors who go around testing faith.

The "institutional" qualifier and the capital "I" in Inquisitors in the preceding paragraph are important because the church *culture* certainly does police orthodoxy, and we do have lower-case inquisitors who go around testing faith. The measure of orthodoxy changes constantly and failing the orthodoxy test, however determined, can mean you are never asked to speak, not called on in class, and excluded from certain callings (teaching the youth, for example). Not measuring up can mean your Mormon neighbor doesn't talk with you, and parents of children in the ward won't let their children play with your children.

Like shibboleths, the culture's reaction to orthodoxy and heterodoxy is something you can't choose or control. You can choose to get away from the whole thing. You can choose not to care. But if you are choosing to live on the inside of the edge—appropriate to this book—there is a good chance there's something about your beliefs or practices or attitudes that your neighbors can find fault with, and it's highly likely they are watching.

Survival in a judgmental society entails three levels of consideration. First, you need to do the internal work that amounts to not letting them decide for you. Staying or going, participating or remaining quiet, should be your decision, not compelled by the ward or the worldwide church or your next-door neighbor. Yours alone. This is the differentiation work that runs through this whole book, but now it's you versus the community. This book has both a *Working with the Institution* section and a *Working with the Culture* section for this reason.

Second, you need to make decisions about how you're going to interact and how you're going to present yourself. There are options. You can choose to stay quiet. Almost always there are plenty of introverts on the back bench who never raise their hand and politely decline to give prayers and talks. You can hide there. Because there's almost always a quiet group, staying among them seems a perfectly workable survival strategy. I count a ten-year period of my life when I was among that group; in those years I would have predicted it would never change.

In a transition or middle ground, you might practice your Mormon vocabulary; that is, practice sounding orthodox. If it is genuine on your part, it can probably work for the long term. But if it's a mask, a device to get along and not make waves, it may be more work and more stress to try to sound orthodox than to stay quiet or get out. Simply "passing" does not appeal as a long-term strategy.

Eventually you may want to speak up with progressive or radical or provocative ideas and learnings. You can be gentle about it, crafting comments that are not threatening to the orthodox but open the possibility of a second or third way for a few. "Gentle provocateur" has a nice ring. Church leaders have spoken out against the idea of a loyal opposition, but we already know that church leaders are not going to decide everything for us. For some of us the very reason for staying is to be that provocateur, including to make room for others to ask questions, and including to stand up for marginalized people. However, it takes time and effort and a modestly thick skin to make waves. My overall impression is that the culture in many places can tolerate the gentle provocateur for the long term, but it's like surfing a big wave or walking a tightrope—it requires skill and close attention and even so there's a high risk.

Then there's the aggressive flame thrower version of heterodoxy. It may be tempting, and it might even be the right and necessary choice in certain circumstances, but it's not a survival strategy. The culture will kick you out. Hence the stoicism recommendation in the chapter on Anger.

Third, you need to do the external work that determines where the current lines of orthodoxy are drawn regarding issues and topics that you're likely to talk about. You need to have at least a well-grounded theory when you choose to speak up. If you don't have a theory and some confidence in your theory, that would be a good reason to sit quietly and observe for a while. In any event, determining the lines of orthodoxy is a hard problem. The lines are redrawn constantly. They change from time to time and place to place. There is no rule book and no reference site.

My working theory and opinion is that cultural orthodoxy is a hyper-local phenomenon—not dictated by the central church and more like a ward or stake definition. Just for example, here's a short version of what I see as orthodoxy requirements in the latter half of 2021 in my ward in Utah. This should not be taken as authoritative or correct or even more-likely-than-not. Not even in my ward, where I would guess at least a third of the ward members would disagree. Rather, think of this list as a thought starter or as an outline to start your own discussion for your time and location. As you read, if on three or four lines you say "not for me, not where I live," you get the point.

- Sustain the historicity of the Book of Mormon and the foundational story of the Restoration, with gold plates and Angel Moroni and priesthood restoration.
- Sustain the current Prophet, relying on and expressing confidence in him.
- Support the Plan of Salvation, including a pre-existence, a time-of-testing earth life, and a multiple-degrees-of-glory afterlife.
- Support a traditional version of God and the godhead—the expected yes to the first temple recommend questions, "Do you have faith in and a testimony of God, the Eternal Father; His Son, Jesus Christ; and the Holy Ghost?"
- Consider The Church of Jesus Christ of Latter-day Saints to be the one and only place where the priesthood authority and keys are held. Consider priesthood functions and keys to be limited to worthy male church members.
- Agree that same-sex marriage, abortion, and any kind of sexual relations outside a one-man-one-woman marriage are forbidden.
- Support the idea that the (U.S.) Republican Party is basically aligned with gospel principles, and the (U.S.) Democratic Party is not.
- Consider the Church to be color blind.

With this outline as background, what follows are four special topics in the field of Church orthodoxy.

THE VOICE OF MY SERVANTS

A common orthodoxy is that the words of the President-Prophet of the Church are the words of God.

Upon review, the "voice of God" orthodoxy is not really that the words of the prophet are the words of God. The orthodoxy is that we *say* the words of the prophet are the words of God. If asked for a source, Mormons will cite D&C 1:38. If pressed, many will acknowledge that scripture does not really say the words of the prophet are the words of God. Furthermore, most of us know there are teachings of modern-day prophets that have been disavowed or ignored or buried. In back rooms we talk about polygamy and race and the Adam-God theory, and whether man is as God once was. And it's not just the dead prophets. Current and recent past prophets say enough different things that most of us know of things said in our own lifetime, in our own hearing, that our neighbors disagree with or have decided to ignore.

It's like the whole culture has agreed to say to each other that the words of the prophet are the words of God, while everybody knows, but says under their breath, *except when they're not*, and comes up with various rationales for why they don't accept everything at face value every time.

The heterodox statement, the one that gets you left out of polite Mormon society, is that prophets are just men and make mistakes. Everyone knows it, but we don't say it out loud.

THE ENDOWMENT

The temple endowment presents a creation story, like a third version to add to Genesis 1–3 and Abraham 3–5. A common orthodoxy is that the temple version is literal, historical fact, about creation, about Adam and Eve, about God the Father and Jesus Christ. This is often read back into Genesis and Abraham, so the overlap or consistencies with the temple endowment are also treated as literal historical fact.

It's not clear whether culturally sound orthodox Mormons would stand up to questioning or would openly assert literal historicity. Although there is modern encouragement toward more discussion, there has long been a strong cultural prohibition on talking about any part of temple practice.[1] In part this is extrapolated from explicit prohibitions on talking about some parts of the temple ceremony, but in part it's the nature of gnostic teachings—secret knowledge about how things really are is generally kept close and shared with the inner circle only. But my best guess is that yes, orthodox Mormons would stand up to questioning. In practice, I watch self-satisfied side comments in the middle of a debate about evolution, or a discussion about how other religions portray deity. Side comments that say "but we really *know*, don't we."

Anything you say that contradicts or disagrees with the temple endowment brands you as heterodox. It isn't necessary to reference the endowment or point out the inconsistency. The endowment is baseline, and statements that vary from that baseline will be recognized.

THE ESSAYS

In late 2013 the Church started issuing essays on church history and gospel topics. They were issued one at a time, without fanfare. Over time the essays have been added to the curriculum for seminaries and institutes and referenced in official guides and member materials for adult Sunday School. In 2016 the essays were added to the Gospel Library app (the location has changed once or twice; currently they show up under the Church History tab in the Library app).

---

1. Elder David A. Bednar, "Prepared to Obtain Every Needful Thing," April 2019 General Conference.

Because the essays were issued by the Church, theoretically they changed or could change the lines of orthodoxy. In my twentieth century experience, if you knew something about Nauvoo polygamy or multiple first vision accounts, or had questions about the source for the Book of Abraham, you didn't say anything at church. Today you might think it possible to talk about Nauvoo polygamy discussed in the *Plural Marriage in Kirtland and Nauvoo* essay, or multiple accounts of the First Vision discussed in the *First Vision Accounts* essay, or discuss the Book of Abraham with some of the questions raised in the *Translation and Historicity of the Book of Abraham* essay. You might imagine your fellow ward members thinking you progressive, but nonetheless expect them to include you in polite church conversations.

It is not clear the essays have made that kind of space. Anecdotally, many members have not read the essays and many do not know they exist. The essays, and the issues they address, are often cited by people who leave the church. Those people are not contributing to classroom discussion, which means a higher percentage of the people in class have not read the essays and do not use them to reset boundaries. Tallying my personal experience, I remember classroom discussion about the several accounts of the First Vision; I have heard general but still hushed agreement that Joseph Smith had multiple wives; and in my limited circle I haven't heard anybody interested in discussing the Book of Abraham analytically.

More importantly, my read of the culture around me is that traditional orthodox members want to feel settled in the belief that there is a satisfactory explanation, but don't want to spend a lot of time on those subjects.

SCRIPTURE STUDY

Scripture study is supposed to be a bedrock of church experience. It might be thought that any scripture study activity (hermeneutics), would be accepted and lauded. But it's not the case. There is orthodox hermeneutics and liberal or radical or even dangerous hermeneutics.

Genre in the scriptures is obvious and sometimes explicit. Verse as in a poem or song (the Psalms, for example) is not the same as a letter answering questions (Paul's letter to the Corinthians, for example). Sunday School discussions often allow for some amount of identification and labeling. However, genre as it applies to scripture has low status. Psalms are poetry until a line or a word is needed to make a doctrinal point, and then that line or word or whole psalm is the transcribed word of God. A story in the Pentateuch can be almost mythological until it is repeated in the New Testament or the Book of Mormon or in the temple, and then it is literal history. Many scholars talk about Jonah as satire, but once a General Authority uses the story in a talk, its meaning becomes whatever the General Authority said it was.

Orthodoxy tends to promote one standard meaning for each verse. Often this is the meaning ascribed to the verse by a General Authority in writing or at a General Conference. This kind of orthodox scriptural interpretation looks like eisegesis, where the speaker or the church brings meaning to or inserts meaning into scripture. To inquire into what the scripture really says—a form of exegesis—is a perfectly legitimate scholarly approach, but often outside Mormon orthodoxy.

When we do discuss what the scriptures say, most conservative traditional Mormon discussions look for the original author's intended meaning by examining the words, the translation mechanics, the historical setting, and the textual setting. This *historical-grammatical* approach is likely to be billed as the most literal or faithful to the text as we receive it. It is common among mainstream conservative Protestants and Catholics, and Mormons. The generally conservative mainstream approach also tends to view scripture as influenced by God, i.e., as *revealed*, meaning it contains more refined knowledge and better accuracy than any human writer alone could produce.

By contrast, the approach taken by more liberal Protestants and Catholics, and sometimes by heterodox Mormons, looks for a primitive or original meaning for the text, including by taking account of the broader social and historical context. This *historical critical* approach can suggest multiple meanings and even meanings the original author did not intend or was not aware of. The same liberal exegesis is also relatively more likely to take an approach that is *rational* (as opposed to revealed) which considers scripture as a human oral and written tradition.

If your scripture study includes attention to genre, if you look for meaning in the scriptures rather than scriptures to quote to make a point, if you take a critical and rational approach in your interpretations, you may find yourself outside orthodoxy. If these methods of study lead to a contradictory interpretation and you say it out loud, you may find yourself canceled from further conversation.

CONCLUSION

It's been clear to me for decades that I am not orthodox by Mormon standards. I have been silent for many years. I have been afraid for many more. The culture is powerful, and it will shut you down.

You can't beat the culture. You can only decide what to do about it. Distilling the advice above, do the differentiation work that gets you to a place where you make the decisions. Don't let the cultural definition of orthodoxy tell you what to believe or what to do. Make conscious choices about how to be present in the community. If you need time to figure it out but you want to be present, choose silence. If you are going to speak up, whether to express your own version of orthodoxy, or to try to pass as somebody else's version, or to open the way to new ideas, tread lightly. There is no standardized rule book, and the map wanders all over place and time.

SPIRIT OF CONTENTION

In the modern social media world there's a common meme that starts with "Cancel my meetings" or "Can't sleep" or "Give me a minute" with the punchline "Somebody's wrong on the internet." This is the world of Mormon speculative theology, doctrine, and practice. We have ideas, we are confident in our beliefs, we know how it works, but we are not agreed. I am right, you are the "somebody" who's wrong—at church or on the internet.

I'm not talking about orthodoxy (see the previous chapter) where there is a broad enough consensus that taking a particular position becomes a me-against-the-crowd contest. The speculative world is more like me against you. Or a few of us against a few of you. Admittedly the line between heterodoxy and speculation is fuzzy; we've already talked about how difficult it can be to define orthodoxy. Rather than reworking the distinction, it might be easier to come at this from the judgment end of things. One common breakdown for how we judge each other is between morality, sociability, and competence. When you're thrown out for heterodoxy it's a moral judgment—we don't like your ideas or your behavior. When you're thrown out for contention, it's a sociability judgment—we don't like the way you treat us.

Have you heard arguments about any of the following?

> Salvation is free for all, but the real goal is exaltation in the Celestial Kingdom with every member of the family included. That takes work and obedience and commitment and endurance.
>
> **VS**
>
> This life and the eternities are both times of agency and progression. What we learn here will stay with us. What we don't learn here we will learn and progress to in the next life. Eventually everyone who wants to return to Heavenly Father will get there.

> Deacons must wear white shirts to pass the sacrament, priests must get every word of the sacrament prayer right, and members must take the bread and water with their right hand.
>
> **VS**
>
> Young priesthood holders should act respectfully and reverently in preparing and passing the sacrament, and members should do the same in receiving the sacrament.

> Blessings come to the righteous as a reward. Punishment comes to the wicked.
>
> **VS**
>
> Bad things happen because Satan causes them.
>
> **VS**
>
> God allows bad things to happen because that's the only way to preserve agency.
>
> **VS**

Everything happens for a reason. God's plan is never defeated. There is purpose in the divine plan for everything that seems good, and everything that seems bad.

Nephi was a prophet and when he says his brothers did him wrong, it must be so.
vs
Nephi was a younger brother. Let's take that into account when he says his brothers did him wrong.

Jesus is distinct from the Father.
vs
God is one.
vs
God exists as three persons but one being.
vs
The Father, the Son, and the Holy Ghost are aspects of God.

Only ordinances performed under the direction of one who holds the keys are valid and efficacious. Ordinances performed here are recorded in heaven. Ordinances canceled here are canceled in heaven.
vs
When understood properly, ordinances lead to a change in understanding, spirit, and actions of the participant that can be neither forced nor taken away.

The (new) *For the Strength of Youth* pamphlet talks about principles and the real world answers or application of the principles are found in the (old) *For the Strength of Youth* pamphlet.
vs

The (new) *For the Strength of Youth* pamphlet talks about principles and we really mean it. There is not a one-answer-for-all-circumstances reply to should I or may I get a tattoo.

The purpose of human life on earth is for God to test our obedience.

vs

The purpose of human life on earth is to learn and experience.

vs

The purpose of human life on earth is to form families and have children.

If you recall arguments about some of the items above, you get the point of this chapter. If you respond to some of the items above as "of course" correct and others as "of course" wrong, you are very likely engaged in this contentious world yourself. If you just opened your copy of the General Handbook or reached for a well-thumbed *Mormon Doctrine* or looked up Adam Miller's or Teryl Given's most recent work, it's a sure thing you are a player. Citing authority is the first and most obvious tell in this game.

Not surprisingly, we're not going to settle any of the issues above. This is a survival book, not a catechism. For survival purposes there are three things you need to learn or settle in your mind:

1. You are not going to win. You will not persuade the world. They may be wrong, but you can't fix it.
2. For so long as you want to stay on the inside of the edge you need to think about relational issues first. Not about being right but about how you interact with your neighbor.

3. Contrary to 1 and 2 above, sometimes you go to battle anyway. These issues are not all arbitrary or meaningless—some are life-and-death-level important.

When I hear an assertion that doesn't ring true, my very first inclination is to fix it. Tell the speaker how it really is. Correct the doctrine. Be the authority. Teach the Truth. The urge to correct can be overwhelming and I can easily rationalize fixing things. It is for their own good. It will help the rest of the class. It will minimize continuing harm. People will ultimately be happier when they have a clear understanding of good doctrine. I am that guy up all night because somebody got it wrong on the internet.

The first problem is that the opening position is usually asserted with authority, and authority seldom backs down. Once in a while the speaker really is proposing a question or a possible answer for purposes of discussion or of learning something. Most of my good experiences of this sort have been one-on-one private conversations or in a very small group, but it does happen sometimes that a class member will volunteer a point of view or a possible response that opens the door for real discussion. On the other hand, where the teacher or the know-it-all in the back row or the senior priesthood leader in the room makes an assertion, there is usually limited space for argument and almost no space to change the result.

A second problem is that people are seldom persuaded to change their preconceptions and prior judgments. You might win an argument, but that's a far cry from changing belief or behavior.

A third problem is that unless you are in a power position—making decisions, setting the agenda, teaching the lesson—you get limited opportunities to speak up in the best case, and even fewer opportunities if you're seen as disagreeable. I'm remembering a Come, Follow Me (Gospel Doctrine) classroom. The high-status men who wanted to participate got two comments, and sometimes three. Women got one. Men who were known to disagree with the teacher got none. I've also been in much more egalitarian, mutually respectful classrooms. But it was the teacher, not me, who made the difference.

Given all these problems, the survival strategy is to play the long game where you maintain relationships as best you can so you can participate in meaningful discussions tomorrow and the next day and the next. This means picking your battles and maintaining a reserve strategy.

My reserve strategy is to write my book. It's a notional book for now, a book that tells how things really work. It's got all the right answers—all *my* answers, of course. When I fail to persuade, or choose not to engage, or learn something new, it all goes in the book. When I'm frustrated or disappointed or angry with the things being said, my correct version goes in the book. My book is an obvious mental crutch, but it works for me. It's the way I get the last word without making enemies or acting the bully.

Picking my battles is all too often about what annoys me. But I keep reminding myself that there are some issues that really matter. Issues that will send someone away from the discussion sufficiently hurt that they never return. Issues that further marginalize people who should be welcome. Issues that if not addressed will make me feel invisible or disrespected. When the lesson turns to LGBTQ issues, it's likely there is someone in the room who has a vital personal stake in the discussion. When the discussion turns to any of the widely recognized commandments, it's likely there is someone in the room feeling guilty right now. When the topic is family relations, it's likely there is someone in the room who was abused by a family member.

When to speak up is ultimately an ethical question for me. When is it more wrong to be silent than to be contentious? Your answers do not need to be mine or anything like mine. Your answers are your own. But it's likely you have answers, i.e., limits beyond which silence is not OK. At the very least, you should think about it.

It's worth noting that the flip side of hurting listeners, i.e., hurting the speaker, can also be a concern. Sometimes the speaker has a vital personal interest in the question being discussed. They may be worried about their eternal soul and their standing in the Church. They may be feeling guilty about something they have done or failed to do. The point of the lesson may be self-justification. A theological debate can start looking like a blood sport.

Playing the long game comes down to basic civility. It's a matter of social awareness, politeness, and good discussion techniques. There's nothing special here; just recognizing that the Mormon culture, the ward, the Sunday School class, is a society, a social structure with social norms. Using an "I" phrase ("my view is", "how I learned it", "maybe that works for you, but I have a different approach") is usually preferred over direct confrontation ("you're wrong", "here's how it is"). A "yes, and" ("here are some additional views", "in this other source it's described differently") is usually better received than a challenge ("check your sources", "prove it"). Tabling ("let's continue the discussion") might be a good idea when what you really see is an impasse.

In Mormon-world debates it is unusually common to appeal to authority. Think about your possible responses in advance, when the next person delivers a "President Nelson said" clincher. A common reply is another general authority quote; some people carry prepared material tucked into their scriptures or stored on their phone for common debates. For me, answering a quote with another quote feels contentious. It reminds me of bible bashing—matching verse for verse—that I was taught not to do when I was sixteen years old. When I'm in a good place for myself, and nobody around me is being hurt, I'm more likely to take the deflection or tabling route. Some kind of "I hear you; that's enough for today." The point here is merely that General Authority quotes as a *coup de grace* happen a lot and you need a plan.

CONCLUSION

Mormon culture is strongly avoidant of disagreement of all kinds. The cultural norm is to smile and nod and let the conversation continue. Disagreeing with anything disturbs the equilibrium of the group. I remember shocked looks and quiet resentment when I forgot myself and brought my law professor Socratic dialogue techniques into a Sunday School lesson I was teaching. When I told a class member "no, that's incorrect," I think it was the first time anybody in the class had heard those words in a church meeting. We police this avoidance of disagreement by describing almost every disagreement as contentious and accusing the speaker of having a "spirit of contention," which we treat as sinful. Notwithstanding every socially aware culturally astute discussion technique, anybody who speaks up with a contrary opinion runs the risk of being thought contentious.

For a survival guide, the proper place to end this chapter might be with advice to not engage, to avoid contention by avoiding disagreement. There seems to be little or no survival value in having an argument or being known as argumentative.

However, I can't let it rest there. My sense of survival is not simply to make it to another day, but to proceed with my soul intact—with a feeling of self-respect and at least an attempt at discipleship. To achieve that kind of survival, there are times when I must engage. Times when it is more wrong to be silent than to speak up and disagree, even at the expense of being seen as contentious. Those times are very seldom about me. If it's just an all-about-me issue, I put it in my book. The times to speak up are when other people might be hurt, people who should not be collateral damage without a fight.

AFFILIATION

Sometimes it's an explosion. Sometimes it's a slow burn. The Church—sometimes members or local leaders, but often the central church—makes you feel angry or dispossessed. The feeling comes in different flavors.

- I am embarrassed to be known as a Mormon.
- I can't be in the same room with that man.
- The Church makes me angry.
- I feel violated—my sense of integrity is contradicted by actions or decisions the church makes.
- I don't belong. It is simply incorrect to call me Mormon.
- I want no part of the harm the Church is causing.
- They don't want me.
- I don't even like these people.

I count half a dozen times in my life when the Church took a position or made a decision or failed to act, when I felt so distressed that I wanted to get out. One such event for me was discovery of the

Exclusion Policy[1] in November 2015. Because it is relatively recent, and because it led to several friends leaving the Church and many more questioning their continued participation, I use it here as a case study.

An outsider to my feelings might say, laugh it off, it's not a big deal, this will blow over. But it is not small or minor stuff when you're in the middle of the distress. My wife's 2015 poem *beyond Beyond*, with a reference to me in the last lines, says it better than I ever could:

BEYOND BEYOND

Romans 8:26 (NRSV): Likewise the Spirit also helpeth our infirmities: for we know not what we should pray for as we ought: but the Spirit itself maketh intercession for us with groanings which cannot be uttered.

Integrity
And obedience—
Their pressures building
beyond Beyond—
Collide mid-cosmos
Shearing.

The shrapnel
Pierces us all.

---

1. In 2015 the LDS Church made a policy change regarding same-sex married couples. The policy was leaked and then confirmed in early November 2015. Commonly referred to as the Exclusion Policy by people who disagreed with it, the policy declared the married couple apostate, and required children living in the household to disavow the marriage and stop living in the household at age eighteen or older before they could be baptized. Key parts of the policy were reversed in 2019. Details of the policy and the reversal are not further explored here, because the emphasis is not on the policy itself but its effect on me and many others.

LIVING ON THE INSIDE OF THE EDGE

The walls
Of our hearts
Rend, Rip
Ragged, shattered.
Sirens screech,
Megaphones
Skew words:
"Love" hisses;
"Protect" hits
Its bleeding targets

with precision.
"Depart!"
The harsh, rash command
from all sides.

And oh, the wailing, weeping,
Moaning
And oh, the hollow lungs
And the bones
leaking marrow.

I seek for Jesus
in the smolder,

And my husband
Curls and cries,
Grief in his beard,
With groans
too deep for words.

SLOW DOWN

Let's begin with an acknowledgment that such an event might be a reason to leave. This chapter is not a *no, never*. But it is a *slow down, let's talk about it first*.

Start with differentiation. Unless you manage to completely bury your ego, there will come a time when the Church says *march right* and your ego says *not me*. If your identity is intertwined with the Church, the *not me* experience will register as an ultimatum—time to leave. However, if you are well down the path of differentiating you will be able to step aside from the ultimatum and consider multiple paths. Take a sabbatical. Rehearse the parts of the Church you do like and bracket the part that troubles you. Move to a new neighborhood. Turn in your temple recommend in protest. Agitate online. And yes, one option is still to leave.

When the Exclusion Policy came to light, one thought that came to my mind was that somewhat parallel statements and actions by the Catholic Church would make me just as angry if I were Catholic. That simple perspective allowed me to step aside from the (Mormon) Church as dominant and controlling in my life, and to see it as "just" a church. In effect, I turned Simon Peter's question "to whom shall we go?" (John 6:68) on its head. Not "where else can I find truth or peace?" But "won't I find the same angst, sooner or later, anywhere else?"[2]

Of course, the Catholic Church example is not the whole picture. There are other churches, not LDS and not Catholic, where LGBTQ issues are more to my liking. That kind of alternative may become important in the slower consideration of what to do next. But right

---

2. Elder Ballard's "Where Will You Go?" talk was delivered a year and a half later, in the April 2017 General Conference. I heard the talk as speaking to this very same topic but making the first point, i.e., "we are the only place with the Truth," rather than the second point, the one that mattered to me in the moment, i.e., "they are all just as bad."

at the start the value of differentiation is just to avoid reflex action, the flight-or-fight reaction that comes too easily, too quickly, to a person whose identity is wrapped up in their church.

I think of differentiation as necessary but not sufficient. Without differentiating, people break. But even with differentiation, there is a lot to think about. The next steps are to measure the problem against possible solutions and against your reasons for participation.

Some problems can be localized or dimensioned in a way that may suggest solutions. A bishop passed judgment in an offensive way. An ex-husband still attends the ward. You lost money in a Ponzi scheme built on trusting relationships with a couple of local church leaders. Early morning seminary has become intolerable. (Unfortunately, every one of these examples is notorious and damaging.) The initial reaction may very well be fight or flight; the whole Church must be destroyed or remade, or I must leave. But reflection may size the problem differently. People move to change wards. People change schools to be in a different part of the country. People stop participating until their local bishop changes. People ask to be released from callings. On one such occasion I turned in my temple recommend and refused further interviews. These responses are not free or easy, and there may be no middle-way response that works for you or is desirable in your circumstances. But the possibility of a measured response ought to be on the menu for consideration.

The size and nature of the problem also should be measured against your reasons for staying. Trivially, if the problem is huge and your reason for staying is weak, you probably leave. The converse is also likely—if you have a robust reason for staying, and the problem is relatively small, you probably stay even while thinking creatively about ways to deal with the problem. However, measurement is not simply gross size, but also shape. If you still feel God wants you in the Church, and the immediate occasion for distress has nothing to do with that spiritual insight, you might continue to feel pain but choose to stay. On the other hand, if you rest on a testimony of the value and importance of the several ordinances, and the immediate occasion for distress is a cascade of questions and doubts about the restoration of the priesthood, even relatively small discoveries or doubts may cut at the very core of your reason for staying. If you have been staying to effect change from within, the immediate occasion for distress might be irrelevant to the change you desire. Or it might strike right at the heart of that change, taking an opposite direction or pushing the likely timetable beyond anything you can tolerate.

Both the size and shape of the problem are relevant because what matters is how it affects you, in your personal and unique situation. The power of finding and understanding your reason for staying—your own call—is that you can distinguish among the various events. Some matter a lot. Some matter not at all. And different for you than for me.

With respect to the Exclusion Policy, friends of mine found that their reason for being in the Church was to make room for LGBTQ members to participate and flourish. In some cases, it was specifically for their gay son or daughter. The Exclusion Policy cut so close to their reason for staying that they resigned. Another friend identified her "truth" of the gospel as the ward, i.e., life among local members working together as a small community. Because the local ward was relatively progressive on LGBTQ issues, she was distressed in a big Church sense but not overwhelmingly affected in a local ward sense. For my part, I realized that I had already moved so far to the outer edges of the Church, in reaction to prior shocks, that ironically there was nowhere to go. I was already there.

The Church would tell you to avoid gospel hobbies, meaning don't become a one-note member and don't let any one issue drive you out. The most common reference is to Quentin Cook's "Looking Beyond the Mark" in the Ensign, March 2003. This seems good pragmatic advice if it can be followed. The problem is that for many of us "no gospel hobbies" translates as not caring. In my experience, not caring is much easier said than done, and even when I can get past my immediate distress the pain is real and big. I reflect on my wife's words in *beyond Beyond*. Having cried with groans too deep for words, I cannot make a place for *just don't care*. But I can and have made a place for *not this time, not for me*.

The Church, or some church leaders, would also tell you that if you stay you should sit down and shut up. I don't expect any different from the institution. But the go or stay-and-shut-up binary is a false binary. There are many in-between options. When I decided to stay, notwithstanding the Exclusion Policy, I also wrote up and made public a 10-point list of ways to protest from within. That was part of my deal with myself.

Differentiating, scoping the problem, and measuring against your call, puts you in a frame of mind to make thoughtful, reasoned decisions. Sometimes that's enough. Sometimes there are additional difficulties, including when a choice is forced, when you experience holy envy, when you feel like a social misfit, and when they don't want you.

FORCED CHOICES

The threat of church discipline can force an individual choice. Schism can force a group choice. It's more complicated than stay or go. I haven't experienced either one directly and shouldn't be opining about how it works or what you should do. For myself, I am reasonably confident a threat of church discipline would cause me to leave on the spot, and I suspect a schism would cause me to choose neither but to get out completely. A possible exception would be finding that one group or the other in a schism included most of my friends and family.

A slightly less acute case that still feels forced is when the church expels a group of people. The experience of "there go my friends" or "the church is hurting my friends" has been devastatingly difficult for me. This is the Exclusion Policy, and the September Six, and the Priesthood Ban, and more. It is a big reason I hold the Church at arm's length. A big reason I am on the edge. Without differentiating, the experience would quickly become a binary choice between Church and my friends. By taking advantage of psychological space between me and the Church, so far I have been able to find middle ground. But it hasn't been easy and I have no confidence I will always find a middle ground in the future.

HOLY ENVY

My church does not ordain women and I believe it will not change in my lifetime. There are churches that ordain women and include women in responsible leadership roles. My daughter has taken herself and her daughters to one of those churches. An apologist will argue that other church doesn't have the priesthood and doesn't offer a sealing ordinance and doesn't have a living prophet. However, because this is an important issue for me, there are days when holy envy takes hold and tears at my heart.

The apologist's argument works for some people. We hear many strong statements of confidence in The Church of Jesus Christ of Latter-day Saints and its ordinances and practices that seem to satisfy the speaker even while they acknowledge a kind of holy envy about other religious traditions. I imagine it is even possible to have such a comprehensive testimony of the Church that holy envy doesn't come up in the first place. However, in my experience people on the edge—readers here—are questioning those very confidences, and holy envy can feel like a big deal.

The obvious cautions are all the old saws, all of which have a kernel of truth. For some of us the grass appears greener over there (but really isn't). For some of us the grass really is greener over there but only because we haven't adequately cared for our own field. For some of us a single gospel hobby can make us forget there are many differences, and a balanced or more comprehensive view might lead to a different conclusion than tunnel vision on one issue. Change is costly. Community has value. History and tradition count for something. For all that, sometimes change is the next step in an individual's journey, and holy envy might be a good guide for a direction to take. Rather than feeling like an escape from a bad situation, following the path of holy envy can feel like moving toward a good, like seeking after something virtuous, lovely, of good report, or praiseworthy.

SOCIAL MISFIT

Based on stories I hear, the social misfit case might be the most common tension for people on the edge. To put it in personal terms, for many of my friends and business associates I am the only Mormon they know. Before they get to know me, Mormon means homophobe, racist, polygamist, or Mitt Romney. I don't want any of those labels. When the church is in the news, there is often a new label, and it usually feels even worse.

Notwithstanding my aversion to the labels, the risk of being a social misfit ranks low on my list of concerns. Partly that's because I'm old and well established and most of my reputation is mine alone, not closely related to my church or my school or my parents. But I'd like to think I am reasonably well differentiated, and whatever they think about the Church, it doesn't stick to my sense of myself. I am quite relaxed about saying "that's not me, not even close." I do work on scripts to make that conversation move along briskly.

As a result of my personal low-level concern, there's a risk of under-estimating the power of the social misfit case for others. I acknowledge that it might be a big deal for you. I do suggest some differentiation work rather than giving in to a flight or fight response, and that's the essence of the Slow Down advice of this chapter.

THEY DON'T WANT ME

For me, the misfit-from-the-inside problem is much bigger than being a misfit on the outside. I want to be wanted, liked, welcomed. It doesn't take very many sideways glances and rude comments to get the feeling I am not wanted. They will say "don't take offense," and that might work when it's just one person being rude, and the rest of the group is welcoming. However, the words of a leader or representative, or a group-wide rejection, or even a subtle but pervasive shunning would drain me of desire to stay. If I ever leave, it's likely "they don't want me" will be one of the last straws.

On the other hand, in an otherwise neutral to positive environment, I have found one person reaching out a hand and saying "I'm glad you are here" is enough to keep me going for months.

WORKING WITH CIRCUMSTANCES

TRIBES AND RESPECT

From the very beginning, when this book was not much more than a title and an idea, I looked for additional voices who could speak to circumstances and challenges I can't. I reached out to friends, and people who have become friends, for contributions in their own voice, consistent with the overall objective of survival on the inside of the edge. The perspectives here are wonderful. I have come to think of the whole of this book as a vehicle to deliver the following chapters.

I am somewhat comforted to find that I recognize and empathize with much of what is said in these chapters. It turns out I am not blind to the world around me. But these are not my stories and I could not speak to the several situations with the same potent authenticity. There is one exception. Having raised three children in the Church, for many of those years as an inside-of-the-edge person, I feel that I can speak to the circumstances of raising children in the Church.

Although the following chapters represent different circumstances and individual voices, I see two common threads. Not everywhere or every time, but common enough to generalize here: it seems that we need a tribe and we need respect.

A TRIBE

Susan Meredith Hinckley says, "Having other women share and validate the challenges unique to Mormon women can be strengthening and healing. There is real relief in talking to other women and realizing you are not alone in your struggle." James Jones says, "You need a community of people that understand you, empathize with you, mourn with you, and validate you because the Church will not or cannot always do that." Mara Haslam says, "There's a saying that friends are the family that you choose.... Gather the people around you that you need to build love and support into your life." David Doyle says, "Especially try to become friends with some queer Mormons; they'll get you in a way others won't. Online friends count—they're still friends."

Speaking as a straight older white man, it goes for me too. The Church offers the elders quorum as my tribe. In almost fifty years as a Melchizedek Priesthood holder, there have been two years when that group felt like my tribe. It can work, but I wish it worked more often. I formed several men's groups in the 1980s and '90s and have participated in online groups of inside-of-the-edge type people for twenty-five years now. I have been in search of a tribe for most of my life.

I wonder whether everybody needs a tribe, a group of people who know and are known to each other, who love and are loved by each other. The local Relief Society or elders quorum might serve. Most wards are of a size that they could be that place, and there are storied wards, often with charismatic bishops and a common purpose, that are experienced and recalled as a place to belong. However, over and over again, I observe people looking for something more or different than a church organization.

RESPECT

We want love and approval from the Church, but we need respect. We would like the road to be made easy, the difficulties to be eased, the stumbling blocks to be removed, the Church to change, and the people to like us. However, for survival we need to be recognized, acknowledged, seen. At an important juncture in my journey a friend of mine said "I don't agree with you, but I welcome you on the pew next to me." I needed that.

The sad truth is that life on the inside of the edge and approval from the church and the bishop are not compatible. We're not going to get it, at least not on the time frame and in the manner we want and deserve. I'm not sure we should even try. Certainly, some bishops and some members understand and speak up. Some bishops and some members do approve and affirm. Roulette works in both directions. But approval has never been something I can count on and it's not an attainable goal I can recommend.

Asking for approval is to re-enlist for a parent-child relationship with the Church. An important determinant of differentiating is to find approval in self-worth or being valued by God, and not from an institution or a parent substitute. If you find yourself desperately seeking the approval of a man in a suit in a church office, it is worth some time to investigate your motives, your needs, your desires. People who constantly seek approval tend to conform (to score approval) or leave (because approval is not forthcoming).

Demanding respect stands on a different footing. Demanding respect is very simply to say:

> I'm for real; I'm an adult; I know what I'm doing; I belong because I want to, not because you give me permission.

It is a perfectly reasonable expectation to be treated as a responsible adult, as a legitimate member of the community. It is not reasonable to be treated as a child or as clueless or ignorant. It is not reasonable to be hounded for change. Yet all these things happen. People living on the edge do live with the reality that respect doesn't always happen and may never happen.

In fact, I imagine a woman or an LGBTQ or BIPOC person reading this saying to themselves "that's fine for a straight older white man with church experience, but I can't imagine it happening for me." I believe you. However, I also believe that we, all of us, should demand respect anyway.

There are two critical differences between seeking approval and demanding respect. The first is that respect is in fact possible. In negotiation terms, respect is a yes-able proposition. Even bishops who feel tightly constrained about giving approval can give respect. It is well within their capacity, as a church leader and as a caring human being.

The second is that demanding respect is necessary for survival of your soul. To be constantly ignored or diminished or expected to leave tends to become self-fulfilling. More importantly, treating oneself as not worthy of respect is damaging to the essence of being. The end of that road is not just "I'm out of here" but "I am nothing."

Respect can happen. It's within reach, it is possible. The Church might need a revelation to ordain women, but we could respect women more by listening to women's opinions, including more women as speakers, quoting women, and including more women in more councils. We might need a whole new church to take temples and temple ordinances off center stage, but we could respect responsible informed members who do not have a temple recommend by including them more in the central life of the ward community. The Church isn't moving in the direction of authorizing same-sex marriage; if anything, we are moving in the other direction. But we could respect civil marriages and recognize the couple and their children as a family.

Speaking about myself, working at living on the inside of the edge, it hurt when I heard "middle way" in a church meeting used like a swear word. On the other hand, a short time later a senior church leader said to me, "The choices you're making are like living on a knife edge. That's a hard road. I respect that you're making it work." It can happen.

Demanding respect may not be a good survival strategy. It might not come in this lifetime. But asking for and expecting respect is a grown-up differentiated responsible adult thing to do, and necessary to maintain personal authority and self-respect. Do it anyway. Save yourself. Quoting Mary Oliver in *The Journey*:

> One day you finally knew
> what you had to do, and began,
> though the voices
> kept shouting
> their bad advice —
> . . .
> as you strode
> deeper and deeper
> into the world,
> determined to do
> the only thing you could do—
> determined to save
> the only life that you could
> save.

ONE WOMAN'S PERSPECTIVE

SUSAN MEREDITH HINCKLEY

This chapter acknowledges that everything in this book applies to women as well as to men, while also making clear there are additional considerations for women. It is not an attempt to be exhaustive, but merely a nod to some readily visible, widely acknowledged but also commonly ignored hurdles we face at church. More than one woman reading this book will have a point at which she thinks, "Yes, but—" and then finish that sentence with an experience of her own, something that points to challenges existing for women that the man writing the book—and the ones running the organization—do not understand or appreciate. Some things are simply outside the experience of even the best of our brothers.

Tasked with detailing specific challenges that have come with the territory in my life as a Latter-day Saint woman, I'm required to highlight negatives. I'm uncomfortable committing these thoughts to paper, afraid the result may be perceived as a laundry list of personal complaints. Women's individual experiences will vary, so I can only speak about my own and then attempt to draw from them a few larger conclusions. I've been a member of the Church all my life, which means I've also been a girl in Primary, a teen in the Young Women's program, a young mother and an older one in Relief Society. I've loved so many aspects of my life as an active Latter-day Saint and continue to pursue my faith in this church by choice. But I have also felt undervalued, underappreciated, underserved, and misunderstood at some critical points along the way. Now that my daughters are grown, I find I raised them in an organization that somehow did not, for them, add enough value to earn a permanent spot in their lives.

If we want to remain in the Church, women simply must be willing to accept, overlook, and in some ways sacrifice more than men do. There—I said it.

To begin with, the Church appears more interested in keeping you around if you're a man than if you're a woman. Look at historical budgets for boys' and girls' programs, or our historical emphasis on preparing boys to serve missions, or years of General Priesthood meetings with no women's equivalent. Consider that there are more women in our pews than there are men to marry, and marriage is not only expected, but doctrinally mandated. Or just look around in almost any meeting and realize that the whole thing is run by men; the organization must invest in keeping them, if only so there's someone to sit on the stand.

Despite being in the majority, to be a Latter-day Saint woman is to almost never have a voice in decision making. Having had the vote for so many years in the secular world, it's hard for women to feel valued in an organization where our leaders are never chosen by us. Even in cases where a few members are asked for leadership recommendations (such as selecting a new Stake President), no women's opinions are sought. Not only do we not hold decision-making roles in our local wards and stakes, but women are rarely even in the room when decisions are made. We hear them as announcements over the pulpit. Nor are we anywhere near equally represented in the general church leadership. Important policies pertaining to women's roles have been written without any input from women. The semi-annual General Women's meeting has been discontinued, but even while it existed half was devoted to talks written and delivered by men. As of this writing it is unclear what effect the elimination of this session will have on the number of women's voices we hear at General Conference, but it's safe to say many female leaders who could address us will not be given the opportunity. Since Relief Society discussions center on General Conference talks (some given by women but the majority by men), even when a woman is not actively hearing their voices at church, she is often discussing men's thoughts and ideas.

Yet there is a narrative popular at church that says women are more inherently spiritual than men are. If that were true, wouldn't members want the ones most in tune to be highly visible and influential, both speaking and deciding? The overwhelming preponderance of male voices makes the story ring a bit hollow. But that hollow ring is precisely the kind of thing you learn to accept as a woman in the Church. Some things are so obvious, to survive you must stop paying attention to them, or at least expertly compartmentalize. To be engaged with a reality that is clearly one way while the organization insists it is another is crazy making.

From the time a girl is young, the messaging is different for her than it is for her brothers. For boys there is an emphasis on missions and priesthood. Although recent changes to age requirements increased interest among young women in serving a mission, such service has always been presented as non-essential, with the clear understanding that marriage is always a desirable first choice.

Boys receive the priesthood as young as age eleven and are publicly acknowledged as they participate in administering the sacrament weekly, and later progress through its various offices. Eleven-year-old girls have no corollary. "When will it be my turn?" is a question for which there is no satisfying answer.

Modesty is overemphasized in our teachings for girls and women, beginning at a young age and centered almost solely on dress. Although updated in 2022 to focus on principles rather than specific recommendations, for years our official guidelines for youth offered many more details about what is appropriate and expected for girls to wear than for boys. Boys don't endure years of lessons about the importance of covering their bodies, nor are they socialized to feel responsibility for provoking girls to engage in sinful thoughts and actions. Boys don't ever have their hemlines measured, and are allowed to dress appropriately for the activity in which they're engaging. Even at official ward or stake activities boys wear swimsuits to swim, for instance, without having to wear shorts or a t-shirt on top. While updated guidelines will hopefully help equalize youth lessons and activities, it will take more time for our culture to adjust its focus away from modesty in girls' dress than it took to rewrite the pamphlet.

Messaging around future choices for youth is different too. Beginning in Primary, girls hear a lot about their divine role as mothers and nurturers, and much less about pursuit of worthy personal goals like becoming an attorney or engineer. A college education is seen more as preparation for plan B than as a desirable end itself. From too young an age, this focus on motherhood as the ideal role can feel demoralizing for a girl who has neither interest in nor opportunities to date boys. Never mind that she has tremendous potential for academic success or other personal achievement. She can begin to feel like she has failed before her adult life has begun.

Though most young Latter-day Saint women now expect to work outside the home, their educational preparation is often targeted not in pursuit of natural interests, aspirations, or abilities, but to qualify them for jobs that will be flexible to accommodate the responsibilities of motherhood. There seems to have been no shift toward realizing personal fulfillment or sharing parenting roles, to accompany the shifting reality of likely employment.

In fact, there is little to no expectation of self-actualization for the Church's women. No officially promoted model for a woman's life outside the one well-defined role of mother. If that role doesn't fit, your Church life may also feel ill-fitting. And even if you do spend part of your life as a full-time mother, that's not likely to provide a lifetime of personal fulfillment. What comes next? Young wives continue to sacrifice dreams of future accomplishments and pursuits to support a husband's education and career. They feel pressure—because that pressure is still explicit—to have children very young, often before they have finished their own schooling. Their choices to prioritize education or work experience for themselves are frowned upon by other members who are vocal in those criticisms, in their families, in friendships, and over the pulpit. These things are improving but remain well behind societal norms. There persists a definite picture for what it looks like to be a valiant Latter-day Saint woman, anxiously engaged in fulfilling her divine role. A woman who chooses to prioritize career, who chooses not to have or finds herself unable to bear children, or who does not marry for whatever reason, can experience a profound disconnect with other LDS women, as well as with the teaching coming from correlated Church materials, and general and local leaders.

Although many women feel they do much of the heavy spiritual lifting in their homes and with their children, a woman is not given ultimate authority in her home, according to official Church proclamations and direction. So long as she is married to a priesthood holder, no matter how well she succeeds in emulating the ideal role model, she is said to be an equal partner with her husband, yet her husband presides. Different marriages may reflect various practical answers to the conundrum of "equal partner" and "husband presides," some more egalitarian than others. Still, the intent of the official message feels clear.

Beyond the doctrinal and cultural reach into her personal and home life, what of a woman's experiences in her Church life? The power differential with a male leadership is real and present in every interaction a woman has with the institutional Church. She does not perform even her individual calling under her own authority. Decisions must be approved, and if she follows the chain up to final approval of an action or decision, it always rests with a man. In many cases, priesthood leaders overreach to exercise control over what lessons are taught in Relief Society, or to approve the program in a meeting or activity planned by and for women. Women are not allowed to be in ward buildings alone, not allowed to work or meet with men alone, not allowed to be with their young women at camp alone. To put it most simply, Latter-day Saint women are subject to and supervised by men at church.

The power differential is nowhere so stark as in the bishop's office. Here a woman is expected to discuss intimate details of her life with a man who is in a position of authority over her. A man has power to officially certify her worthiness and approve her participation. This begins young. It is uncomfortable, but by the time she becomes an adult, a woman will have sat through many interviews with men, behind closed doors, where she may be questioned about the most personal and intimate details of her life and choices.

Turning to doctrine and practice, there are easily identifiable challenges for women. The temple is one of those challenges. Despite ongoing updates that have improved some wording over the past several decades, the temple ceremonies remain difficult for some. For those who attended the temple regularly for years before the changes, the earlier wording is fixed in memory. It is difficult to erase phrases we have committed to our minds through ritual, but agonized over in our hearts. Those sore spots remain sore.

The temple bears reminders of polygamy, the sorest of all doctrinal spots for many women. Of the things a Latter-day Saint woman is required to set aside—or just try not to think about too much—as she participates in her religion, polygamy is the biggest. Besides the difficulty of the practice itself and some of the less-than-faith-promoting history surrounding it, there's the silence that accompanies it today. Our inability or unwillingness to talk about polygamy as a collective church still very much living in its shadow, means that women have nowhere to seek relief. The total lack of any official forum to unpack all our uneasiness with it, our anger over it, our sadness and bewilderment about it, increases the weight of the load. I've heard countless women over my lifetime express some version of the idea that they have faith they'll somehow deal with polygamy in the next life, if they're required to do so. It's a way of stepping around it, and it works to create enough immediate distance for many, if only barely. But countless women feel the pall of the practice in their relationships here and now. An unresolved disagreement over personal views about polygamy can result in a sort of permanent, silent stalemate that hangs over a marriage. As a result, many husbands and wives don't talk about it, and it doesn't feel safe to talk about with people outside of marriage either. Yet some of our scriptures still preach it, and many men—including Church leaders—practice an eternal version, as they are sealed to subsequent wives after they lose the first.

Disparity in the policies for men's and women's sealings is problematic and continues to inflict real pain in women's lives and relationships. A woman who wishes to have a sealing dissolved does not have power to finalize that choice. She cannot be sealed to a subsequent husband if she loses the first. She doesn't always have control over the sealings of her children. These policies that pertain to a future life complicate family lives here and now. When it comes to sealings, women simply have fewer options and less control over their own than men do.

Patriarchy is codified not only in our history and doctrine, but in our current organization and practices. In this the Church is hardly alone—patriarchy can be seen as a natural consequence of men organizing a church during a time when women were considered little more than property.[1] However, as the world continues to make progress in correcting inequality between the sexes, the Church lags. Because women do not hold the priesthood, there is little chance for truly meaningful change in this area. Even eleven-year-old priesthood holders have authority that women lack. And many women feel the fastest way to marginalization, if not expulsion, would be to become vocal in her insistence on equality to the point that she demands ordination. There is nowhere currently for a woman to safely express the opinion that ordination should be available to both men and women. In fact, it may be the only topic that remains more taboo than polygamy. So, a woman who desires to remain a member in good standing will have to accept not only the patriarchal structure of the Church, but the near total inability to publicly express any dissatisfaction over it or to agitate for real change.

Our doctrine includes a Heavenly Mother, but she is simultaneously offered to us and silenced, making her little more than a shadow in the background to which we give an official nod. Here also, a woman is confronted with the question of polygamy—is Heavenly Mother a solitary figure, an equal partner to the Father in all ways, or is she one of many? While some women find this doctrine of Heavenly Mother, however incomplete, to be one of the ideas that makes Mormonism unique and compelling, a woman who desires to talk about or pray to Heavenly Mother will find no encouragement to do so, and in fact will be met with official discouragement. The lack of any relationship or reliable portrait makes our acknowledgement of a Heavenly Mother feel half-hearted if not disingenuous. As a result, many women are seeking further light and knowledge in this area for themselves. In an organization where the search is officially discouraged, and where we have no power, the quest can insert real tension into a woman's relationship with the institutional Church.

---

1. In 1839 Mississippi was the first state to allow women to own property in their own name.

True independence in thought or action can feel out of reach on a doctrinal, cultural, and practical level for women. The Church is not supportive of single adult women, especially divorced women. This includes those who are effectively "single" for Church purposes, who have a non-member or not attending spouse. Women have a respected and recognized place in the community mostly as the spouse of an active LDS man. Furthermore, many Latter-day Saint women rely on a husband for the bulk of their financial support, a result of having forgone a career to raise a family. In practical effect, a woman may feel locked into a Church marriage. This can put her in a difficult situation should a real disagreement with Church policy or doctrine stress the marital or the Church relationship, where they may feel like one complex entrapment.

The culture does not encourage thoughtful exploration of doubt. If you're struggling at church, it can feel particularly difficult to find support from other women. To a distressing degree, women are complicit in their own marginalization, perpetuating cultural norms and eagerly defending and enforcing some of the very policies that are most problematic. It can feel distinctly unsafe in a group of women at church to express disagreement or disillusionment. We grow up grappling with, side-stepping, and learning to ignore or shelve so many real inequities in our church lives. After carefully constructing your life around an ideology, practicing years of avoidance and years teaching children the same, admitting there may be flaws is an enormous challenge, an affront to self-image that requires a deconstruction or rearrangement of belief. Some are not willing or able to do this work. When it feels like some women defend the status quo as if their life depends on it, perhaps those women believe that life as they know it actually does. But if your experience leads you to find the status quo indefensible, feeling empathy for women who defend it does not make it easier to live with.

For a woman to admit to problems or decry damaging policies also leaves her in the position of having to address those issues.

Should she advocate for change openly, risking disfavor or even discipline, or sit in silent anger, risking her own mental and/or spiritual health? Considering the responsibility that could come with acknowledging hard truths about a Latter-day Saint woman's life may be enough to keep many from engaging with those ideas at all.

Seeing these things spelled out in succession does give me pause. Why stay?

There are as many reasons women stay in the Church as there are women who make that choice. Why you were baptized to begin with, how being a Latter-day Saint has figured into your story and the life you've built since, and your own set of personal experiences and relationships all figure into the solution of how you might make it work, and even more fundamentally, whether you want to make it work. Are you the only member in your extended family, or one link in generations of active members? Are you married to a Mormon? Have you raised your children in the Church, and have they carried that activity and beliefs into their adult lives?

The pull of children, spouses, or extended family members can be strong, and I have found that my own answers around remaining active have evolved as my family has. For instance, so far in my life the biggest challenge to staying was having my adult daughters leave. So much of the church narrative centers on family; when your family no longer shares those views or beliefs, that narrative can lose its power and even its appeal. The biggest surprise for me was that rather than wanting to lure my children back to LDS Church participation, I felt satisfaction that they were at peace in their lives. They trusted their own feet, and their feet led them out. The fact that my feet continued to feel rooted while theirs did not made me take a hard look at my roots in a way I never had before. The vague feeling I carried that I had no choice was suddenly replaced by the realization that I did indeed have one, and that my future Church involvement would need to be for purely personal reasons if it was going to bring peace or happiness.

I had to answer the question, "What's in it for me?" Although I find it hard to believe now, I'd never asked myself that question. Most of my Mormon life had been spent thinking about ways my membership and activity impacted others, either through callings or personal relationships and responsibilities. As I have worked my own path and talked to other women who have asked themselves similar questions, I've found some answers that seem to come up repeatedly.

Many women value the opportunity to serve that church involvement provides. It's not that they couldn't otherwise find ways to serve, so much as their engagement at Church plugs them into service automatically.

There is inertia and a commitment that accompanies sunk cost; once a woman has invested much of her life and resources in Mormonism and its teachings, it can be hard to change, or even want to. Staying may feel like the easier option. Having raised children in the Church creates another layer of entanglement, particularly if they've embraced it in their own lives and wish to continue. For many women, the desire to be able to attend their children's future sealings or accompany them through the temple is enough to keep them active for years beyond their natural desire to continue.

Some women feel their marriage would be threatened if they were to leave. The value of keeping peace with a spouse you love and share a life with may simply rank above the value of personal religious satisfaction. For some, lack of financial independence may complicate this too, as previously mentioned.

Some women value the community and social involvement the Church brings to their life. A particular program or practice, such as participation in Relief Society, can also be a draw.

Some women have had spiritual or other personal experiences connected to their Church lives that remain meaningful to them, so choose to stay engaged even when doctrine or policy becomes problematic. For other women, a particular doctrine or teaching—such as eternal sealing or a connection to ancestors—may remain deeply resonant when other interests have faded. Many women find at church real hope or relief from the pain of losing parents, children, or a spouse.

I think figuring out how the Church adds value to your life as a woman is step one to figuring out how to stay active in it. Then what? How might a woman find a fulfilling spiritual life in an organization she feels is deeply flawed? Flawed specifically in ways that require women to accept complexities that may not only cause cognitive dissonance, but also very real pain?

In my experience, finding a place to talk about troubling issues is invaluable. Whether an online group, a therapist, a trusted friend, or family member, having other women share and validate the challenges unique to Mormon women can be strengthening and healing. There is real relief in talking to other women and realizing you are not alone in your struggle.

Serving in a calling from which you derive satisfaction is also a practical way to increase enjoyment of the Church experience. Emphasizing any aspect of the Church that brings you happiness can make the difficult things easier to live with. If you love family history, or sacred music, or working with youth, or teaching children, or personal study, lean into it. Letting the rest go may not be entirely practical, depending on what stage of life you're in, but giving yourself permission to take what works and leave the rest is the most helpful advice I can think of.

It may be particularly hard for Latter-day Saint women to give themselves permission to take charge in all aspects of their spiritual lives, and for that reason alone I advocate trying. There is truth to the idea that others have only as much control as we give them, and women in the Church have given men a great deal of control. Staying requires a willingness to cede control of some big stuff, but I'd argue that a spiritual life must always be at its core personal, and Church participation need not be an all-or-nothing decision.

Being in the process of staying involves a combination of the above strategies for me. I feel rooted and drawn to helping other women find their place here too. I have enormous hope for the future women of our church, for a Heavenly Mother who will at last have her say, made real for us all by the collective yearning of a generation who finally grieve her absence deeply enough to insist she be given her rightful place. For a sisterhood strengthened by what has been required of us in the past and committed to realizing a more equitable future. A Relief Society that welcomes expression of the full range of women's thoughts, needs, and experiences, our diversity of hearts and minds knit in a collective desire to mend, lift, and grow. Not only each other, not only our families, but the Church organization, and the world in which it exists. Things are getting better. Not as fast as I'd like, but the direction is hopeful. I see in the ever-enlarging vision and expectations of our youth further reason for hope, as the Church and its women inch uneasily forward together.

THE INSIDE OF THE EDGE FOR SINGLE ADULTS

MARA HASLAM

We've all seen them, the images of a happy nuclear family. They appear in the church magazines and the Gospel Art Kit, in our church libraries and in our heads: the images of a happy couple standing in front of a temple, where they have supposedly just been sealed; the images of a father, mother and children reading from the scriptures together; the video clips of a parent and children walking on the beach or through a meadow. Church leaders frequently quote the Proclamation on the Family that marriage is "ordained of God." Recent emphasis on the concept of the covenant path[1] further points to temple marriage as the culminating ordinance on that path. There is no mistaking that this is the ideal we are expected to aim for in our church: a nuclear family with a father and mother and children.

But what happens when your life doesn't fit the ideal?

---

1. See, for example, Elder D. Todd Christofferson, "Why the Covenant Path," April 2021 General Conference.

It's a legitimate question because there are so many of us who don't fit the ideal. I, for example, have been attending church my whole life and am now in my 40s. Despite attending singles wards and activities, dating, and "putting myself out there," I have not found anyone that I thought would make a good marriage partner for me. And I'm not the only one; many of us, regardless of how much longing, prayer, fasting, dating, and energy we have put into creating a family, are living single. The adult membership of The Church of Jesus Christ of Latter-day Saints across the world is now more single than married, according to statistics quoted by Elder Gerrit W. Gong in the April 2021 General Conference.[2] Active women of the church outnumber active men[3] and the gender gap appears to grow wider as the members of the church get older.[4]

In The Church of Jesus Christ of Latter-day Saints marriage and family are often presented as the solution to all of life's problems. It seems that everyone has heard stories about returned missionaries who get married just a few weeks after coming home from their missions, or young people who get engaged after dating for only a few months. The pressure to marry seems to come from all sides: family members, Young Men leaders who promise that fulfilling a righteous mission will get you a "hot" wife, ward members who ask if you're dating, mission presidents who present marriage as the next step at your exit interview, bishops who check up on your dating life, and talks from general authorities counseling young people not to delay marriage. Some singles feel like the Proclamation on the Family is used like a club to beat home the teachings that you should try to make your life match the document as much as possible, as soon as possible. The overwhelming message is that marriage is the goal.

---

2. Elder Gerrit W. Gong, "Room in the Inn," April 2021 General Conference.
3. Jana Riess, "Worldwide, only 25 percent of young single Mormons are active in the LDS Church," *Religion News Service*, October 5, 2016.
4. Arielle A. Sloan, Ray M. Merrill, J. Grant Merrill, "Gender Distribution of The Church of Jesus Christ of Latter-day Saints Worldwide," *BYU Studies Quarterly* 53:1.

The next step in the logic is this: if marriage is the goal and you're not married, then something is wrong. Something is wrong with your dating technique; something is wrong with the people you've been meeting; something is wrong with your faith and priorities; something is perhaps deeply wrong with *you* that makes you undesirable or unsuitable for marriage. You're a "menace to society."[5] And because of this feeling that something is wrong, single people are often pushed to the margins, treated as a problem to be solved, and made to feel as if church and church activities aren't for them. Even worse, *we* begin to believe we are failures.

Still further, singles are made to feel as if we aren't full adults because we aren't married. We are often juvenilized to the point that some units require that YSA activities be chaperoned by a married "adult" (who may very well be younger than some of the single people in attendance). The recent expansion of the roster of callings available to single members of the church highlights the fact that singles weren't previously considered capable of handling these callings. Some single women get the cold shoulder from the married sisters in their ward because of the misguided assumption that the single sister would steal their husbands. Strict boundaries about married people and single people of the opposite sex not spending time together mean that single LDS women often don't get the same number or quality of mentoring opportunities from their married LDS bosses and therefore don't progress in their careers.

Perhaps most sadly, those of us who don't have the support that comes from an immediate nuclear family find that extra support from the Church is often lacking when we need it most. I've heard from more than one divorced member of the Church that they simply stopped hearing from ward leaders or ministering sisters and brothers, as if divorce were contagious. One sister in a Facebook group posted that she was made to feel unwelcome at a stake activity

---

5. Chris Brough, "Seeing beyond Single," *Ensign*, June 2004.

because the seating arrangements had been organized for couples and her presence as a single "messed up" the number of people at the table.

It's hard to be single in a church and culture that treats you as less than an adult, that sends the message you have failed at achieving life's primary goal, and that makes you feel fundamentally flawed because you haven't married.

So what do you do if you are single and want to stay?

DEALING WITH JUDGMENT

First, please know that your single status is not automatic confirmation that there is something wrong with you or that you are not faithful enough (not praying enough, not going to the temple enough, not serving enough, etc.) This logical fallacy stems from the vending machine view of religion. The idea is that God is like a vending machine: if you put in the right coins (for example, righteous deeds) and press the right buttons (for example, a certain amount or quality of prayer and scripture study), a certain blessing will come out. The real situation is much more nuanced.[6] As Sheri Dew once said, "If fasting and praying could get you a husband, I could pick anyone I wanted."[7] It's often not helpful when people try to comfort you about your single status by saying things like, "We don't know all the details, but it will all work out after this life." But you can actually embrace that very teaching and turn it to your advantage: we don't have all the answers about the details of how each case will be handled, so you are free to have some of your own beliefs about your specific place in the plan of salvation. For example, what kinds of sealing are possible? What kinds of matches can or will be made in

---

6. Elder Dale G. Renlund, "Abound with Blessings," April 2019 General Conference.
7. Doug Robinson, "Sheri Dew: Living the unexpected life," *Deseret News*, October 28, 2002.

the spirit world or during the Millenium? Will people who are dissatisfied with their sealing partners be able to split from them? What will happen to those who are sealed to someone who didn't qualify for the Celestial Kingdom? Though our religion has a relatively robust set of teachings about the afterlife, there remains much we don't yet know about exactly how things will work for individuals in certain sets of circumstances. The Heavenly Parents I believe in will create as many opportunities as possible for each child to return to Them. You are at liberty to understand the less transparent areas in the plan of salvation in ways that build you up rather than tear you down.

Chances are good that well-meaning members will sometimes insinuate that something is wrong with you or your choices if you are single. In addition to the faith-connected judgments I listed above, you may encounter judgments or pressure about your attractiveness, education, age, number of children, financial status, etc. My advice is to prepare your responses in advance. Some options might include responding verbally in the moment, simply ignoring the comments and walking away, removing yourself from contact with the person making judgmental comments (including asking for a release from a calling that places you in close proximity), moving from a singles ward into a family ward, and/or talking to the person one-on-one and explaining how hurtful such comments are. You may also choose to follow up with a church leader (or a different church leader, in the case that it was a leader who made you feel judged). Each situation may require a different kind of response.

When these kinds of judgments are so prevalent in the culture we engage with, it is easy to internalize them to the point that we may feel that there is something wrong with us that makes us unsuitable for marriage. I have found mental health therapy very useful at helping me to overcome internalized judgment against myself.

FINDING YOUR VILLAGE

Just because we are single does not mean that we are unworthy of fulfilling relationships and supportive networks. Our current church culture often promotes a 1950's-style nuclear family as the ideal, but historically and outside Western culture, people have often lived in multi-generational families together with or close to extended family members. There's a saying that friends are the family you choose. Don't feel you need to conform to one style of living. Gather the people around you that you need to build love and support into your life. These might include a circle of roommates, siblings, a gaming group, extended family members, a choir, yoga buddies, or any combination of the above. Find a way of doing life and relationships that works for you.

The well-known relationship therapist Esther Perel commented on the evolution of expectations we have of marriage in Western culture: "Marriage was an economic institution in which you were given a partnership for life in terms of children and social status and succession and companionship. But now we want our partner to still give us all these things, but in addition I want you to be my best friend and my trusted confidant and my passionate lover to boot, and we live twice as long. So we come to one person, and we basically are asking them to give us what once an entire village used to provide."[8] Don't feel compelled to wait for one partner; find your village. Some church programs for singles are provided to help us find like-minded people, but you may need to look outside the church and its programs to find the members of the village that *you* need. The Proclamation on the Family presents a goal for family life, a sort of ideal to aim for, but real life is seldom ideal. The Proclamation itself says, ". . . other circumstances may necessitate individual adaptation." Finding your own village and surrounding yourself

---

8. Esther Perel, "The secret to desire in a long-term relationship," TedSalon NY2013.

with people and relationships that work for you is a powerful way to practice that individual adaptation.

DATING AND MARRIAGE IN AND OUT OF THE CHURCH

If you're like me, you've wondered whether you should date people who are not members of the church. You've probably heard stories of people who marry a nonmember only to have that nonmember join the church later: the ultimate "flirt to convert." I do know some people whose lives turned out that way, but there is no guarantee that any person you date or marry outside of the church will want to convert.[9] I don't necessarily see that as a problem; many people have fulfilling interfaith relationships.

Latter-day Saints have so much riding on marriage; we believe that it affects not only our earthly life but our eternal exaltation as well. But there are many other possible reasons for marriage including sanctioned sex, having children, companionship, having someone to depend on, and more. I have gone back and forth about whether I wanted to date only members of the church or whether I was open to dating people outside the faith. I've heard lots of women say that men they dated outside the faith treated them better than the Latter-day Saints they dated. Personally, I have decided that I would like to have a fulfilling romantic relationship now, even if it doesn't necessarily lead to an eternal relationship. You can consider if you want to be married, and if so, what kind of marriage you would like to have, and why.

Here are some questions that you may consider when deciding whom to date and marry. I present them as examples of normal

---

9. Jana Riess, "Why Mormons Have the Lowest Rates of Interfaith Marriage," *Religion News Service*, May 7, 2013.

questions that people may think about in these situations. Your answers to these questions will be individual.

- How important is it to me to be sealed to my marriage partner?
- Can I talk freely with my partner about the things that mean the most to me in life, including my religious beliefs?
- Does my partner respect my boundaries (religious, physical, and otherwise)?
- If we plan to have children together, how will we raise those children (in terms of religious principles)?
- What kinds of potential dating partners are available to me in my church units and geographical location?
- How comfortable am I with online dating versus meeting people in person?
- How comfortable am I with the possibility of having a long-distance relationship with someone I meet online as opposed to dating someone in close proximity?

THE SEX TALK I WISH I'D HAD

As a friend of mine put it, there is a vacuum of discussion when it comes to singles and sexuality. I have encountered the belief in members of the Church that sexuality is something singles don't have to deal with because we "don't know what we are missing." I find that point of view to be naïve. If you're like me, you've experienced sexual desires since puberty and have to deal with them whether you are single or married. But for some reason, or perhaps many reasons, the Church is relatively silent on principles that adults can use to guide our sexuality. Since many of us are interested in finding a romantic relationship at some point, I'd like to offer some principles that can help with this process.

When I say sexuality I mean the whole range of human sexual and romantic feelings and behavior, including things like kissing and holding hands and sexual thoughts as well as the act of sexual intercourse. It seems that sexuality is something that has been given to almost all of our Heavenly Parents' children, so it's important for us to have some principles to guide our use of it at all stages of our lives. The LDS marriage and sexuality therapist Jennifer Finlayson-Fife said, "I would like to help single members of our faith community forge a strong relationship to themselves (inclusive of their God-given sexuality), solid relationships with others, as well as a strong relationship to the highest principles in our faith. In other words, as Christians, I hope for all of us (marrieds and singles alike) to approach our sexuality in line with our moral commitments and ideals, in a way that fosters a strong sense of self and a capacity for intimacy with others. To love self, to love others, and to love God: This is the point of all of the commandments, remember."[10] In the same presentation, she encourages singles to use their power to make choices in their sexuality, whether that choice is to express it or not express it in a certain way in a given situation.

There are rules, of course, but rules without principles behind them often don't make much sense. A rule without an explanation of the underlying principle can often be misinterpreted and taken to mean something other than the rule originally intended. We singles are often referred to *For the Strength of Youth* for information about how to deal with romantic parts of our relationships, but the rules in that book are made for teenagers and don't come with many principles behind them. As a result, I think it's easy for those rules to be misapplied and misunderstood. Instead, or in addition, I would refer to the principles discussed in the chapter on *Sex* in this book, and reinforce the following two principles:

---

10. Dr. Jennifer Finlayson-Fife, "Sexuality and Singledom—Navigating with Clarity and Integrity," podcast transcript at Finlayson-Fife.com/blog/, May 30, 2015.

- Sexuality deepens the connection between partners.
- People are not objects.

SEXUALITY DEEPENS THE CONNECTION BETWEEN PARTNERS

If you think about the many different kinds of relationships that exist between people in the world, marriage, as defined by our Church, is unique in that it is the only kind of relationship in which sexual relations are sanctioned. Why would this be so? In our friendships, working relationships, relationships with ward members, and so forth, sexuality is not prescribed. But in marriage, it is generally accepted that the married parties will have a sexual relationship. Adam was told, "Therefore shall a man leave his father and his mother, and shall cleave unto his wife: and they shall be one flesh" (Genesis 2:24). Becoming "one flesh" can be interpreted to mean sexual acts such as intercourse. And I believe it is through these acts that the people involved "cleave" to each other. In other words, a sexual relationship creates the deep bonding that we want to exist between people in a marriage—deeper, for example, than the relationship between a child and parents, as referenced in the scripture from Genesis.

In fact, the word "marriage" does not indicate simply a wedding ceremony, but rather two people entering a bonded relationship. We speak, for example, about the "marriage of minds." If you want to create a marriage, a deeper kind of relationship, it is natural to want to use different kinds of sexuality to strengthen that bond. My advice here is to make sure that the level of sexuality that you express in the relationship is appropriate to the level of the relationship.

Here are some questions you may be wondering about as you consider what level of sexuality is appropriate for your relationship:

- Are there differences between casual dating, serious dating, engagement, and marriage as far as what level

of sexuality is appropriate? If so, what are those differences?
- What ways are there to explore sexuality and sexual compatibility with a person in addition to intercourse?
- What ways of expressing love and affection are most meaningful to me and my partner?

PEOPLE ARE NOT OBJECTS

Sexuality feels good. Everything from a long, lingering hug to a kiss to more intense sexual actions can be mutually pleasurable for the people involved. But there is also a way to use sexuality for your own pleasure, to take more than you give, to treat people as objects for your own use. I believe that the appropriate use of sexuality involves treating your relationship partner as a whole person and not as an object.

In modern culture women bear the brunt of objectification to the point that men feel comfortable telling women on the street to smile so they are more pleasant for the man to look at. Women and girls are given long lists of "modesty" rules about covering up their bodies because a man may be excited by looking at them, while men are given much looser clothing rules or no rules at all and are not taught to handle their own sexuality when they see someone beautiful. Women are disproportionately treated as if they are decorations, arm candy, beautiful shells instead of whole people. To the men reading this chapter, I plead with you not to make the mistake of seeing women as objects. Of course, women are not off the hook either, but the objectification of women is such a common practice in our society that it deserves special mention.

Anyone with a relatively normal sex drive is going to sometimes see someone that they find attractive and experience a sexual response. I don't see this as evidence that something is going wrong but rather that something is going right! It means our sexuality is operating in a normal, healthy way. How you deal with that activation of your sexuality in your thoughts and in your actions is your responsibility. Don't make the mistake of blaming others for your sexuality.

Another application of this principle is to not let anyone treat you as an object. You should not feel pressured into participating in any behavior that makes you uncomfortable. If someone you are in a relationship with is treating you as an object or using you for their own pleasure, set appropriate boundaries, which may very well include not seeing that person any more.

Finlayson-Fife said, "As a faith community we need to do a better job of addressing single adult sexuality . . . and the way to do it is to talk differently about sexuality in general. We need to create an ethic around sexuality in which we teach the value and potential goodness of our God-given desires, as well as the importance of channeling our sexual energy toward choices that forge our strength and benefit those we love, depending on the relational context we are in." [11] The principles offered in this section are an attempt to guide you on your personal creation of an "ethic around sexuality." More excellent principles and questions to ask yourself are found in the chapter on *Sex* in this book.

CONCLUSION

As singles in The Church of Jesus Christ of Latter-day Saints, our lives probably aren't going to fit the "cookie-cutter" checklist. I argue that this is not a bad thing. Instead of trying to make your life conform to a mold that doesn't work for you and being frustrated when it doesn't, I encourage you to embrace your personal path and gather people around you who can help make that path a happy and

---

11. Candice Madsen, "Expert Q and A: How singles can embrace both chastity and sexuality," *Deseret News*, December 29, 2015.

fulfilling one. Often people on the inside of the edge are accused of not living the gospel as well as others do, but I feel that edge-insiders are often coming from a place of deep commitment to faith and personal integrity. The ideas in this chapter are presented with the hope that they will help you consciously build a life that is happy and aligned with your faith. Taking responsibility for creating the life you want will help you to build a flourishing life while being resilient to judgment or pity from others.

LIVING ON THE INSIDE OF THE EDGE— A LATTER-GAY PERSPECTIVE

DAVID DOYLE

I have checked many of the boxes one might expect of an active member of The Church of Jesus Christ of Latter-day Saints. I served a full-time mission. I attended Ricks College and Brigham Young University. I taught at the Missionary Training Center. I have held callings ranging from Primary pianist to elders quorum president. The one notable box I haven't yet checked is marriage.

To be fair, it wasn't even a possibility for me to marry until 2015 when the U.S. Supreme Court legalized marriage for gay couples. In response to the court's decision, a letter from the First Presidency was read at church. I heard many members speak of their fear, their worries, and their disappointments at the expansion of marriage to gay couples. Many comments were unkind and insensitive. I went home and cried.

Later that year the Church implemented a new policy labeling members in a gay relationship as apostates and mandating that they face disciplinary councils; it also forbade their minor children from being baptized and becoming members of the Church. I was hurt and angry at this new policy and ready to walk away. I yelled at God, "Why did you let me stay in a church which clearly doesn't want me?" I got the answer that it's fine to leave, but if I am willing to stay there is a special work for me. That work includes helping leaders better understand, and helping queer Mormons learn to accept and love themselves.

I decided to stay and was immediately asked to serve as the stake executive secretary, which means when a General Authority visits and meets the stake presidency, they also bump into a gay man, and sometimes they invite me to visit with them when I travel to Utah.

I have a Tumblr blog where I started writing about my experiences, thoughts, and feelings as a gay church member. In 2017, I wrote a post about telling a Seventy that I'm gay, and the kindness and love he showed me. The post went viral, over 500,000 views, and resulted in many people sending me questions. I've replied to nearly 2,000 of these messages. And what is the question I get asked the most?

"Why do you stay?"

I get this question from queer people and from non-queer people, from active members and from those who've left.

It's unusual to come across a queer individual who still attends The Church of Jesus Christ of Latter-day Saints, especially one who isn't still in their 20's. Most queer people leave the Church, and for good reason. So why do I stay?

- I stay because these are my people.
- I stay because this is where I learned to communicate with the Divine.
- I stay because it makes things easier with my family.
- I stay because it's familiar.

- I stay because of inertia.
- I stay because there are queer kids who need someone.
- I stay because I'm stubborn.
- I stay because Jesus invited me to.
- I stay because I will not be erased. My presence means the Church has no choice but to recognize queer people exist.
- I stay because I feel like I make a difference.
- When I was not out, I stayed as part of trying to pass as straight.
- I stay because I want to increase understanding.
- I stay because it gives me credibility with LDS parents of queer kids.
- I stay because sometimes my soul is stirred at church.
- I stay because humans have a need for religion as evidenced by the many religions we have created since time immemorial.
- I stay because this is my church, too. I claim a seat for as long as I want to belong.
- I stay for the meaning it makes in my life.
- I stay because it helps me be better and do better.
- I stay because I am unwilling to cede the space to bigots and retreat to only queer-friendly places. I do not believe segregation will ever improve things.

People seek religion because they have questions. I have many unanswered questions. But queer people generally find fewer answers than others. If I stick it out and am faithful all my life, what blessings are in store for me? What's my place in heaven? Our church emphasizes families, so why am I expected to go without a family of my own? What's old age going to be like if I don't have children or a spouse? Fundamental questions and choices about faith and love and life aren't limited only to LGBTQ+ people, but we're faced with questions in a painful and ongoing way.

The choice to leave is always in front of me—it doesn't go away. It can be exhausting. I certainly feel dissonance as a queer member. I have to swim upstream to stay in this church; sometimes it's really tough. It would be easy for me to float away. Do I ever want to give up? Yes. I've considered leaving, but I'm not ready to go away yet.

I really wish I fit and could live the Mormon dream. However, I am regularly reminded that I don't exactly belong, that I'm second class. Even my presence at church can make some people uncomfortable.

When LGBTQ+ topics arise in church, they're always linked with restrictions. Queer members don't often hear messages of love and hope regarding our situation. In some important ways, I'm not sure I can reach my full potential as a human being inside the Church.

I love the Church and its people, yet that love is unrequited. I don't want to be merely tolerated. I want to be embraced. I want to be respected as a peer and a fellow child of God, accepted for being on the path of discipleship with the body of Christ—all of us together. I want to be understood, loved, and included.

The intersection of being queer and religious is stressful and messy. Let me get very real with you. Here are some of the effects I deal with from being a queer Mormon.

- I have wanted to unalive myself.
- I'm pretty sure I have an eating disorder.
- I deal with low self-esteem.
- I have symptoms of PTSD.
- I used to self-harm.
- I have social anxiety disorder.
- I'm lonely.
- I spent years suppressing my feelings.

Being in this space means being wounded. Surely this isn't what anyone wants for their loved ones. Sometimes the wounds inflicted by others at Church are intentional, sometimes they're unintentional. Really, it doesn't matter what the intention is. It hurts.

Often, it's like getting a papercut over and over and over. I've been told it's inappropriate to mention I'm gay and I shouldn't say I'm gay if I'm not having sex. In answer to the Sunday School teacher's question of what's an example of people calling evil 'good,' people answer 'homosexuality.' I hear the Family Proclamation used to diminish queer people. I sit through many lessons about the covenant path when I'm not allowed to complete that path. Those small wounds add up.

Then there are times when the cut goes much deeper, such as when apostles speak of queer people as enemies, or suggest queer people will be relegated to lower kingdoms of heaven. I can't think of a more rejecting teaching than that I'm to be forever separated from my loved ones simply for being gay, something I didn't choose and can't change.

I share all this in hopes people will understand that while I may be an active member of The Church of Jesus Christ of Latter-day Saints and do my best to make it work, it's difficult. All the time I feel pushed to the periphery.

—

This book is a survival guide for those living on the inside edge of the Church. I want to share thoughts and lessons I've learned as a queer person in the Church. I hope queer members will find something helpful to them, to build their resistance and ability to stay for as long as they want to stay. And I think many of these thoughts and lessons should be of value to all of us children of God.

This is not an ordered list. Some is practical advice, some is observations about who we are, some is reframing how to view the Church.

—

Being queer is okay. Queerness can be found throughout the animal kingdom. God loves diversity. God created me as a glorious, eternal being. The same is true for the person who is transgender, asexual, panromantic, or any other person in a queer category. I don't know how we fit into God's plan, but God knows. Our situations are part of the natural variations of the human condition.

—

When I accepted that I'm gay, it transformed how I understood myself and the world around me. It changed how I view the Church. It changed my faith, pushing me to a more complex version of faith.

—

If you're young, and even if you're not so young, it helps to have a safe trusted adult in your life with whom you can ask questions and talk about your feelings, doubts, and fears. Ideally this would be your parents, but if there are subjects you can't talk to them about, find other quality adults who can fill this role.

—

There will be people who can't see your worth. Don't let yourself be one of them. If other people say they have a problem with you being queer, they're right—it's THEIR problem. Don't let them make it YOUR problem.

—

Be gentle to yourself. Words have power; say positive things about yourself. List the mental and physical things that are positive and healthy in your life; recognize the skills and qualities you've developed.

—

Developing your talents and skills is not selfish. Investing in yourself will be a great gift to yourself and to others.

—

Nothing blooms all year long. Do not expect yourself to do so. Take time to nurture yourself. You are your longest commitment so make caring for yourself a priority.

—

Jesus said "as ye would that men should do to you, do ye also to them likewise" (Luke 6:31). But the Church and its members do not treat queer people as they would like to be treated. I dare say if they were asked to do all that is asked of queer people, this would be a very small church.

—

You can't pray the queer away; it doesn't work that way. You are meant to be who you are. God already knows you're queer, and God wants you to succeed. This is a part of His plan for you. Accept it. Enjoy it.

—

What you can pray for is to know this is your path. Don't worry that you will mess up God's plan for your life. You are not that powerful.

—

God doesn't single out individuals or groups for different treatment. God says all are alike. I wish we as a Church really believed this because it feels like we spend a lot of time distinguishing between who is allowed to receive this blessing, who gets to participate that way, who gets to be involved and who doesn't.

—

No one has the right to say you aren't loved by God, or that you aren't loved as much. That is contrary to all the scriptures. Don't you believe it. Rather than take someone else's word for it, pray and ask if God loves you.

—

When Jesus interacted with people on the peripheries of His society—those who didn't have political or social power—they always felt Jesus' love. People were seen and heard; they were touched. They left Jesus with more dignity than when they started. I'm not sure queer people can say the same about their encounters with Mormons. But for us as individuals that's a worthy goal, to leave people feeling uplifted from their interactions with us.

—

Push back against the negative messages. Speak up to challenge the rejecting things said about you and about queer people. If you can't speak up, then think positive messages to yourself to replace the negative ones.

—

Find ways to affirm yourself. This is especially important if you're not fully out to the people in your life. You could wear something that is subtly queer, something that non-queer people likely don't recognize, something other than the Pride rainbow. For example, a pendant or earrings with the colors of pan, or trans, or bi, or ace. In whatever way you're queer, there is something there for you.

—

Focus on Jesus and the overarching themes of the gospel. The Church is human, the Church is flawed, the Church is part of this temporal world. Focus on the gospel and not the Church.

—

I don't believe our Heavenly Parents forgot about queer people in Their plan. I believe I'm included in God's plan, even if not in the Church's version of that plan. I believe and hope there's more to be revealed. The idea that the Heavenly Parents who made me gay didn't also make an accommodation for me to return to them is nonsensical. How is this loving or fair or hopeful? That isn't the God I know.

—

Jesus knows what it's like to be mocked and rejected. He was called names and betrayed. I find it helps knowing Jesus understands things I deal with. I can go to Him for comfort.

There is more to be revealed. The Restoration is ongoing. The artist is not finished with His masterpiece. Just because the painting looks a certain way now doesn't mean the artist intends for it to look that way forever.

The Lord says His yoke is easy and His burden is light, and I laugh at that. Maybe it's not His burden I'm carrying but the burden the Church puts on me. It's important to differentiate between the gospel and the Church.

—

God wants you to live! You may find yourself in a dark place but remember our Heavenly Parents do not want you to unalive yourself. If choosing life means leaving the Church, choose life. It may sound dramatic, but many queer people face these feelings. Please get help if you find yourself here. There are going to be some hard times. Mental health issues are common for people like you and me. Seek therapy when you recognize you need help. If you're in college, you could see a therapist on campus. That's something you likely already paid for as part of your fees. If you have insurance through work, it may cover sessions with a therapist.

—

Being Christ-like is more important than ordinances. All the saving ordinances can be performed for an individual in a few hours, but it takes a lifetime to become the kind of person who can abide a Celestial glory. We may be denied some things in this life and unable to complete the covenant path, but ordinances can be added later.

—

Maybe you can't participate in queer spaces due to your current circumstances, but you can try to limit the time you spend with people who aren't supportive of LGBTQ+ people and cut some of that bigotry and negativity out of your life. If you must interact with such a person, draw boundaries around topics you will not discuss with them.

—

Each of us can receive personal revelation. Each of us can work out our path in life with God. I have heard church leaders say that personal revelation will never contradict church teachings, but that has not been my experience. I have gotten the message that I'm not broken at a time when the Church taught that I could be 'cured.' I have received the clear message it's okay to seek a relationship. These personal revelations have been very clear and accompanied by strong feelings of warmth and love, the feelings that I feel when the Spirit testifies.

—

Find other queer people to be friends with. Being around queer people helps me feel normal. When I'm with queer people, I don't have to edit myself as I do with Church people. Especially try to become friends with some queer Mormons; they'll get you in a way others won't. Online friends count—they're still friends. As much as straight people can love and support you, in some ways, they can't fully understand you. They've never had their existence come into question in the same way.

—

There will be people who say if you sustained the prophet and apostles then you need to obey them and do what they say. That's not how it works. I sustain plenty of people in my local congregation and it doesn't mean I will do whatever they say no matter what. If I think the top Church leadership sometimes get it wrong, why would I still raise my hand to sustain them? I guess it's more a vote of hope. I hope they're listening to God, and I hope the answers they're getting reflect the love and acceptance that I think God would have for His children.

—

Queer people have been part of this church from its earliest days. A drag queen was one of the founders of the general young men's program.[1] A lesbian couple were central to the beginnings of the General Primary Association, the Children's Friend magazine, and Primary Children's Hospital.[2] Queer people contributed hymns we sing and paintings distributed in our magazines and hanging in the Church's museums and offices.[3] A transgender woman designed

---

1. B. Morris Young - General YM Program (https://en.wikipedia.org/wiki/B._Morris_Young)
2. Louie B. Felt, first general president of the Primary, and May Anderson, board member - General Primary, Friend magazine, Primary Children's Hospital (https://en.wikipedia.org/wiki/Louie_B._Felt#Same-sex_relationships)
3. Evan Stephens - multiple hymns (https://en.wikipedia.org/wiki/Evan_Stephens); Katharine Lee Bates - America the Beautiful (https://en.wikipedia.org/wiki/Katharine_Lee_Bates#Relationship_with_Katharine_Coman); Judith Mehr - painter (https://archive.sltrib.com/article.php?id=3463749&itype=CMSID)

many of our temples and the Missionary Training Center in Provo, Utah.[4] Our Church would be much poorer without their contributions. There is a legacy of 'pioqueers' that you can claim. Both the LDS culture and the LGBTQ+ culture are rich and beautiful, full of history and tradition and heroes, and you are a full member of both and allowed to interact with and claim those histories.

—

Look for moments of queer joy. These are moments of happiness related to your queerness. This includes being on a date and anticipating hands touching and getting all the feels. Getting to be with someone when they receive their driver's license with the correct gender marker. When someone trusts you enough to come out to you. Getting complimented for the rainbow pin you're wearing.

—

We know who we are in a way most non-queer people never will. Queer people have had to figure out how we are different, what that means for us, and how that changes the narratives we've been taught. Because we had to wrestle with the concepts of identity, sexuality, gender, gender roles, biology, and our place in the world, we know who we are. This is truly one of the great blessings of being queer.

—

Music can really lift a mood. You can include gay anthems in your playlist and most non-queer people won't even pick up on it. It's easy to find Pride playlists on Spotify or by doing a Google search. Likewise, a good arrangement of a hymn can bring peace and nurture our spirituality.

—

4. Laurie Lee Hall - architect (https://archive.sltrib.com/article.php?id=5522210)

When I read the scriptures, I try to liken them to my queer self. What lessons are there for me? It turns out there are quite a few. Jesus sided with the poor and the outcasts. He fought gender inequality, racism, political corruption, hatred, and injustice. I can act in faith by following His example and teachings. Moses, Ruth, Nephi, and Sarah each had to grapple with what to do. They didn't know the end of the story and how things would play out. I don't know the end of my story, and that's okay. I'm not perfect and God can still use me. Life is messy. Life doesn't wait until we're perfectly prepared and feel totally up for what's ahead of us. We do our best, learn from our mistakes, and try to do better.

—

Time and again God shows He is not beholden to the customs of this world, particularly those that restrict who can receive His blessings or favor. The second born gets the birthright. The youngest son becomes ruler over older brothers. It is more difficult for the rich to obtain blessings and enter heaven. Women are worthy leaders. The Gospel is not limited to nationality or race.

I wonder what other traditions will be knocked down by our merciful Lord.

—

Read stories with queer representation. Here are a few suggestions:

- *Autoboyography*, by Christina Lauren
- *Aristotle and Dante Discover the Secrets of the Universe*, by Benjamin Alire Sáenz
- *Everything Leads To You*, by Nina LaCour
- *Simon vs. the Homo Sapiens Agenda*, by Becky Albertalli

—

I know how it feels to be on the margins and I can empathize with people in their struggles. I've been used by God to befriend the friendless and comfort the comfortless. He guides me to people who need to feel His love.

—

You determine your relationship with the Church. Despite what Church members often say, it isn't an all-or-nothing proposition. You can participate to whatever degree works for you. You can accept or refuse callings. You can attend Sundays but not activities, or only attend activities. You can come for sacrament meeting but not the rest. If you like that sense of community, participate enough to retain that feeling of belonging.

—

When things are said at church that bother me, I ask myself:

- Is it consistent with the God I know?
- Does it fit with the greatest commandments of loving God and each other?

Those questions identify a lot of things I can dismiss.

—

You can have questions and doubts and still have a testimony. You can have opinions that differ from the Brethren and still be a good member. You can disagree with Mormon cultural norms and still be LDS.

—

Sometimes a good cry really is cathartic, can help you get all the feelings out that you have but can't express. Crying is healthy.

—

If this truly is God's church, then all of God's children should be included and loved. Right now, it's clear that not all are included and loved. I see the hurt and harm the Church does to queer people. Most queer members leave; very few queer people will convert. The gospel is meant to be good news, and for queer people it often is presented in a way that it is not good news. As the scriptures say, judge a tree by the fruit it bears, and the fruits the Church produces for queer people aren't good. Until the Church is a good place and welcoming for all Heavenly Parents' children, there is work to do.

—

You are not your problems. The dark and terrible things you deal with usually are things that come at you from outside, but many of the good things in your life come from within you.

—

I don't know what the future holds. I don't know what heaven will be like for me. I focus on what I can do now, and trust God will take care of the future. I believe the Lord is doing work in the world today and I want to be part of that. Instead of asking "what would Jesus do?" I choose to ask "what can Jesus do through me?"

—

There's nothing wrong with being in the closet. Sure, it can feel like you're holding in a huge secret, but it's safe there. We all come out in our own time. Every queer person faces the decision of when is it better to be safe and when do I want to be more authentic about who I am and how I experience the world.

—

People and institutions change and grow.

—

Queer people don't seem to fit in the plan of creation as it is taught and understood by our apostles, and yet we exist. How many more queer people must God create before the Church realizes He wants them here?

—

I wish my church and my orientation were more compatible. I don't believe I am incompatible with God.

—

It's interesting that the Church has rules and policies and doctrines about queer people without revelation or scripture to base them on. Where is the revelation to oppose same-gender marriages? When did they get a revelation that gay people shouldn't have companionship and love? Where's the revelation that God doesn't want me to fall in love with another man? Where's the revelation that God doesn't want someone to express their gender identity? Maybe the answer is that the Church does not have revelations about individual situations, but that is our job.

—

I've shared a lot of thoughts about staying. That doesn't mean it's the right choice for you. Church can hurt. Stepping away can be the healthy decision for many queer people. You can be a good person without the Church. Heavenly Father will help guide you to do good no matter where you are in your life. You can also be a good person while still affiliated with the Church. You haven't disowned the queer community or ignored the realities of the twenty-first century Church if you stay for your own good reasons.

BLACK AND MORMON: ACTIVISM TO SURVIVE

JAMES JONES

Affirming the marginalized is a pursuit I've been involved in professionally in one form or another since the murder of Trayvon Martin in 2012. If there was a moment that activated my generation, that was it. In a previous career I did it with art. Currently, I do it with the word. I've been a member of the Church my whole life. I have long been aware of the awkward and dangerous positions the color of my skin can put me in as I occupy predominantly white spaces. I've long been aware that the Church is one of those places. Though I credit the less than ideal experiences I've had for my current professional and academic trajectory, I also don't wish them on anyone else and dedicate a significant amount of time and energy to affirming the marginalized.

I co-host a podcast that centers the marginalized in Mormonism by reading the Come Follow Me lessons through the lens of the marginalized. I needed such a resource and knew others would too, so I created it. The podcast and the opportunities it gave me to further share my voice eventually brought me to Union Theological Seminary, the birthplace of an interdisciplinary concentration called Black Liberation Theology. As of now, I'm the only person to pursue this particular academic discipline from a Mormon perspective, and part of my goal in pursuing it is to add that Mormon perspective. As a member of The Church of Jesus Christ of Latter-day Saints and someone who has a testimony of its most fundamental truth claims, I have a vested interest in making the Church more hospitable to Black souls. Not only will my experience be less lonely, but I also know that the restored church of the same brown-skinned Jesus Christ who was lynched by a corrupt state will not be the church it is supposed to be until Black folks feel like the Church was made with them in mind.

Before proceeding further, my positionality as a straight able-bodied cisgender educated large Black man has to be named. All these characteristics permit me additional energy and privilege in predominantly white spaces. I can say things and move in spaces that others without such privileges cannot; at least I can do so with fewer negative consequences and less risk to my social standing, physical safety, and emotional health. The joke within the Black community is that straight Black men are the white people of Black people, the implication being that in the Black community, people like me will have the most blind spots. Consequently, I will imperfectly try to address issues and will not always or properly consider the intersections of anti-blackness and misogyny, ableism, queerphobia, and more.

All that said, I'd like to share just a few recent examples that evidence that The Church of Jesus Christ of Latter-day Saints is a less than ideal church for Black folks:

In March and April 2019, just days before the Notre Dame Cathedral caught fire, three Black churches in Louisiana were burned down via arson. However, President Nelson only sent a message of comfort to Pope Francis. There was no mention of the Black churches.

When the November 2015 terrorist attack in Paris happened, there was a statement put out by the Church and many Mormons on social media added French flag overlays to their profile pictures. When the terrorist attack in Kenya with more casualties happened earlier that year, or the Beirut bombings happened that same week, no statements were released and very little performative solidarity was displayed.

When a mass shooting killed 9 black people while they worshiped, the Church was silent. But when a mass shooting took out 61 people at a Las Vegas music festival, the Church put out a statement.

I was tapped to teach a class on the history of race in the Church to my elders quorum a few years back only to have it derailed by a few members of the quorum who seemed profoundly offended by the mere suggestion that Brigham Young was racist, even though, definitionally and functionally, he was racist.

In 2016, a friend of mine, a Black woman, sat in a congregation in a metropolitan area on the Sunday following the deaths of Alton Sterling and Philando Castille. The ward had several Black members in it and they were in mourning. For most of the sacrament meeting, no one said anything about the deaths or the pain that Black America was in. Prior to the conclusion of the meeting however, the counselor conducting the meeting stated that the bishop wanted to say some words before the closing hymn. There were audible gasps in the congregation, anticipating some words of comfort or joint mourning. The bishop took the podium and began his remarks with the words, "I'd like to share what I learned during a trip my family and I took to Idaho . . ." The bishop, the ecclesiastical steward of his congregation which included Black souls, spoke no words to the pain they were experiencing.

In most meetings I had with bishops as a young man, the bishops expressed pleasant surprise at my intelligence and manners. I wondered why their expectations of me were so low as to be surprised. Later I was criticized by other young people in my ward and high school for being unwilling to embody their ideas of Blackness. One young White man was so bold as to ask why I 'talked white'. While the question makes no sense, I knew what he was getting at, although I wasn't sharp enough to grasp and articulate how problematic his words were. Arguably this was innocent coming from a child, but he likely grew into an adult with these same misguided ideas about Black intelligence and Black behavior. The adult becomes a teacher of Black students, an ecclesiastical steward of Black souls, a parent of Black children, cops in Black neighborhoods, and the list goes on. The point is they become people in positions of power that can do harm to Black people without a proper understanding of and respect for Black people.

Every race related issue I have come across in the Church has come down to an ignorance of, apathy about, or hostility toward Black people and their experiences. In the history of our Church, we have never socially or politically required otherwise. For far too much of our Church's existence, being spiritually and socially violent toward Black life was an institutional feature. It's true that as of 2021 the Church has demonstrated a more regular and vocal stand against racism, but none of this has yet translated into any specific institutional strategy or policy that makes racism costly or teaches members how to be deliberately anti-racist. This is obviously a problem in a church with our history of spiritual and social dispossession of Black people, a church that has yet to make proper restitution for that dispossession, a church with so few Black people, and a church that is consistently late to minister or totally absent in the face of Black oppression. This makes for a less than ideal environment for the Black body.

Surviving (and even thriving) in this space however, is not impossible. And for those of us who desire to do so, whatever our reasons, here are at least three things that help. These suggestions have an unintentional but direct analogue to what President Hinckley said every new convert needs: "a friend, a responsibility, and nurturing with the 'good word of God'."[1] Every Black member needs three things: to find a tribe (a friend), to work for change loudly (a responsibility), and to affirm your life with the word (nourished by the good word of God).

FIND A TRIBE

As the African-American proverb states, "We all we got." There have been times, particularly in the midst of Black death at the hands of law enforcement officials or white vigilantes, where I knew I wouldn't have a chance of lamenting properly at church unless there was another Black person I knew in attendance. There are congregations in metropolitan areas that have a significant and even, in rare cases, predominantly Black membership, where these issues can't really be avoided. In fact, even though there are no institutional structures in place to facilitate lamentation, sometimes such spaces are created anyway by or at the request of Black Saints in the congregation. For me and the majority of Black Saints who don't have congregations like this, we're able to have our grief acknowledged through communities of Saints online. There have even been whole events created for the purpose of acknowledging us, our contributions, our resilience, and our pain (e.g. the annual Black LDS Legacy Conference, Black Lives Matter to Christ). Just as Christian discipleship isn't intended to be lived in isolation, so it is with Black Mormonism. You need a community of people that understand you, empathize with you, mourn with you, and validate you because the church will not or cannot always do that. Most of the time, they probably won't, and if they do, it'll probably be too late. #BlackLivesMatter was first said on social media in 2013. The first time a General Authority in the Church said it was October 2020 and the Church has yet to use the phrase, put out a statement, or directly condemn racism in or out of

---

1. President Gordon B. Hinckley, "Every Convert is Precious," *Liahona*, February 1999.

the pews with any real specificity. Your best chance of being validated, heard, and nourished is within a community of Black believers.

MySpace saved me as a youth, introducing me to a network of Black Latter-day Saints my age and older. These Saints taught me how to process the priesthood ban and introduced me to the likes of Darius Gray and Marvin Perkins. This resource held me over until I got to BYU, where there was an actual Black Student Union and I could go to Genesis on the first Sunday of each month. These days, if you don't have access to spaces like Genesis or a Black student union at a Mormon school, you can find communities online like Black LDS Legacy and others that prioritize the Black experience in our faith. Through these communities, members often find new resources to help us navigate our journey and new friends to bear us up. It was through these channels that I first learned about Black Liberation Theology and consequently learned just how affirming Mormon theology can be for the Black soul. With these resources, including the community I joined, not only can I stand in my faith, but I can also give back to the community of Black Mormons and many others, in ways I wouldn't have been able to otherwise. I can do for others what was done for me as a youth.

AFFIRM YOUR LIFE WITH THE WORD

The Bible is the original weapon of racism. Throughout the history of the United States and colonialism worldwide, self-proclaimed Christians have been the progenitors and perpetuators of racism. Overseers of the enslaved would quote scripture as they abused their hostages. If the Bible was preached among the slaves, it was from a heavily redacted version, the so-called Slave Bible, usually with a focus on the words of Paul, in which several passages, even a whole book (Philemon) could be transformed with a slave master's eisegesis. Many complicated and extensive works of theology were written to justify both chattel slavery and racial segregation. When people did fight against slavery and segregation, the most violent and vociferous defenders of the racial hierarchy were Christians. In short, white supremacy and Christianity are deeply intertwined and, consequently, traditional Christianity is not primed to affirm Black life.

There are scriptures in the New Testament, and more in the Book of Mormon, such as 2 Nephi 26:33, that affirm equality of all persons regardless of their immutable identities. We can and should use these scriptures to affirm the value of Black lives, but many churches don't yet live into those ideals, as evidenced by the long delayed response to the pattern of police brutality against Black people; the response to atrocities in overseas European countries but no similar response in America to atrocities that happen to Black people; and by the lack of Black bodies in congregations, in leadership, in the office buildings, etc. You cannot outsource your understanding of what God's word means for you in your Blackness to leaders who haven't, at the very least, demonstrated a knowledge of your Blackness. Therefore, it becomes necessary to learn the scriptures in a way that is specific in its affirmation of Black life.

Get used to reading the scriptures through a Black lens. Read the scriptures in a way that affirms you. Considering how effective Bible-based racism was in spite of how antithetical slavery, segregation, and racial hierarchies are to the gospel, one can imagine how much more effective and plentiful are Bible-based affirmations of Black life. For example, Alma 60 is often read in the context of the chapter that follows it as a lesson on how to not overreact to harsh words or ill-informed personal attacks. But through a Black lens, Captain Moroni's words hit differently:

> 5 But behold, great has been the slaughter among our people; yea, thousands have fallen by the sword, while it might have otherwise been. . . . Yea, great has been your neglect towards us.

> 6 And now behold, we desire to know the cause of this exceedingly great neglect; yea, we desire to know the cause of your thoughtless state.
>
> 7 Can you think to sit upon your thrones in a state of thoughtless stupor . . . while they are murdering thousands of your brethren—
>
> 8 Yea, even they who have looked up to you for protection, yea, have placed you in a situation that ye might have succored them . . . and have saved thousands of them from falling . . .
>
> 9 But behold, this is not all—ye have withheld your provisions from them . . .
>
> 10 And now, my beloved brethren—for ye ought to be beloved; yea, and ye ought to have stirred yourselves more diligently for the welfare and the freedom of this people; but behold, ye have neglected them insomuch that the blood of thousands shall come upon your heads for vengeance; yea, for known unto God were all their cries, and all their sufferings—

In just a few of Captain Moroni's opening words, Alma 60 becomes a cry of Black America and a damning indictment of complicity or participation in White supremacy.

Learn from Black theologians like Esau McCauley, Willie James Jennings, Howard Thurman, Kelly Brown Douglas, and James Cone. Cone once said, "Trying to understand Christianity from a white point of view is like trying to understand Jesus from a Roman point of view." Many of the most life-giving readings of sacred texts, therefore, are from Black theologians, for Jesus identified with those on the margins; so much so that he declared our treatment of them was our treatment of him (Matthew 25:40). Having drawn the parallels between the humiliating brutal state-sanctioned death of Christ on the cross and the regular state-sanctioned lynchings of Black bodies, I'm personally convinced that there is no American who is able to embrace and teach Jesus like the Black American. Our experience as Black people provides a profound hermeneutic through which we talk about and experience the divine and ourselves. This alone is why the church needs us so urgently. They will never truly know Jesus until they know us.

WORK FOR CHANGE LOUDLY

The scriptures also teach us that we should work for justice. Many people use the lack of institutional power as an excuse to resign themselves to inaction in the face of oppression. I know several members of the Church who acknowledge that there's a race issue in the church, problems with how we address questions surrounding LGBTQ folks, and more, but when time comes to directly address homophobia, racism, or other kinds of bigotry in our pews, they're quiet and motionless. Mere hours before sitting down to write this sentence, I was sitting in a Sunday School lesson with homophobic words being spoken and no one but me and the only queer person in the room spoke in defense of our queer siblings. We have to be better than this for a couple of reasons, but perhaps the biggest and most overarching reason is that it's our covenant responsibility. Bigotry is a sin and treating it like an unsavory personality trait rather than a sin is itself a sin, for it allows the sin to be perpetuated. To refuse to bear testimony of the *imago dei* in our marginalized siblings is a deliberate turning away from our discipleship and our covenants.

The limited institutional power most members and leaders have (even those in the upper echelons) will not bring about necessary institutional changes by the acts of one alone. However, every individual member of the church has the power to change the spaces they occupy simply by taking up space, being present, demanding recognition. My friend Derek, an openly gay and unafraid Latter-day Saint theologian, doesn't have any administrative callings in his ward. He does however command respect anywhere he goes, because he knows who he is and that God validates his identity. When he's asked to speak on or teach about LGBTQ issues in his congregation, he states his expectations where his respect is concerned and politely yet firmly checks those who don't meet those expectations. If homophobia happens in a lesson that he's not teaching, he does what Paul did to Peter and interrupts it immediately so as to prevent anyone from getting the impression that the homophobia is normal or acceptable (Gal 2:12–17). Oftentimes, he only has to do this once for those around him to get the message. He knows he doesn't change everyone's mind all the time, but he does know that those in the spaces he occupies will at least think twice before they imply that Derek is not entitled to the same blessings straight people are entitled to by virtue of orientation alone. In other words, Derek makes the spaces he's in safer by speaking up. You don't have to be a theologian, an academic, or be in any presidency or bishopric to disagree with bigotry in church spaces, but you do need to disagree with it and do so loudly and unmistakably. It was probably very uncomfortable for Paul to disagree with Peter so loudly and publicly in Antioch, but "the truth of the gospel" (Gal 2:14) compelled him to do so. Not his office, not any degrees, but the simple truth that the gospel of Jesus Christ had dissolved hierarchical distinctions between Jews and Gentiles, a point he would state plainly in the following chapter: "There is neither Jew nor Greek, there is neither bond nor free, there is neither male nor female: for ye are all one in Christ Jesus" (Gal 3:28).

Not only are we allowed to hold our institutions accountable for how they live into the truth that all are alike unto God, but we are covenantally obligated to do so. You could even argue that our survival depends on it. The Levite Uzzah was struck down for steadying the ark, but what most people don't acknowledge as they condemn the 'ark steadiers' for criticizing church leadership, is that the reason the ark needed steadying in the first place is because David, the leader, didn't transport the ark properly. He did not seek the voice of the

Lord and he did not consult the Torah which had spelled it out. Uzzah could have spoken up, at least that's the impression we're given when David blames the Levites for what happened to Uzzah, but he didn't, and paid for that omission and David's negligence with his life.

Unfortunately, those who aren't directly affected by our oppression (i.e. white people) are less likely to know that holding our leaders accountable for how we treat those on the margins is part of our covenants; even if they do, they're less likely to act on it with the required urgency. Though it isn't fair and theoretically shouldn't be this way, the lot will fall on Black members to lead out and call the rest of church membership to repent for attitudes and actions of prejudice. Our ability to exist in church spaces safely and with dignity will depend on it.

In saying all of this, I acknowledge how difficult it is for Black folks to be disagreeable, considering how white people tend to be threatened. A few weeks ago, a white woman broke down in tears because I politely interrogated her homophobia. A few months before that, the same thing occurred when I pressed a white woman to name the power dynamics present in a seminary class where a racist incident occurred. As a Black man, I know that if a white person, especially a white woman, simply feels threatened by me, I'm in danger, socially and physically. It may not always be prudent to be disagreeable. Today I watched a white presenter tell a Black doctor during a live broadcast that her hair reminded him of an Alpaca and he wanted to pet it. She laughed it off, but it was an awkward laugh that communicated she was laughing only to protect her career. It's a situation that way too many of us know. I'd be a rich man if I could charge for every microaggression I experience in the workplace.

I don't believe there is a one-size-fits-all answer for how and when to acknowledge racism, but I believe our best chance for survival is to be actively involved in dismantling oppressive structures. Survival is simply not sustainable if the Church remains as it is or if we lie to ourselves about our needs for affirmation.

COMPLICATED FAMILIES: RAISING CHILDREN ON THE EDGE

CHRISTIAN E. KIMBALL

My children are all adults, all married, all have their own children. They should tell their own stories someday. But I get asked for the Mormon score because my break with standard Church practice happened when my children were 10, 13, and 16. So here goes: Including spouses in the count, there are four Seminary graduates, two missionaries, one Peace Corp volunteer, one BYU graduate, one temple marriage, four active (LDS) Church members who hold and have held the whole range of callings one might expect at their respective ages, two active in another church with responsibilities that would not be available in typical Mormon practice, seven grandchildren being raised in the (LDS) Church, and four being raised in another church.

That's the Mormon score. It's mixed. My own scoring looks like this: six well-educated, happy, productive, contributing members of society. Three happy marriages. Eleven grandchildren. Eleven college and graduate degrees including all three women with graduate degrees and careers. Six thoughtful, considerate, churchgoing, independent thinking adults whom I would trust to run the world.

Raising children in the Church is supposed to be great. That's what the programming is about. There is a lot of support and attention for families. Families with minor children are the core class of members, which is patently clear to everyone who is not in that class.

Reality does not live up to theory, in so many ways. This is not the place to discuss or solve all the many gaps between the ideal and the real for families generally and for families In the Church. Whole books have been written on rebellion, on discipline, on gay children, on childlessness, on addicted children, and so on and on almost to infinity. My focus here is on the special concerns of an inside-of-the-edge parent with minor children in the environment of The Church of Jesus Christ of Latter-day Saints.

There are at least four flavors of special concern:

1. My children outed me.
2. My children came home with ideas that troubled me and doctrinal statements that I didn't agree with.
3. My children are walking their own road. They ask many of the same questions I have, and come to their own answers. They decide whether to stay or go and how they relate to the Church, and their decisions are not always the same as my decisions at their age or now.
4. Church folk judge me by what my children do.

OUTING

Peter raises his hand in a Primary baptism prep class and challenges a picture: "my Dad says Joseph Smith wasn't looking at the plates like in that picture, but put his face in a hat and said the English words out loud from there." That statement comes right out of the *Book of Mor-*

mon Translation topic in the Church History collection, but seven-year-old Peter coming out with that line labels me, his father.

Generalizing, if it doesn't happen in Primary, it's going to happen in Seminary or in a bishop's interview or in the middle of a youth activity. You are going to be outed.

Of course, it might not happen. But there are too many stories, too many examples, to place bets on getting through your children's Primary and Youth experience in the Church without being told on.

Some people try to hide from their children. Practice an outward appearance of orthodoxy and orthopraxy in their home as well as at church. I suspect hiding from the children is common. I'm more confident it is a long difficult slog for the parents, and likely to fail anyway. Children are notoriously observant. They know. Hiding is not a long-term survival strategy.

Some people teach their children to hold family secrets close. As a child of such a family, I recognize a bias, but in my opinion, holding family secrets close is damaging to the children, the parents and the family altogether, in the long run. And likely to fail anyway. Making children keep secrets is not a long-term survival strategy.

The only survival strategy I could come up with was to proactively out myself. I considered it one of the costs of living on the borderlands of the Church and having children at the same time. A modest silver lining is that my children—while sometimes embarrassed by me—are smart and wise, and with knowledge about me were able to calibrate and moderate the way I became known through them. By the time my children were in their mid-teens nobody was surprised. Not my children. Not the ward. Not our local leaders.

QUESTIONS

On the way home from Church, Christina asks, "Why was that last speaker talking to just the boys about missions?" Answering Christina's question was complicated and multi-layered. There's history and change over time. There's the whole topic of what we teach young men different than young women, including a sexist way to talk about it and a feminist way to talk about it. The way I talked about it was different when she was eleven than when she was eighteen. However, to be frank, the question never had a satisfactory answer.

We rejected the idea of saying nothing, and we rejected the idea of pulling Christina out of Church. We weren't going to lie, by commission or omission. And we were interested in encouraging a life in the church. Not demanding, but encouraging.

For a more general response, I suggest starting with the question of what you want for your children. If you want a by-the-book literal believer who goes on a mission, gets married in the temple, and never looks back, the standard church programs are designed to help you get there. My non-scientific anecdotal observation—lots of evidence, but not anything like a double-blind test—suggests the programs do work to the point of getting an uncommonly high percentage of our teens on missions and into the temple. However, "never looks back" is much more difficult and much less predictable.

If the strong loyal literal believer is what you're after, chances are you respond to difficult questions by biting your tongue and agreeing that's just the way it is (not a particularly good survival strategy for yourself), or by introducing a small amount of nuance, like an explanation "that's how it sounds but this is what it really means."

At another extreme, perhaps you want someone who thinks like you do (because you are right, because you know best, because you are the parent). In that case you are more likely to launch into an explanation of what's wrong with the teaching and how they should think instead.

What I wanted for my children is neither of those extremes, but I wanted them to grow up to be fully functioning mature adults with their own ideas and opinions and choices. With respect to the Church and religion generally:

- In the long run, I want my children to make their own decisions and come to their own truths. I want them to own their religion, whatever form that takes.
- In the short run, I want them to be smart, educated consumers of and participants in the Mormon experience. I want them to know when they might shock people, when they are going with the flow, when a question has both a rote answer and a deep answer, and all while being intentional and knowing about how they participate.

With those goals in mind, I tried to avoid simple binaries—two options only. Instead, I tried to introduce multiple points of view and alternate answers. By default, I would take a stab at the standard out-of-the-manual church explanation, labeling it as such. I might add a riff on what a very conservative old school Seminary teacher might say. Often, I would project what a liberal or progressive Sunday School teacher might want to say, in a tolerant or open-minded class. If I thought it could be relevant, I'd try to pull out of deep memory what I was thinking at their age and compare it with what I think now. I sprinkled in "I don't know" and sometimes even "I don't think anybody knows." Most importantly, I tried to label everything. Not suggesting that any one view is the truth or the right answer, but making it clear there is more than one view. I think labels themselves were an important part of the education, and I found that using good labels and describing more than just one or two options set me free to have my own opinion and express it. It mapped a middle ground between stating my beliefs as revealed wisdom and avoiding saying anything at all about what I believe.

JOINT PARENTING

This can sound almost easy when using singular pronouns—what *I* would do with *my* children. However, while my wife and I work well together and have much in common, even about the Church, we are different people with somewhat different goals and expectations. I'm aware that having two parents who are divorced or separated complicates matters, and that grandparents and uncles and aunts, teachers, and even babysitters, can try to take on some aspects of parenting, including responsibility for religious education.

Such responsibility turns out to be especially difficult even with just two parents. First, that role is not well defined by culture or by the Church. It is very common for parents to have different expectations about who does what with respect to religion. Second, unless parents agree to default to an outside standard—usually the standard church narrative—they confront the fact that no two people are in the same place at the same time in their beliefs and practices. To compound the problem, a common characteristic of people living on the inside of the edge is that we are not willing to default to an outside standard. One of our answers was the same labeling mentioned above: "Here's the standard Sunday School line, here's what I think, and here's what I think your mother thinks but maybe you should ask her."

Extended family members have their opinions too. Opinions about how much they are entitled or expected to contribute to their grandchildren's or nieces' and nephews' religious education. And opinions about the content of that education. I have seen grandparents try to take over. And I have seen adult children cut their parents—the grandparents—out completely because they were so at odds about religious education.

My children grew up geographically far distant from their extended family on the Mormon side. We didn't have a lot of competition from grandparents and uncles and aunts. Flipping the script, now that we live closer to my siblings, I have become the suspect edgy uncle who sometimes shares heterodox ideas with a niece or nephew. I'm not sure my siblings appreciate it, but at least it comes labeled as an outlier point of view.

AGE-APPROPRIATE TEACHING

I talked with my young children—six and seven years old, in the process of baptism preparation—differently than I talked with eleven-year-old children starting into the Young Men's program and Young Women's program where priesthood differences (for one example) and puberty (for another) show up. I took a different approach with sixteen- seventeen- or eighteen-year-olds at the height of individuating and mapping a personal agenda.

The idea of age-appropriate teaching seems obvious when distinguishing between Primary-age children and Primary graduates in the Young Men or Young Women programs. I would probably add quite a bit of content and detail at every level to the standard church programs, and still more at the middle grades than primary grades. Where things get most interesting is at the older teen high school age. All too often church programming holds the curriculum at about the same level from age eleven/twelve all the way through high school. I think this is intentional. In the modern era this style of church education is often attributed to Elder Packer's teaching. One notable example[1]:

> You seminary teachers and some of you institute and BYU men will be teaching the history of the Church this school year. This is an unparalleled opportunity in the lives of your students to increase their faith and testimony of the divinity of this work. Your objective should be that they will see the hand of the Lord in every hour and every moment of the Church from its beginning till now.

---

1. Elder Boyd K. Packer, "The Mantle is Far, Far Greater Than the Intellect," Address to the Fifth Annual CES Religious Educators' Symposium, 1981.

Another way to describe standard church programming is that it is not designed as an expansive learning experience, but rather as a funnel directing teenagers into missions and temples.

By contrast, for my mid-teens (beginning high school or secondary school) I did not intentionally hold anything back. Whether sex or politics or religion, I shared all the complexity I know, all the different ways of thinking I could muster. That's a personal decision and opinion, which I come to from listening to high school students as they posed sophisticated questions about Mormon priesthood, about sex and marriage, about epistemology, about crime and punishment. I once heard my son talking with his friends about the use of humor in tragedy, in Hamlet, and it woke me to the possibilities for conversation and understanding. I know a few things that only experience can teach, but I can't think of anything that can be put into words that I wouldn't talk about in an appropriate setting.

This book is not the place to recommend or encourage for or against my approach with high school-age teenagers. Rather, it is the place to consider costs and benefits in advance, so that informed decisions can be made. In the nature of counting the cost, my approach with high school-age teenagers can come off as dangerously counter-cultural. I think it made my teenagers something of outliers in their church community (although they think any outlier-ness was 90% their own doing). My sense is that believing parents and believing church teachers don't want me anywhere near their teenagers and probably were suspicious of my children as teenagers.

SUMMING UP

There is no one magic answer for how to respond to teachings your children bring home. The best answers will be driven by what you want for your children. Depending on the choices you make, there may be costs in social capital, in reputation, in respect in the community. I am not neutral on this subject. I have opinions about what I would do and did do with my children. I do not have similarly strong opinions about what you do with your children. But I do believe and encourage the view that what you do with your children should be all about their best interests, and not about what society or the Church or individual church members think about you, the parent.

JOURNEYS

My daughter has been a happy and productive member and lay leader in another church for more than half her life. My older son is sometimes embarrassed by the things his father says. Sometimes that's because he thinks what I consider edgy opinions are obvious and I'm calling attention to myself for no reason. My younger son is a very thoughtful nuanced Mormon bishop who asks my advice but holds his opinions close.

Eventually your children are going to walk their own road. They will ask many of the same questions and come to their own answers. They will decide whether to stay or go, and their decisions may not be the same as your decisions at their age or now. That's what children do.

It is somewhat notorious that traditional believing all-in Mormon parents are pained if their children leave the Church. There is a peculiarly Mormon version of the pain, where parents worry that the promises of the sealing ordinance will be broken. However, as I listen to parents in this position, most of the pain is about rejection and distance and loss of a family feeling.

For the purpose of maintaining some equilibrium, it is useful to remind yourself and to be reminded that the rejection pain is common to all sorts of children-separating-from-parent situations. Being a nuanced, thoughtful, understanding parent doesn't prevent it from happening. Being out on the edge of the Church asking hard questions doesn't cause it to happen. Holding tight to the center would not have been a panacea. Children grow up and take their own journeys.

For the same purpose, it is useful to remind yourself that your hard-won answers are not everybody's answers. You may have a heterodox view of the Church or of some specific doctrine that took you hard decades of study and trial and error to achieve. You may be every bit as certain in your heterodoxy as your 100% believing neighbors in their orthodoxy. Notwithstanding your certainty, your children may reject you. They may find a different path altogether. They may find questions where you find certainty. They may find certainty where you have only questions. They may think you are hopelessly naïve. A middle way, nuanced, heterodox approach—even a very big tent—does not guarantee that you and your children will end up in the same place.

I take difference as inevitable. What I want for me, and my children, is not sameness or agreement but love and mutual respect. Of the two, love comes without effort for me. I love my children, I am proud of them, I like their company. Mutual respect requires some attention and feels like a higher calling. We are different and we do not try to fix that difference or force agreement. Respect is not trying to fix, not forcing agreement. We are independent, differentiated adults who can respect each other, spend time together without fighting, and feel like family. That is what I wanted all along, and I've been blessed.

JUDGMENT

The Mormon world has a sweeping model of the righteous family. Ostensibly doctrine but clearly cultural, the picture is of an extended family where everybody is a devoted church member, everybody serves a mission, everybody marries in the temple once, for time and eternity, everybody holds a current temple recommend at all times and attends regularly, senior missions are common, and there are a few General Authorities in the mix. The picture is so comprehensive and the standard so high that almost everybody can find gaps in almost every family.

I have been blamed for my failure to live up to the ideal of a Mormon patriarch. I have been blamed for my children not fitting everybody's imagined model of a Mormon child or young adult. It is a fair assumption that somebody will blame your edgy behavior and choices for every family failure. The only clear way out is to have an even blacker black sheep in the family. I'm afraid this is a grin-and-bear-it observation. I have no solutions to suggest. Just commiseration. My children are wonderful and I'm more than ready for them to take over and run the world and the Church—as they are in fact doing. But my Mormon score is mixed at best. I clearly do not measure up to Mormon standard. My children don't want me to say that. I think most of all they don't want it to be true.

COMPLICATED FAMILIES: RAISING FEMINIST BOYS IN A SEXIST CHURCH

ANNE BENNETT

In many respects, being a woman in the Church is harder than being a man in the Church. This is explained at some length in *One Woman's Perspective*, above. I assumed it would be harder to raise daughters than to raise sons in the Church. I am discovering that the latter brings many unique challenges. As the mother raising three sons (and a daughter) in the Church, I find myself distraught at the realization that what I want my boys to become and believe in terms of gender relationships and abilities is very different from what will happen by default in the Church. As it currently stands, to be active in this Church is in many respects to perpetuate and prop up patriarchy, a concept I deeply hope they will reject. I want them to be active participants and leaders but concurrently reject the patriarchy upon which leadership authority rests: a tricky line. Let me describe this problem below and provide a view of the thin line I've found to walk as I navigate this problem.

But first, what about the daughters? Sadly, girls quickly realize that nearly all spheres of life will be more difficult for them because the world and the Church do not work like they should. Girls and young women learn they have to be careful where they go alone and how they dress. Later they learn that pregnancy and childbearing considerations will weigh heavily in professional decisions and may drastically affect their pay. While it always hurts and always feels wrong, many women see sexism everywhere and are not shocked when they see it in the Church as well. Girls see it, and learn to cope, within a generally sexist world, workplace, and church.

By contrast, boys can grow up in a sexist world and church without even seeing it. At church the sexism is systemic and taught as doctrine (see 1 Corinthians 11:3, 1 Timothy 2, and D&C 132). It is always present, and seems to be unchanging on the scale of a boy's and young man's life experience. The apparently fixed nature of sexism in the Church is key. The sexism, based on patriarchy, that is practiced in the Church would seem egregious if encountered in any other sphere of society. Can you imagine if you enrolled your children in a co-ed school and were then told that women could work the lunchroom but only men could become teachers, administrators or principals? We would reject that school immediately and move on. I would be horrified to have my children educated under those conditions. Yet somehow, I keep taking them to church where they only see men in positions of authority.

When boys face sexism in other aspects of society they can often see change. In teaching children about sexism the curriculum is often to discuss debunked sexist ideas of the past. Lessons often highlight accomplished women in society to demonstrate that there is no limit on a woman's potential. Children learn how to respond when they face sexism. I am grateful for these lessons but as an LDS parent, I often find myself in the uncomfortable position of needing to include the asterisk of Church, where these lessons of equality simply do not apply.

In many aspects of society we see men using their privilege to help women rise up or be recognized. A boy can pick a girl partner in science class, insist on equal representation at a workplace meeting, or advocate for maternity leave. In the Church, however, this is not an option. Feminist-minded men cannot use their position to bring up women. At least not in any structurally meaningful way. I would take a feminist bishop over a misogynist bishop any day, and a bishop can certainly increase a women's visibility or shut down messages of sexism from the pulpit. But he cannot confer priesthood authority on a woman or include a woman as a counselor in the bishopric or even advocate for equal representation of women in church leadership or quorums. I believe patriarchy hurts men almost as much as it hurts women. Patriarchy prevents both men and women from being their best, most Christ-like selves. It is anathema to the fundamental teachings of Christ. It is as if all the Savior's teachings on the last and the least of these doesn't apply when it comes to gender. For this reason, I have significant anxiety about raising boys in the Church, where they will be awash in and raised up to participate in a patriarchal structure.

That being said, my closest experiences with men in the Church are overwhelmingly positive. When I think of men I hope my boys will emulate, I remember a blessing circle around my daughter Paige, thinking of her father and her uncle and her grandfathers. I know because I have seen in real life that the Church raises up good men—men like I hope my boys will become. I think the Church can give men a sense of community and friends, often very elusive for adult males. I think the Church encourages fidelity and commitment to wife and family and encourages a focus on children—two factors which heavily influence the happiness and success of a marriage. So many of my non-LDS friends complain about how uninterested their husbands are in their children or family life. The Church certainly provides ample opportunity and pressure to serve, which I think is a much better use of time than watching football or getting drunk. (Just avoiding alcohol saves countless men from terrible life choices and consequences.)

The Church isn't just helpful for men but for boys, too. I love it when my boys learn lessons about peacemaking, prayers, choices and consequences, gratitude, sacrifice. So much of societal boy culture is geared toward battles, superheroes and villains, and video games; I am grateful for the exposure church provides to counterbalance this. I am also grateful that other adults are invested in my boys. I am so pleased that they sing together in Primary and are exposed to music. I think the Church is an important place to go as a family, where we all participate and learn about the same things: Christ, becoming better, repentance, and loving those around us. The Church is where I learned the gospel, which I believe is the ultimate source of happiness and growth in life for men and women. I think the Church is a pretty great place to raise boys.

If you follow the several paragraphs above, you will note a dissonance. I have significant anxiety about raising boys in the Church, where they will be awash in and raised up to participate in a patriarchal structure. And I think the Church is a pretty great place to raise boys. How do I teach them to participate in priesthood ordinances and church life (as exemplified by the men in their life) as a source of goodness that will bring them and those around them joy, and at the same time teach them that I think patriarchy is evil? I feel legitimately stumped; and a bit like a hypocrite for raising them in the Church.

I do not want them to feel guilty about embracing the priesthood and using it to serve others. They should feel good about the service. But I think it is downright wrong that it is denied women. I don't think it is any one particular person's fault that patriarchy exists, but every time an 11-year-old boy is given the priesthood and a girl is told to prepare for marriage, the problem is perpetuated and becomes more ingrained. The patriarchy is given a new root to spread and flourish through that boy's life and future family. I'm not sure what to do about that. If the boy says "I refuse unless you also ordain the girls in my class" he is essentially cutting himself off from the church for life.

I am not a man and cannot speak directly to the choice to be part of a patriarchal priesthood system, but I am one of the few people I know who has said "I put my foot down, this line I will not cross, patriarchy will stop here with me." And yes, I am paying a price for that decision (if you wish to see it that way) and its ripple effects are clear through my family. I am not sad about my choice (although I am sad it had to be made), but I feel sad if I think about my oldest son refusing the priesthood as an 11-year-old or if I think of my next son refusing the opportunity to be a bishop because that same opportunity is denied to my daughter. My heart does sink to unfathomable depths, however, when I think how I will answer their questions of "Why is Paige not getting the priesthood? She's 12."

I think both accepting the priesthood and accepting a calling such as bishop would help them become better people through service. I do hope that if they accept callings extended to men only they will use some of that power or authority to push the envelope, raise some noise, and speak up against the dangers of patriarchy. I hope they will get summoned to the stake president's office to explain why they called a woman to a position requiring priesthood authority or asked to justify why they signed off on a woman blessing her baby in a Sacrament meeting. My hope would be that their response would be confident, genuine and ring true to what they were taught at home.

I hope they will recognize that when little boys and girls, and grown men and women, see only men on the stand they know who is in charge, they see patriarchy working. When I was a child I saw the men on the stand and thought "people tell me girls are just as loved as boys and have just as much potential, but everyone up there is a man, so I guess they are lying to me." Actions speak louder than words. A sense of being lied to leads to anger, anxiety, and distrust.

Not exactly the feelings I am hoping my children will get from church. How do we tear apart the entwined truth and untruth of patriarchy and gospel? A question for the ages.

So should we just wallow in the difficulty of this conundrum or are there solutions? I think part of the solution lies in the messages we teach our children. I want to raise boys who are aware of the issues highlighted above. I want my boys to hear me say that girls are just as important as boys and actually believe me, even though I keep taking them to this Church where boys are obviously more important than girls. I don't want them to draw the same conclusions I drew.

I guess I need to be very explicit about what I celebrate and what I disdain. I don't want them to end up like so many men I dated: reasonably good and "righteous" men but with a subtle undercurrent of sexism. Those men saw my strengths, accomplishments and ambitions as a threat, or worse, as an insult, rather than a gift that would bless both my life and his and lead to a stronger partnership. Many marriages are stifled by this undercurrent of sexism, leading to resentment and failure to realize the potential of the relationship for both partners. I would never want that for my boys, or for my daughter.

I want to raise boys who embrace the good of the gospel and participate as fully as they are able but reject vehemently that which corrupts by masquerading as truth, in or out of the Church.

I want to raise boys who can discern this difference and are strong enough to act with integrity when the choice is between obedience or conformity and their own integrity.

I want to raise boys to see that they have been given much and to respond by giving of themselves.

I want to raise boys who recognize, celebrate, and are grateful for the fullness of a woman and her ambitions and accomplishments.

I want them to see a woman as having a price above rubies, not because she is a virgin, submissive, or good at cooking, but because together, as equals, they can bring out the best in each other and create sources of goodness that would not be possible alone.

I want to raise boys who know and feel in their heart that following Christ will lead to happiness.

I want to raise boys who are emotionally healthy, who do not have to do mental gymnastics to reconcile what they are doing or saying at Church with what they have been taught at home.

I want to raise boys who have self-esteem and can accept they have flaws but know that they have the power to overcome and grow and could say that that process is familiar to them because they saw their parents go through it.

I want to raise boys who can see a better world than the one they were born into and devote their actions to creating that reality.

I want to raise boys who see in themselves the potential to bring joy and comfort to others.

I want to raise boys who will be the engine, not the head, of a strong loving family.

I want to raise boys who feel gratitude and humility for a world of profound joy and beauty.

I want to raise boys who know that they are deeply loved by their parents and that they have infinite potential.

Despite the horrible rope of patriarchy which must be deracinated in order for us to move forward as a church, I think the Church is the best place I know to teach the gospel principles of faith, love, and happiness. I am going to stay and keep my family here. I will stumble down the thorny path of church history and painful conversations as my children mature. I'm sure I will spend some moments apologizing, others defending, some begging, and many wondering whether this is still the right decision. In the end, I will do my best and simply hope that they can withstand the vertiginous dissonance between patriarchy on one side and the equality spoken of by Christ on the other side. I will try to keep my focus and energy on the teachings of Christ. Hopefully, the arc will continue to bend slowly and surely towards truth and they will find a happy life in a church which looks similar but distinctly better than the one they see now. And if they don't choose this church, whether they believe me or not, I'm going to love them just the same, and there's nothing they can do about that.

COMPLICATED FAMILIES: LGBTQ CHILDREN

SHARI SIEBERS CRALL

If I didn't believe the Church would change its stance on our LBGTQ family, I wouldn't stay. Of course, it would make staying a lot easier if for once we were at the forefront of change.

How do I know it will change? Because God is in the paradox and he has shown me that over and over.

Once, and this is a simple example, I was in charge of our stake play. As with all things theatrical, time was pressed, rehearsals tense, and resources inadequate. We were to have our final run-through at the stake center, but lines got crossed and a stake leadership meeting began gathering in the chapel. Suddenly we were told we would have to move, but final run-throughs really need to happen on the actual stage. I could feel the morale of my troupe flagging as they felt all their time and effort was being disrupted and disrespected. The stake leaders wanted an inspirational play, but insisted on taking the room on dress rehearsal night?

I had been studying about God and paradox, and to look for Him when two contradictory or seemingly opposed ideas presented themselves as truth, like faith and works, or "don't eat the fruit" and "multiply and replenish the earth." In this very concrete situation, I said a little prayer and then stood back to see what God would do. I believed God thought both were important, and a way would be shown to transcend. It was.

The actors dispersed to side rooms to run through music numbers while the priesthood session used the needed larger chapel to begin. Then the leaders dispersed to the smaller rooms for sessions, and the actors returned to the main stage. It was simple, yet when folks were at loggerheads with tempers rising and both insisting they needed the larger rooms, the solution could not be seen.

It was a wonderful object lesson for me. The rooms, the time frames, were always there, but hidden by our pride, no one saw them. Yet, with just a little softening, just a little nod that both needs were legitimate, an answer was easily found.

I pondered that in my heart. The visual was of myself as a pin dot on the earth, limited in what I could see and God looking down on the pin dot that was earth in the universe, seeing all. From God's viewpoint, human contradictions were often resolved just by telescoping out. God transcends paradoxes.

Understanding my son was gay was a process of telescoping out and moving from my head to my heart. During the teenage years it was all head, working to make sure the cognitive dissonance didn't kill him. It remained in my head as he served a mission, returned to BYU and dated a woman for 18 months. After that relationship ended with both acknowledging they did not want a mixed orientation marriage, the process finally moved to my heart. I realized this wasn't going to be some nifty church narrative where we wrote a book and bore our testimonies. Rather, my son really was gay and the Church did not have an open pathway for his progression or even membership. At that point, I decided I needed to lift my anchor of testimony and set sail to see what I would find. Would my boat of belief actually float?

Over many months of examining my thoughts, feelings and beliefs, I sailed back into the harbor marked Mormon. I loved the Book of Mormon. King Benjamin's address had shaped my life and career. I loved Moroni and Ammon, and especially King Lamoni's father. I believed Joseph Smith really saw God our Father and Jesus Christ. I felt intense devotion to my pioneer forebears for their hardship, their hunger and thirst and filthiness and bug infestation and soreness as they made the trek across oceans, rivers, and plains. I just couldn't turn away from that. Even the polygamy they endured. I couldn't turn away.

After the November 5th policy of 2015, my cousin who is lesbian called me. She hadn't gone to church in decades, but her name was still on the records. What should she do now? Should she ask to have her name removed because she was married? In the sacredness of the conversation, we also laughed. I joked that our great-great-grandmother must have made a deal with God on polygamy, that if she did it her children would remain in the Church through the seventh generation. Well, we were the sixth generation, so we were stuck. But I don't joke anymore because the seventh generation is leaving fast.

I also used to joke that God was raining LGBTQ children onto Mormons, because there were so many queer Mormons in my congregation and among my friends, and I kept making new connections and friends through the Mormon LGBTQ community. I don't joke about that anymore because secretly I think it's true. The absolute best and brightest among us are queer, and it breaks my heart to see us running them into exile. Alas, like my pioneer ancestors sang, "By the rivers of Babylon there we sat down, yes, we wept, when we remembered Zion." I have great belief in that Zion where all are welcome and nurtured and loved. But right now, I weep.

So how do I stay? From simple to complex, from self-preservation to self-examination, from practical to ethereal, here are my tools.

First, I lost my smugness. There are many times I hate that it is gone because it was such a comfortable, luxurious place. Even though I miss it, I know I am better off. Constantly pulling that beam out of my eye, as painful as it is, I see better.

Next, I got satisfied with what my friend Jenn called a sunbeam testimony. God made the world, it is beautiful, I'm in it, you're in it, love each other. That's it. I hang out in Primary where the doctrine is simple.

It also helped that we landed well. We have lived in one place a long time, where the community has grown around us, but we are well known old timers here. Our priesthood leadership has been unfailingly supportive, of us, of our children, of our advocacy for LGBTQ acceptance. I remember asking my dad how he made it through the Black exclusionary years. He said simply, and very uncharacteristically, he didn't listen to "those idiots." We have been incredibly lucky not to have priesthood leaders who were idiots. That has saved us. Our stake president has talked us into remaining in the pews after several general conferences.

Once I sought out my bishop after a particularly grievous Relief Society lesson to ask him which parable I needed to apply? Was I Eli, unwilling to look at wickedness in my son? Was I the blind man's parent, in John 9, with a congregation ready to oust me and asking Christ, "Master, who did sin, this man, or his parents, that he was born blind?" Was my son destined to wait, like Gentiles in Christ's day, to be content with the crumbs handed out by heterosexuals? Was he the laborer in Matthew, who, dejected and rejected until the eleventh hour, was finally selected, and paid the same? Was he the last who would be first? Would the "kingdom roll forth" and steamroll over me, without looking back, or would the "kingdom roll forth" to include me, and my son, and my family, sealed in the temple and hoping for eternity too?

My bishop was sweet. He didn't know. He just assured me I belonged there, in the Church, in the ward, and that I should feel free to get up and leave if someone or something was getting too much. He hasn't been my bishop for years, but I still follow his counsel.

I have sought out other LGBTQ folks to give me understanding. They have given me articulation for my feelings. They have taught me how to process. They have illuminated the questions and answers, the dilemmas, and the simplicities. Nathan Kitchen, President of Affirmation, gave a powerful speech at the 2021 International Affirmation Conference, calling on the Church to remember LGBTQ people are our children, our fathers, mothers, siblings, cousins, and friends. They are not strangers, but our own, and we must stop casting them out. If we followed the Savior's admonition to love one another as well as the advice of Harvey Milk, to come out, come out wherever you are, we would see our congregations filled with LGBTQ family members sitting next to us.

In *The Whole Language, The Power of Extravagant Tenderness* (Simon & Schuster, 2021), Catholic theologian, Father Greg Boyle, wrote, "We hear in the gospel, 'No room in the inn,' and we think Motel 6 and "No Vacancies." But actually Joseph went home. These were his people. So, everyone who said no were probably blood relatives. They were cousins and uncles and there was no room for the shame and disgrace of Joseph's 'fiancée,' big as a house and ready to burst. Tenderness finds room. Church at its best."

I am selective about what I read and hear. Whereas General Conference used to be a feast, it is now a buffet. I am impressionable. I can hold a grudge. My mother used to tell me, "Don't put yourself in situations you can't handle." I apply that to Conference or other talks. I don't watch or read talks that speak negatively of LGBTQ people. I am old now and not as limber. I can't do the mental gymnastics required to square all that.

For instance, I did not watch my beloved Elder Holland speak of musket fire in August 2021, when speaking to BYU faculty, referencing those who opposed BYU's stance on LGBTQ relationships as firing muskets on the truth and perhaps the fire should be returned. Ironically, he spoke directly to the paradox of love and the law, unable to apply even one of the many transcending parables Jesus taught on this topic.

I seek out other religious folks who struggle with their faith traditions, such as Father Boyle, Sister Helen Prejean, Brian D. McLaren, Mormon thinkers and writers, and of course, Jesus. They give me ways to think about my path to God, to think about what is required to live a life seeking justice and giving mercy. I want to live as Colossians 3:14 taught, and I love the language Eugene Peterson used in his translation, titled The Message: "And regardless of what else you put on, wear love. It's your basic, all-purpose garment. Never be without it."

All the things I have been taught through a lifetime in the Church, the skills I have learned, my fluency with the language of the Spirit, have served me well. When my heart beats with that burning in the bosom when someone says something hurtful in the LGBTQ realm, I raise my hand, I get personal, I bear my truth, and feel we all transcend.

I also tell people, soon after meeting them, that we have a gay son and a transgender grandchild. I give them a heads up so they can check their speech and remember that most people in our congregations have LGBTQ loved ones. I'd much rather they talk behind my back if they have something negative to say than say it to my face. If my presence serves as a moderating force in quelling anti-LGBTQ rhetoric, that's a win.

Another big piece is my children, none of whom remain in the Church, but who have not become offended by my continued participation. I have friends whose children have confronted them about continuing to give money and time to an institution that has cast them out. If my children felt that way, I would have to reconsider.

I read the scriptures. I read Paul, in Romans: "Who in the world do you think you are to second-guess God? Do you for one moment suppose any of us knows enough to call God into question? Clay doesn't talk back to the fingers that mold it, saying, 'Why did you shape me like this?' Isn't it obvious that a potter has a perfect right to shape one lump of clay into a vase for holding flowers and another into a pot for cooking beans? . . . Hosea put it well: I'll call nobodies and make them somebodies; I'll call the unloved and make them beloved." (Romans 9:20–33, The Message).

I feel absolutely committed, as I was taught in Young Women's and Sunday School and Relief Society, to hold my beloved Church to the gospel standard that God is love. That there is no conflict between love and the law. That we are all fellow travelers. That if God made people L or G or B or T or Q or I, who am I to question the potter's hands? Really, who are we to challenge the worth of God's creation? I picture the day when our current prophet is challenged like Peter by all the Corneliuses among us. Then all the antipathy, the self-righteous rationalizations, the imagined holding to the rod will dissipate like so much sound and fury.

The day cannot come soon enough. We see Elder Peter M. Johnson, who is black, and his wife, Stephanie, who is white, profiled in the Church News, and we no longer blink. Someday we will see an LGBTQ couple and no one will think anything of it. In the meantime, I mourn for all those who we have alienated or worse, lost, to pharisaical prejudice. Like Jacob of old, I hold tight to the angel and will not let go, wrestling for the blessing.

For now, I know I will remain until I don't. I am aware a final straw may come. I no longer define enduring to the end as remaining an active Mormon. I take more responsibility for finding my way back to God than following a culturally prescribed path.

President Barack Obama said, "Hope is not blind optimism. It's not ignoring the enormity of the task ahead or the roadblocks that stand in our path. It's not sitting on the sidelines or shirking from a fight. Hope is that thing inside us that insists, despite all evidence to the contrary, that something better awaits us if you have the courage to reach for it, and to work for it, and to fight for it. Hope is the belief that destiny will not be written for us, but by us, by the men and women who are not content to settle for the world as it is, who have the courage to remake the world as it should be."

Like Ether (12:4), I believe in God and surely hope for a better world. God is in the paradox, and I know in whom I have trusted. I am watching now for doctrine to telescope out, to see how Christ will transcend this. I expect it will unfold with wondrous simplicity as we all remember who we are.

COMPLICATED FAMILIES: PUSHING ORTHODOXY AS A SEMINARIAN'S DAUGHTER

KAJSA BERLIN-KAUFUSI

When I was a little girl, I was sure my father had one of the most important jobs in the world—he was a seminary teacher. When I would tell someone that, eyebrows would raise and often I would get a respectful "ohhhh" in response. In the heavily Mormon community where I grew up, this immediately put me in what I thought was a somewhat prestigious circle. As a daughter of a church educator, I was privy to seemingly endless amounts of gospel knowledge as well as insider perspectives on whatever was the current hot topic in our church community, be it excited conjecture or scandal. Frequently, people sought out my father to ask his opinion, certain his perspective held higher value than the average congregation member because he worked for the Church.

I never questioned his authority. Never. His views on anything gospel or church related were what my little mind upheld. He led our family in studious righteousness, seeking to fulfill every one of God's laws with exactness, believing firmly that, as popularly taught within Mormon circles, "obedience is the first law of heaven." When I refer to my dad as a scholar, there really is no better term to describe him. He is exactly that in the most classical sense—poring over scholarly books with a kind of holy devotion, meticulously underlining their contents with a perfect line, ever so careful not to damage the page. He would pace the floor at night, Arabic and Hebrew grammars in his hand, brow furrowed, conjugating verbs in their various forms, the guttural and unfamiliar sounds of the Semitic languages filling the otherwise quiet house. His love of the scriptures and the classical, conservative interpretation of the text flowed over into his religious practice. This created a kind of productive tension in our home, because my mother looked at things with quite the opposite perspective, preferring to focus on the spirit of the law and the abundance of grace offered to us through our Lord Jesus Christ. We often joke that had my dad been born in a different time, he would have made an excellent Lubavitcher Rabbi; his passionate zeal for proselytizing and fluidity in Old Testament scholarship with attention to detail made him a worthy candidate.

Despite my parents' differing perspectives, my father was the head of our household. Through his influence, we knew what a good Mormon family did and didn't do on Sunday. We knew what a good Mormon drinks and doesn't drink, eats and doesn't eat, says and doesn't say, how we dress and don't dress. It was clear for me, as a little girl whose gospel education had been very black and white, who was in the righteous club and who was out of it. I loved the confidence that worldview gave me.

My parents frequently told me, with a sense of pride, that one of my first words was "Jerusalem." Time spent at BYU's Jerusalem Center is a highlight of their marriage; trinkets from their experience lined the shelves of my childhood home, photo albums were frequently pulled down and pages turned with a whimsical reminiscing. I was three when my dad went to the Middle East a second time to study advanced Hebrew, this time leaving my mom, my sister and me, at home. Emotions were high as we dropped him off at the Portland International airport, my mom attempting to put on a brave face for her two young girls, my dad trying to be empathetic but also failing to mask excitement for his upcoming trip. I clearly remember his leather study bag which fit snugly over his shoulder. BYU would later publish a picture of him next to the Old City's Western Wall (Ha-Kotel Ha-Maʿaravi in Hebrew), which is considered to be the last portion of Jerusalem's second temple to have survived over the centuries. Sure enough, in the photograph, my dad is wearing his leather over-the-shoulder study bag.

Every job comes with occupational hazards; some are more obvious than others. There are occupational hazards to working in Church Education that intrude into the lives of family members in sometimes hilarious, occasionally traumatic, and often unexpected ways. Being exposed to the scriptures at a young age in a regular and methodical way does things to your mind. It opens up your world and causes you to ask unique and hard questions, many of which, as I have come to discover, have no answers. The scriptures say that "those with eyes to see will see." I was certainly equipped with eyes to see—but once open, my eyes couldn't stop seeing, even if I had preferred them not to.

Growing up in the Berlin family with a born and bred, dyed in the wool, true blue Mormon dad and a Jesus-rooted, Bible-loving, cross-wearing mother was a recipe for some unusual chemistry that led to fascinating discussions in our home and in our community. Word about our passionate and often entertaining dinner-table discussions leaked out to the point that friends would wander by the house just to see what we were talking about. Chances were good that it was something politically charged, doctrinal, historical, or all three.

If you've ever seen paintings of a traditional Jewish family around the table on the Sabbath, my family very much resembled that. Food being passed, hands raised in passionate disagreement, my father presiding with a stern but amused look, arms crossed, one of us maybe losing interest while the rest of us were still at it, with the occasional guest or two staring in wonder at the conversation at hand.

When my family moved from Oregon to Utah, our second house allowed more space for my dad's beloved books. Custom shelves lined his basement office, becoming a home for his religious volumes and various knick knacks from countries he had visited when he eventually left his seminary position and worked as a scripture translation supervisor for 15 years. The books and religious curios didn't just have a place in his office, of course. They were scattered throughout the house, and more than once I noticed a somewhat worried look on the face of a first-time visitor who came into our entryway to see ceramic plates painted with Arabic calligraphy. Their look would become even more confused when they asked about the plates and were told they were quotes from the Holy Quran. While conservative, my dad found it perfectly acceptable to love and study all the Abrahamic faiths (Judaism, Islam, Christianity and their offshoots). "After all," he would remind us, "we are all children of the book!" This idea of "children of the book" is an Islamic idea that demands respect for Christians and Jews, who all claim Abraham as their father. My father's liberal attitude toward other sacred books outside our Mormon cannon would plant seeds of curiosity and respect for the world's religions deep inside me that would later germinate into a life's passion, as well as a critical lens that I often wonder if he regrets nursing, unaware at the time where that trajectory would take me.

Cognitive dissonance grew within me at a young age as I encountered controversial subjects specific to the LDS tradition, such as Nauvoo era polygamy, Blacks and the priesthood, women's roles in the church, etc. Some people would be scared away from further inquiry. I on the other hand was encouraged to study my faith, the greater world-scriptural tradition, and deep questions of the soul.

There was a time when my faith was simple and sweet. I eventually recognized that I have a complex and paradoxical relationship with the scriptures, texts that I deeply love, that feed my soul on a practical level as well as a mystical level. But before that, I knew, I just knew, that all my questions had answers, if I just looked hard enough. The late Rachel Held Evans said that when her biblical worldview began to crack, one crack expanded into many, fissures within the rock of her foundation, questioning in a domino-like effect that took one question about certain Biblical texts leading to biblical accuracy, leading to how the cannon was assembled, leading to questions on church authority, leading to questions on the Holy Spirit, leading to questions on the nature of God. Because Held Evans' story felt familiar to me, I wonder whether this process is similar for everyone who deconstructs the religious tradition of their childhood. Looking back, I see myself deconstructing my faith from a very young age. However, I didn't allow myself to recognize or examine the implications of that deconstruction until nearly twenty years later.

As a young newlywed and a recent graduate with an MA in Biblical Studies under my belt, I aspired to follow in my father's footsteps and work for the Church Education System. Through the influence of a progressive female Dean at BYU's department of Ancient Scripture, I was hired almost immediately and spent five happy years (though not without spiritual and intellectual trauma) working as faculty in BYU's Ancient Scripture department.

Semester after semester of strong student-ratings accompanied by individual letters from my students, expressing gratitude for the unique nature of my classroom (I was known for my open-minded approach to scripture, classroom discussions, and my passion for transformation in Christ) seemed to continuously reinforce that God was with me on this path. Despite the continuous internal discussion I was having with myself on issues of LDS theology, culture, interpretation and practice, my students gave me hope for the future of Zion. Interacting with them, guiding them through the scriptures, and having opportunity after opportunity to bear my witness of the Savior was bread and butter to me.

The courses I taught consisted mostly of Old Testament and New Testament subject matter, and so the increasing strain on my "questions to come back to" mental shelf was somewhat kept at bay for a time. Then, in an unforeseen but almost certainly inevitable event, I was suddenly terminated from my position with BYU in the Spring of 2020. I was teaching a Gospel Doctrine class at the time, and due to my publicly progressive voice that was perceived as a bit too liberal an informal inquiry was established by people who questioned my motives, describing me as a wolf in sheep's clothing. Without including me in discussions of my public voice and written work, it was decided by my priesthood leaders that my ecclesiastical endorsement for BYU employment should be pulled and thus, in alignment with BYU policy, I was immediately fired.

Upon receiving that ominous phone call from the Faculty Relations Vice President, I do not exaggerate when I say that I felt something inside of me split wide open and crumble onto the floor of my soul. And yet, with death comes new growth; with the breaking down, the potential for a building up. No mud, no lotus. In hindsight, while I initially penned those sentiments in regards to my faith journey, I now see that these truths also apply to familial relations, and specifically to the suddenly very vulnerable relationship with my lifelong scholarly hero and gospel mentor, my father.

Due to the fact that my mother is a convert to the church and has always been a nuanced Mormon at best, I received and continue to receive nothing but love, support, and validation from her as I navigate my religious deconstruction. Seeing my initial reaction of hurt and suffering upon being fired from BYU, she raged when I raged and mourned when I mourned. My good father did the same, but always optimistically offered a silver lining to the trauma I was experiencing, sure that both my bishop and stake president would see this situation as a "divinely inspired mess" that would call attention to the need for better training for bishoprics and Sunday School presidencies on contemporary issues and policies surrounding the Gospel Topics Essays. He shared that all CES instructors had been told during an in-service training that they needed to "know these essays like the back of your hand."

Except, that didn't happen. At no point was there any attempt to counsel together and remedy the situation, coming out stronger, wiser, and more efficient as a ward leadership. With each conversation I had with my dad over the course of the traumatic months while I was in limbo as to whether or not BYU would rehire me, I saw the optimism slowly fade from his eyes, replaced by a sweet sadness for my pain accompanied by a sense of unspoken worry as to "what happens now?"

Feeling the chasm between us grow as we began to leave more undiscussed than discussed, I felt the need to be frank with him as to where I was in regards to my childhood faith and my relationship with the Church. This was a few months after it was clear that I was no longer teaching for BYU, nor interested in pleading my case for a rehire. One night, sitting down in our living room with both my mom and husband present, I blurted out the truth of what I had been tip-toeing around for weeks. "Dad," I said, looking into his bright blue eyes that seemed even brighter at the time (something that happened when he had heightened emotions), his brow furrowed and his lips tightly pursed in concentration (an expression that ironically, I mimic with exactness), "it's important for me to know that you know where I'm at with the Church and that you see me for who I am right now, not who you want me to be or who you think I should be." His eyebrows raised but he said nothing as I rushed on, my speech getting more rapid as my heart rate increased. "Dad, I haven't been wearing my garments for weeks now. I'm questioning everything . . . everything!" My arms expanded into a wide spread, emphasizing my words as I leaned towards him. "The history, the doctrines, whether or not I even believe any of our truth claims as a church and what that reality will mean for me in relation to the Church moving forward—" His hand went to his face, covering his mouth as he nodded to show he was listening, not hiding the cloudy expression that was beginning to appear. "Dad, the temple, honestly, means nothing to me right now. I have no desire to return nor do I think I will ever have a desire to go back; everything for me has just changed. Now that I'm no longer required to pretend my shelf items aren't really that big, they've actually crashed onto the floor of my life and shattered into messy, sharp shards—it's like the contents of what I used to hold as my gospel testimony are exposed, rotting as time goes on." His hand remained covering his mouth as his gaze turned more serious, his lungs filling with air as he took a deep breath, exhaling slowly.

Realizing I hadn't been breathing, I suddenly gasped as I sucked in much needed oxygen and felt hot tears running down my face. In a lowered voice, my father posed the question, "Kajsa, there was a time when you said it was your greatest desire to keep people in the Church. Has that changed? I thought you were sure that that was your ministry?" Emotion seeping out of my voice, I snapped, "That hasn't changed, dad. I want to make space for everyone who wants in some way to stay, to let them know that there is a place for them next to me on the pew, regardless of which side of the orthodoxy fence they fall, but it seems that my ecclesiastical leaders aren't comfortable with my public voice, and yet, it's my voice that allows that space to be made and invites folks to dialogue. I refuse to put allegiance to church leaders, upholding a white-washed narrative, and defending the institution, over the relationships I have with individual people and their walk with Christ. I just refuse, Dad!"

A heavy silence sat between us as we gazed at each other from across the room. What I had just exposed to him clothed me in the garment of the scarlet letter. Indeed, something he despised most in this world was now manifesting in his daughter—unabashed apostasy. We eventually concluded the visit with the agreement that there was much more to discuss and that most likely we would need to have many of these meetings in the near future. With a sincere hug and exhausted emotions, I saw him and my mother out the door and back to their car.

What we'd intended never seemed to occur. Perhaps our emotions were too raw, perhaps we both felt that we were defending that which was most precious to us as individuals; for my dad, his commitment to the restored gospel and for me, my authentic voice and discipleship to Jesus, be he God, guru, rabbi, social reformer, or all of them. In even approaching a discussion about my deconstruction, each of us had on our defensive armor, guarding that which we valued above all else. As time passed, the distance between us grew.

One Friday I was listening to my Sunday playlist as I was cleaning the house, using the physical activity to distract from the growing anxiety I now typically felt about the upcoming Sabbath day. One of the songs on my playlist is *Where Is It Written?* from the movie *Yentl*. The story is about a young Jewish woman in the late nineteenth century who is her widowed father's only child. As a rabbi, her father went against tradition and taught his daughter Talmudic studies, realizing that her zeal for religious knowledge far exceeded that of his male students. I often imagine myself as a kind of Yentl, and in many ways, I imagined my dad as a rabbi, his focus and passion on religious scholarship and disseminating that knowledge throughout the community. In the film, Yentl and her father frequently engage in passionate and enjoyable sparring over the biblical text—something I grew up doing with my father and never really stopped doing until recently. I suddenly realized I missed that connection with my dad; "missed" was perhaps too gentle a word. I ached for it, and if my assumptions were correct, he missed it as well.

I know my dad, a recent retiree, missed his students and engaging his colleagues. Now that I was no longer in the classroom, we had that in common. Picking up my phone I dialed his number, making small talk and then getting to the point: "Hey Dad? I've been listening to this great book on Audible by Sue Monk Kidd, *The Dance of the Dissonant Daughter*. I see so much of myself in her lived experience. I know you've been wanting to connect and we just haven't made that happen. Would you be interested in reading this book with me? Maybe once or twice a week we could read a few chapters and then discuss certain points in the text that resonate with us?" The enthusiasm in his voice was tangible as he eagerly agreed, telling me he would order the book that night on Amazon and we could begin next week.

Our first reading session took place over Zoom, and it was immediately evident that both my father and I were in our element. A love of books and ideas was something we shared, and through this text we were able to connect on common ground, using Kidd's words to facilitate discussion on the very subjects I was navigating—religious deconstruction, challenging patriarchy, cultivating my authentic voice, etc. I remember ending the call with elation and a deep feeling of satisfaction and hope. That two-hour reading and conversation had been a more sincere connection with my father than we had had in months. We both said how much we enjoyed the discussion and ended the call with a smile and an "I love you!"

Not all the conversations were congenial; many points Kidd made ruffled my dad's feathers and frequently trod on ideas he held sacred. Luckily, through our academic training, we knew how to navigate tension and hold space for each other's ideas. When it was clear that we were simply going to disagree, we did just that, pressing on through the text, holding to our intent of finishing the book. Through this process, I was able to express my thoughts and feelings on my deconstruction that I needed my dad to hear, allowing the book to act as a facilitator to that dialogue. At the same time, my dad was able to maintain connection to me throughout this journey, making clear his positions on things while also showing sincere intent to "meet me at the table," so to speak, recognizing my positions and letting them stand next to his own.

Since beginning this informal book club with my father, I have added several books to our list. We have missed a week or two due to busy schedules and occasional heightened emotions over "churchy" things that simply cannot be avoided, but we continue to circle back to our intention of working through the books that allow us to connect and dialogue about the things that are most sacred to our souls.

The words of *Where Is It Written* return to me. While thinking about her father, Yentl petitions:

> And why have eyes that see
> And arms that reach
> Unless you're meant to know there's
> Something more
> If not to hunger for the meaning of it all
> Then tell me what a soul is for
> Why have the wings unless you're meant to fly
> And tell me please why have a mind
> If not to question why
> And tell me where
> Where is it written what it is I'm meant to be
> That I can't dare to have the chance to
> Pick the fruit of every tree
> Or have my share of every sweet imagined possibility
> Just tell me where, where is it written, tell me where?

Many times I feel exactly as Yentl felt, pushing against the confines of the system that she was raised in. To use another classic film reflective of Jewish orthodoxy, and in turn, Mormon orthodoxy, I also recognize that my father no doubt feels like Tevye in *Fiddler on the Roof*, seeing the expressions of his daughters' freedoms as a challenge not only to his religious traditions, but also to the way in which he has protected and provided for his family through "tradition!" Tevye anguishes over the separation of his family unit due to the encroaching wave of modernism that challenges the traditional system their people have abided by for centuries. His youngest daughter, Chavaleh, reveals to him that she intends to forge her own path by marrying a gentile, and begs for her father's blessing. This choice would excommunicate her from her Jewish identity, much like willingly no longer participating in temple ritual nor paying tithes excommunicates someone from their Mormon identity. Anguishing over the love for his daughter but also his love for his traditions and the security they bring him, Tevye passionately stomps his foot, raises his fists to the sky and shouts, "some things I will not and cannot allow!" The scene ends with Tevye turning his back on his daughter, rending his garment as she collapses to the floor, hands outstretched toward her father as the scene goes black.

During one of our more tense book discussions, after it was made clear to both of us that we had reached an impasse, my father gently offered, "you know, Kajsa, while many of the conclusions you have drawn here perplex me, I want you to know one thing that I DO know—I know you are walking this path out of your genuine love for God and his righteousness. So what more can I say to that? It is my duty to accept your agency and to love you while you traverse this journey. I will always be here to listen as you explain the perplexities of your heart to me, should you want to share them. I think God wants me to listen in this situation more than he wants me to speak. So I am here to listen, and I will continue to listen."

Upon hearing those words, I felt my heart melt, accepting the peace offering he was sincerely making. While he stands in his place of orthodoxy and I continue to dance on the fringe of that orthodoxy, my good father, with all his conservative patriarchal perspectives, continues to hold my hand, as I, with all my liberal perspectives and passionate stands against the church institution, continue to hold his. In this act we refuse to allow our differences to divide us, but rather, we allow them to move us both together to new places of understanding and perspective, joined by the bonds of familial love which, though it may look different to each of us, we both believe to be eternal in some nature. With each book will come progress on our journey to understanding, service, and love, as we support one another. Our path gives me hope that space can continue to be made for others who think differently than we do, even if perhaps that difference is radical, losing none along the way.

CHOOSE THE RIGHT

Sometimes doing the right thing is a challenge. With the best of intentions, all the good will in the world, acting according to your conscience can require the most sophisticated ethical and moral judgment, and even so end up being heart wrenching.

In the context of religion, and Christianity more narrowly, and The Church of Jesus Christ of Latter-day Saints most specifically, there are two often opposing forces. On the one hand, consider all those promises and commitments and covenants we make. Are they binding and enforceable forever, in all circumstances, no matter what we knew then and what we know now? On the other hand, consider the dictates of our conscience, what we really believe, especially what we believe about human beings and how they should be treated, when our conscience comes in conflict or seems to come in conflict with the Church.

The Primary lessons about choosing the right way or doing what Jesus would do suggest simple straightforward answers, as though all we have to do is choose. Many of us find the real adult world more complicated. The next most simple answer—to follow the promptings of the Holy Ghost—also falls flat too often for too many. For some the promptings never come. For others there are clear answers on occasion, but the heavens are silent in the present. Furthermore, one common characteristic of people on the edge is that we have lost confidence or trust in the Holy Ghost, or more precisely in our understanding or interpretation or reliance on the Holy Ghost.

There is nothing light or easy in this subject. These are seriously challenging problems. These are the problems of people genuinely, sincerely, with the best of intentions, trying to do the right thing.

PROMISES MADE

Most of us want to keep our promises. Most of us really try to keep our promises. The default is: Yes, I will. Yes, I do. We show up for appointments. We tell the truth. We do what we say we will do. Perfectly? All the time? To the letter? Probably not, not most of us, not all the time. But our baseline is a general expectation of saying, then doing. We can take it from the Bible, or lessons at our mother's knee, or a utilitarian analysis of social functioning, or an internal Spirit-led sense of right and wrong.

There is a whole discourse one could write about commitments made under duress, and promises made while deceived, and covenants made without information or preparation. Some of us still feel committed even though deceived or forced, but that kind of obligation smacks of scrupulosity, a pathological guilt about moral or religious issues. The real challenge for most of us involves promises made with full knowledge and sincere intent at the time, that for whatever combination of reasons now feel wrong—something you said ten years ago that you wouldn't say today.

I want my word to have meaning, and I don't want to live in a society where others disregard promises made, where a person's word has no staying power. To operate as a group, we need some amount of reliance on what we say and what others say. Some of us do take that reliance principle to the extreme and feel absolutely bound by promises made twenty years ago, with no expectation about that ever changing. However, for many of us, in real life, there is something longer than tomorrow and less than forever about promises. A sort of half-life of promises where commitments and covenants fade slowly over time. Eventually, sometimes, divorces and separations do happen—in marriage, in jobs, in friendships, and in relationship with the Church. The simple fact that we talk about renewing commitments and attach some importance to renewal is evidence that promises fade. An absolutist, a person who is committed to forever promises with no compromise, may not understand. For the rest of us there comes a time when we are a different person, a larger person who includes the 15-year-old self and the 25-year-old self and more, who is added upon. Where circumstances are different and our world expansive, so much so that the old decision or commitment is in fact the work of a different person in a different time and place. At that point we need a new decision. It might be renewal or confirmation or reiteration. It might be rejection. It might be any number of middle ways. It might come with costs of several kinds. It might dash expectations, even reasonable expectations. There is no free lunch here. But there is a new decision.

Making a new decision will always be a personal choice. This is one of the places where one would hope for help from the Holy Ghost, but even that will almost always be an individual and private matter. The best of friends and strongly pastoral church leaders will wish you well on your journey, wherever it takes you. But that same group of people typically will resist telling you what to do. The more common response from institutions and from people who have come to rely on you continuing as you were, will be to reject or push back on change. Some of that latter group of people may even be promise-forever types and they might not understand or agree that there is even a possibility of change. For all these reasons, deciding what to do about old promises is inevitably a lonely path.

The path is lonely and very often uncertain. Some choices get renewed regularly and purposefully. Some choices fade to such a degree that they hardly matter, one way or the other. Sometimes there is an event that presses a decision to renew or reverse. The whole range of possibilities seems as big as life itself. Not susceptible to a mechanical algorithm. Ultimately this is a wisdom practice.

CONSCIENCE STRICKEN

The sentences start with "How can I...."

> How can I sit here silent while my friend is being judged and excluded?
> How can I belong to a church that looks or is [racist]/[homophobic]/[sexist]?
> How can I stay in a church that tells me I will never get it right?
> How can I give money to a church that already has more than anybody knows what to do with, and there are so many needs in the world?
> How can I sustain a priesthood that will never include my daughter?
> How can I say yes when I don't believe and don't really mean it?
> How can I answer with my version of the truth, when I know it's not their version of the truth?
> How can I . . .

Often the question is framed as one of personal integrity. I know or feel or believe or see something differently than the Church does and the conflict tears me apart. I can't be honest with myself. I can't be honest with the Church. I can't be honest with my friends. My loyalties are torn. One common response is to break the tension by getting out of the Church.

These conflicts are genuine and serious. In fact, for all the problems people have with the Church—whether history or policy or practice or being offended or hurt—in my experience when people do leave the most common precipitating event or last straw is some form of "how can I?"

Leaving might be the right thing to do. Be true to yourself. However, these are feelings we're talking about, and feelings call for reflection before action. Slow down and think about it. The world is a complicated mess and feelings are only part of the whole.

The first "work" is to consider whether you know yourself. Our modern pop culture tells us to "find yourself" or "you do you" or "be real." When we want a gospel overlay, we punch up the idea of agency. This is what we're supposed to be about, i.e., learning and exercising agency, acting on personal revelation, seeking an internal sense of right and wrong.

However, being real is hard. Even if we are free agents in some ultimate sense, to a large degree we are the sum of what we've been taught and experienced. For myself, very often what feels right is what my mother taught me when I was five years old. Robert Fulghum's 1990 book may seem cute and quaint in the twenty-first century, but there is something to pay attention to when he writes "all I really need to know about how to live and what to do and how to be I learned in kindergarten." If we're going to move beyond what we learned in kindergarten we need to study. Study the world. Study ourselves. Study history. Study economics. Read the great works. Listen to the sages. Study philosophy and psychology and the way the mind works and logic and physics and more. It looks very much like the work of a lifetime.

To know what we want to do, we need to develop wisdom and judgment—the ability to think and act using knowledge, experience, understanding, common sense, and insight.

The next "work" is to figure out what the externally provided "supposed to" looks like. The "right" in Choose the Right. The Jesus

Way in What Would Jesus Do? In the Primary version it always seems obvious, so easy. In the adult version, not so fast. Life is complicated. There are many stories, complex circumstances, surprise endings. There are intended and unintended consequences. There are stated objectives and hidden agendas. All too often the naïve version of "right" turns out to be what some speaker wants us to do. Or what a friend tells us to do. Or what will look good in one group or another. All too often the naïve Jesus Way is just exactly what the Church or the parent or the preacher or the advocate thinks would be good for us. But how do they know? The true Right, the real Way, may be somewhat different than it first appears.

If we are interested in choosing the right, rather than simply doing what we're told, we can start with the handful of circumstances where we know what Jesus did. But we are not itinerant preachers in the first century of the common era, and the overlap of circumstances is limited. On the other hand, if we start generalizing from what we read about Jesus, we may end up in the position of a friend who says "'I'm trying to be like Jesus' means I'm making trouble, I'm ticking people off, and I'm doing a fair bit to rabble rouse. Check, check, and check." Probably not what your Primary teacher had in mind when she wrote WWJD on the board. In practice, the inquiry into what Jesus would do or what is right circles back to the same lifetime of study we talked about above. Study. Trial and error. Experience. Wisdom.

Finally, suppose in all our wisdom we come to the place where we began, with what our best self feels (e.g., get out!) in conflict with what external evidence tells us to do (e.g., stick it out, agree, pay, obey). Even so, the choice is rarely a simple binary. Very often there is a menu of intermediate measures. Walk out. Take a break. Speak up. Write a letter. Reject a calling. Turn in your temple recommend. The world seldom serves up ideal situations and perfect solutions. The real world is full of second-best alternatives. Thank God.

WISDOM

In the end, this chapter—this whole book—is not about getting to yes, or to no. It is not about keeping promises, or about changing direction. It is not about leaving or staying. The end of this road is wisdom. The hymnal had it right all along. The Children's songbook "Choose the Right Way" includes answers—pray, have faith, repent, obey. The adult hymn "Choose the Right" gives us the grown-up version:

> Let wisdom mark the way before.
> In its light, choose the right!
> And God will bless you evermore.

AFTERWORD

FORMER BISHOPS

I am a former Mormon bishop. As a 60-something man with a lifetime in the Church, many of my friends, my cohort, are former bishops. At last count in my local ward we have 14 former bishops. We—we former bishops—recognize there is a way we interact with the Church and church leaders that probably wouldn't happen without that experience.

I wish everybody could have the experience of being a Mormon bishop. I wish we all, men and women alike, could be bishops or former bishops. It's not possible, but the desire informs this book. Part of what I've tried to do is convey as much as I can of that former bishop attitude and approach. Irreverently and idiosyncratically, to be sure.

CURRENT BISHOPS

Upon reading an early draft of the Talking with the Bishop chapter, a close friend who is in fact a sitting Mormon bishop exclaimed, "but I want them to talk with me!" Then in a serious tone, "Tell me how I can minister to your readers, to members of my congregation who need and want this book."

Other early readers who are deeply involved with the Church and who want the best for the Church and the members have protested that the Church is changing and improving. That good things are happening.

I believe them all. But I also believe the good things happening don't always reach the stakes and wards and individual local leaders. Not fast enough, not comprehensively enough, not at the granular level of individual members in their homes.

If this book can encourage even one more bishop to ask "how can I minister to your readers?," it will all be worthwhile. For that alone.

FIXING THE CHURCH

Another good friend who read a pre-release version found it frustrating because his focus is on changing the Church from the outside. He asked what effect I imagine this book could have on the institutional church? Of course my first answer is a non-answer because that's not what this book is about, and I suggested he find (or write) a different book. Pressed for something more, I guessed probably zero effect at the top, but if 10 active adult members of a ward read this book and announced to their bishop they were going to apply the principles for themselves and their children, that might have a local effect analogous to a shop floor unionizing.

DEEP CHURCH

In an interview in 1952, C.S. Lewis talked about the deep church as the body of believers committed to mere Christianity. Lewis had his own ideas about mere Christianity. Other writers have defined it differently. But there is always a sense of core beliefs, of essential value and commitment, of mission and purpose that is not narrowly defined by sectarian debate. In Yiddish I would use *mensch*—a real person, a person of integrity and honor—to describe these believers. In common Mormon speak, I might use *true disciple*.

It is possible to read parts of this book to say we are broken people, barely hanging on at the inside of the edge, needing help at every turn. That message is unintended but I feel it myself and it makes me want to apologize.

It is possible that people who adopt an adult-to-adult approach to the Church because they want a life on the inside of the edge will instead be ostracized like a foreign body. I deeply regret that possibility. But I don't expect the institutional church to validate my approach and I don't expect approval for this book or any of the suggestions in this book.

What I can offer, in the end, is my personal, sincere, heartfelt belief—one man speaking about my friends and companions on this journey—that adult members who have doubts and feel a call to stay and grow up and practice wisdom, are the real thing. Part of the deep church. Mensch. True disciples.

CHRISTIAN KIMBALL is a 'retired' bishop, a 'retired' professor, and a 'retired' lawyer. Linda and Christian live in the mountains of Utah and travel frequently to visit their 11 grandchildren and their grandchildren's parents.

Made in the USA
Middletown, DE
05 September 2024

60433677R00183